THE LOEB CLASSICAL LIBRARY

FOUNDED BY JAMES LOEB 1911

EDITED BY

JEFFREY HENDERSON

STATIUS

I

LCL 206

STATIUS

SILVAE

EDITED AND TRANSLATED BY

D. R. SHACKLETON BAILEY

HARVARD UNIVERSITY PRESS
CAMBRIDGE, MASSACHUSETTS
LONDON, ENGLAND
2003

5/0 M-W 7/03 21.50

LOEB CLASSICAL LIBRARY® is a registered trademark
of the President and Fellows of Harvard College

Library of Congress Catalog Card Number 2002024274
CIP data available from the Library of Congress

ISBN 0-674-99604-6

CONTENTS

SILVAE

BOOK I

BOOK II

CONTENTS

CONTENTS

Acknowledgment

Recent decades have been quite prolific in 'higher criticism' of Statius' works. I cannot pretend to be well-read in it, and am the more grateful to Professor Kathleen M. Coleman for her generous and expert contribution (see pp. 11–21). I owe her thanks, too, for permission to reproduce, in Book IV, the plan of the imperial fora that appeared in her edition.

D.R.S.B.

SILVAE

EXTEMPORE POEMS

INTRODUCTION

Apart from a marginal mention by his younger contemporary Juvenal, what is known of the poet's life and personality comes from his *Silvae*. His name, Publius Papinius Statius, is given in his manuscripts. The surname (*cognomen*) Statius was by origin an Italian personal name, and so like other such borne by slaves, who after getting their freedom would take it as a surname and pass it on to their descendants. The poet of course was no slave, neither was his father, whose name is nowhere attested. Statius' father was a native of Velia on the southwest coast of Italy, but moved to Neapolis (Naples), a Greek colony, which remained a centre of Hellenic culture after acquiring Roman citizenship. Here his son was born, probably about 50 AD. He was a savant and a poet, winning prizes for his compositions at the regularly recurring festivals both in Naples (the Augustalia) and in Greece (Pythian, Isthmian, and Nemean Games). He was probably a Knight, but may have lost his qualification because of a financial reverse, after which he made a career as a teacher of literature, especially Greek, and Roman antiquities. According to his son pupils flocked in from far and wide, and Romans of high rank were schooled to fit them for their futures, particularly as members of the great priestly colleges. While planning a poem on the eruption of Vesuvius in 79 he died[1] and was buried on a small property he (or his son) owned near Alba Longa, a few miles from the capital.

Following in his father's footsteps the young Statius won prizes at the Augustalia and later at the Alban festival instituted by the Emperor Domitian (ruled 81–96), where he producd a poem on the founder's German and Dacian campaigns. Probably after his father's death he moved to Rome and competed unsuccessfully at the great Capitoline festival, possibly in 90—the disappointment of his life. That may have had something to do with his subsequent decision to return to Naples, where he will have died in about 96. He married Claudia, widow of a well-known singer and mother of a musically gifted daughter. He himself was childless, but in his closing years he made up for it with a favourite slave boy whom he freed and whose early death he laments in his last extant poem (*Silvae* V.5). But contrary to what has sometimes been assumed from v. 73 of the same, there was no adoption (vv. 10–11).

His *magnum opus,* an epic of twelve books on the mythological theme of the Seven against Thebes, in which he had been preceded by the fifth/fourth-century Antimachus of Colophon, was published after twelve years of work (*Thebaid* 12.811) and torturous revision (*Silvae* IV.7.26), probably in 92. As was customary he had already recited portions of it to audiences (including senators), and Juvenal (7.83–7), writing about a quarter of a century

[1] Not, however, necessarily soon after it but at any rate before March 90; see the discussion in Coleman's edition of Book IV, pp. xviii-iv.

4

later, tells us that these exhibitions were eagerly anticipated and enthusiastically received, but financially unre-
warding—the poet went hungry. However, with his property at Alba and the presumed support of the Emperor and
wealthy patrons, Statius was certainly no pauper. Another
epic, the *Achilleid,* was begun probably in 95 but halted by
the poet's death. The first book and part of a second survives.

The *Silvae,* with probable composition dates 89–96, appeared in three instalments: Books I–III together after
January 93, Book IV in 95, Book V posthumously, probably
in or after 96. The title echoes that of a now lost work of
Lucan. Like Greek ὕλη, *silva* has two meanings: 'wood' or
'forest,' and 'material' from which something is made. In
the present context the meaning comes out clearly from a
passage of Quintilian (10.3.17) concerning speech composition. Some speakers, he says, 'elect to make a draft of the
whole subject as rapidly as possible, and write impromptu,
following the heat and impulse of the moment. They call
this draft their "raw material" (*silva*). They then revise
their effusions and give them rhythmical structure' (Don-
ald A. Russell's translation).

That might describe the *Silvae,* as the author repre-
sents them: collections of occasional, virtually impromptu
(apart from revision[2]), miscellaneous verse compositions,
each taking a couple of days or less in the writing. That the
other meaning 'wood' is relevant, as sometimes supposed,

[2] This must be assumed, though Statius does not mention it.
As my notes will show, a number of passages suggest that marks of
hasty composition survive. The same however is true of the 'tor-
turously revised' *Thebaid.*

5

I do not believe. Nor do I see significance in the fact that the description is not used of individual pieces, in the singular. One fancies that Max Müller did not refer to an item in *Chips from a German Workshop* as a chip.

Each poem comes with a title that definitely does not originate from the author: see K. M. Coleman's edition of Book IV, xxviii–xxxii; she suggests that the editor of Book V added titles to make up for the absence of a full preface and that similar titles were later added in the previous four books.

Nearly all the pieces are addressed to or concern an individual, aside from the Emperor usually a rich patron with whom the poet was more or less familiar. One of them, the elderly littérateur Pollius Felix, seems to stand out as a true and congenial friend. Several meet us again in Martial, who never mentions Statius nor Statius him.

Recent decades have been quite prolific in studies of Statius' works (see the overview below by Kathleen Coleman). His mastery of the hexameter at least is unquestioned,[3] and it surely extends to his hendecasyllables and his two exercises in lyric, though the latter have been customarily decried. For the rest, let readers form their own impressions.

Virgil was Statius' unapproachable idol. 'Rival not divine Aeneis but follow from afar and ever venerate her footsteps': so he takes leave of his Thebais. But at the same time he hopes for his epic's immortality and testifies to her

[3] Housman, the best conceivable judge, gave him credit as a 'superb versifier,' but did not greatly care for him otherwise ('I have not read the *Thebais* more than three times, nor ever with intent care and interest.' *Cl. Papers,* 1197).

warm reception by contemporaries. By the *Silvae* he and they and their posterity no doubt set less store, but Ausonius and Claudian and Sidonius knew them in late antiquity. In the Middle Ages the author of the *Thebaid* was a favourite, Dante's sweet poet, highlighted by the encounter in the *Purgatorio*. For Julius Caesar Scaliger in the cinquecento, so D. W. T. Vessey reminds us in his introduction to A. D. Melville's elegant verse translation (Oxford 1992), Statius was, aside from Virgil ('we should add Homer,' and I for one should no less emphatically add Lucan), 'both of Latin and Greek Epic writers easily the chief'—not after all so lavish a tribute as it sounds. In the shadow of nineteenth-century Romanticism and its aftermath Statius' reputation went into a long eclipse, but the last three decades or so of the twentieth produced a marked revival of interest and appreciation, however parochial, for both parts of his oeuvre.

Text

Except for a tenth-century manuscript L (Laurentianus 29.32), a miscellany which includes the birthday ode to Lucan (II.7), the only manuscript authority is M (Matritensis Bibl. Nat. 3678), from which other extant copies derive. It is a copy commissioned by Poggio Bracciolini of a manuscript, probably of the ninth or tenth century, that he discovered near Lake Constance in 1417 but which later disappeared. This copy too disappeared for a while, but was discovered in 1879 in the Biblioteca Nacional of Madrid. In sending the copy to a fellow scholar in Florence, Poggio deplored its imperfections: the copyist was 'omnium mortalium ignorantissimus.' Copies of this were made in turn, and from one of these, also a bad one, was taken the editio princeps (Venice 1472). Annotations in a copy of this edition by another famous humanist (and poet), Angelo Poliziano (Politian), have been the subject of a complex and protracted controversy, perhaps now settled: see E. Courtney's preface to his Oxford Text of 1990. It seems that annotations that were not taken from M are the product of conjecture or accident. In my critical notes these are attributed to Politian, and as such make an important contribution.

In Courtney's list of 23 editions of the whole work from the princeps to A. Traglia's of 1978 and 1980 I would star those of the Papal Secretary Domizio Calderini (1475),[4] J. F. Gronovius (1653; also his *Diatribe Statiana*), and J. Markland (1728). After them perhaps come E. Baehrens (1876), J. P. Postgate (1904 with G. A. Davies in *Corpus Poetarum Latinorum*), G. Saenger (1909), and J. S. Phillimore (1910). E. Courtney's (1990) is probably the best text so far, including some fine original emendations. Mine was formed independently, but benefited from comparison with his. Even so, differences amount to more than 250, an average of about one every twenty lines in the first four Books and double that number in the ultra-corrupt fifth,

---

[4] Some of the conjectures with his name in my notes ('Calderini, Itali' in Courtney's apparatus, from which I take them) presumably had other authors, but the large number definitely his establish him as an exceptionally acute critic. Perhaps his most notable achievement was to have seen the truth in Martial 11.94.8 *iura, verpe, per Anchialum,* to which a swarm of later hariolators have been obstinately or ignorantly blind.

apart from spelling, typography, and many divergent punc-
tuations. Some discrepancies come from conjectures that
were not available to him, others can be attributed to the
differing character of the two editions; a Loeb editor is ob-
ligated to put a premium on readability and use the obelus
only as a last resort. But Courtney's text is far removed
from conservatism reduced to absurdity as in A. Maras-
toni's (Teubner) of 1961 and 1970, and a high proportion
of my disagreements stems from judgment, not circum-
stance.

In the legion of contributing non-editors from Politian
onwards first place belongs to eighteenth-century N.
Heinsius. Special mention is due to L. Håkanson's *Statius'
Silvae*; one of the twentieth century's most gifted critics is
here at his best, often brilliant and assuredly more often
right than wrong. Housman's article in *Classical Review* of
1935 (*Classical Papers* 637–55) is worthy of its author.

These assessments are personal of course and indicate
my principal debts. In my critical notes, as to information
based mainly upon Courtney's, some corrections adopted
in the text are omitted as too obvious or minor to be worth
recording. ⊊ is used to cover early corrections of unspeci-
fied origin (Courtney's 'Itali'). For the published sources
of emendations assigned to their authors see Courtney's
lists, and add P. T. Eden, *Mnemosyne* 46 (1993) 92–97 and
378–86.

Commentaries

The only modern commentary on the whole of the
Silvae is F. Vollmer's of 1898. Despite his shortcomings as a

critic in this work,[5] it still must be consulted, though super-
seded in Books II and IV by the hugely comprehensive and
generally judicious commentaries of H. J. van Dam (1984,
Mnemosyne Suppl. 82) and K. M. Coleman (Oxford 1988,
London 1998). The notes to my translation include, beside
basic information to make it intelligible,[6] much hermeneu-
tic and/or revelatory matter, such as may concern any com-
mentator to come. Textual items are mostly relegated to
the Critical Appendix.

Translation

Statius' oblique and artificial style makes for ambigu-
ities of word and phrase and divergences among transla-
tors. I hope to have avoided blunders. The following from
the preface to my Loeb edition of Martial (1993) also applies here: 'As translator I have been especially concerned
with fidelity, which of course does not have to be literal.
Readability would have been served if what I may call
mythological aliases had been replaced by familiar equiva-
lents (e.g. "Athenian" instead of "Cecropian"), but that
would have removed a major stylistic feature. Like other
Latin poets, Martial liked such variations, partly no doubt
as giving the versifier more room for maneuver, but also for
diversity and a cultural cachet.'

---

[5] In Housman's judgment ten years later (*Cl. Papers,* 771) it
was one of two in which the criticism of Latin poetry touched its
nadir. In 1930: 'The late Friedrich Vollmer, after an unpromising
start, became in the course of his life a considerable scholar and
even something of a critic' (ibid., 1170).

[6] In the case of names the index may also be consulted.

RECENT SCHOLARSHIP ON THE *SILVAE* AND THEIR CONTEXT: AN OVERVIEW

KATHLEEN M. COLEMAN

The following sketch ranges beyond items devoted exclusively to the *Silvae,* in an attempt to locate the collection within the larger social and cultural context of Flavian Rome. This survey, necessarily brief and extremely selective, concentrates mainly on English-language contributions. Items on individual poems are generally not included unless they are emblematic of an approach to wider issues, but a broad range of detailed studies can be accessed through bibliographical surveys and essays (Cancik 1986, van Dam 1986, Vessey 1986), and in the recent commentaries on Books 2, 3, and 4 (van Dam 1984, Laguna 1992, Coleman 1988, with important addenda to the last in Corti 1991a and van Dam 1992).

A watershed in scholarship on the *Silvae* came in the 1960s with a study in German tackling the rhetorical origins of the twin obstacles to modern appreciation of this poetry: their dense and elaborate style (often called mannerist), and their encomiastic content (Cancik 1965). This was followed by a crucial monograph identifying the *Silvae* with the Greek cultural milieu of the Bay of Naples, especially the practice of *epideixis* (display poetry) (Hardie

1983). Statius' bilingual background, and the training in Greek literature that he received from his father, are of signal importance; we are to think of him as a Greek poet writing in Latin (Holford-Strevens 2000), a poet immersed in precisely those recherché Greek authors who, while not canonical, are shown to have given a sophisticated veneer to the discourse of the contemporary Roman elite (McNelis 2002).

Central to understanding the climate of Statius' poetry is the role of the emperor and his court in determining cultural tastes, a legacy of the Julio-Claudian dynasty (Wallace-Hadrill 1996). Poetry like the *Silvae* holds up a mirror to a society dominated by the emperor, reflecting even the imprint that he has made on the physical fabric of the city of Rome (Darwall-Smith 1996). The figure of Domitian permeates the *Silvae,* and his literary interests as well as his autocratic tendencies have been counted a major influence in their production (Coleman 1986). Although nothing else quite like the *Silvae* has survived, they testify to a cultural practice that is frequently glimpsed in the world of Domitian's successors too; there seems to have been greater continuity in the literary climate under Domitian and Trajan than the patchy surviving record—and the protestations of new-found liberty by Martial, Pliny, and Tacitus—might suggest (Coleman 2000).

The content of the major proportion of poems in the *Silvae* is determined by the interests and preoccupations of Statius' private patrons in and around his native Naples and at Rome (D'Arms 1970, White 1975); indeed, the two circles may have overlapped (Nisbet 1978). Prominent among Statius' addressees are the wealthy and leisured classes practising a lifestyle of Epicurean withdrawal among elegant intellectual pursuits (Corti 1991b, Myers 2000). The most generous of his Neapolitan patrons, Pollius Felix, is portrayed as a paradigm of philosophical harmony that is reflected in the accommodation between his sophisticated Surrentine villa and its natural setting (Nisbet 1978, Krüger 1998). But not all Statius' associates are sequestered in Epicurean seclusion; he writes also for senators and equestrians vigorously engaged in public life, to whose endeavors he lends a suitably Stoic coloring (Laguna-Mariscal 1996).

Statius contributes poetic enhancement to the significant moments of his patrons' lives through the application of a repertoire of *topoi* (standard features) that are visible also in the graphic arts; Pollius' villa provides a vivid illustration (Bergmann 1991). In the *Silvae* landscaping, architecture, and objets d'art are perpetuated in decorative verse in which the veristic is blended with the mythological, and nature is balanced by artifice (Pavlovskis 1973, Öberg 1978). Similarly, Statius' most extravagant compliments to his patrons are expressed through the whimsical conceit of mythological spokespersons, a device inherited from Hellenistic encomium. Within an encomiastic context, it has been argued, the purpose of such spokespersons is twofold: their enhanced status tickles the ego of the recipient, while simultaneously their role entails a suspension of belief that wittily absolves the author of responsibility for his most outrageous extremes of flattery (Coleman 1999).

It is precisely this elaborate flattery that is the feature in the *Silvae* most antithetical to modern taste, and most provocative of radically differing interpretations. In the liberal atmosphere of the late twentieth century one approach interpreted it as covert criticism, either mocking the pretensions of Statius' patrons (including the emperor) (Ahl 1984), or setting them up as a literary model against which to test the superiority of Statius' own poetic program (Malamud 1995, Newlands 1988a). Although the publication of individual items of 'occasional' poetry in a miscellany does not invite the entire collection to be read as a monolithic exposition of a coherent system of attitudes and approaches, this has nevertheless been recently attempted, in a study in which the 'subversive' interpretation of the *Silvae* is modified and refined (Newlands 2002): the books that Statius himself published (*Silvae* 1–4) are viewed as a subtle expression of his disquiet with some of the attitudes and behaviour of the establishment that he was obliged to praise, and a meditation upon the role of the poet in an increasingly autocratic age.

An alternative approach starts from the premise that the poems of the *Silvae* are independent compositions governed not by consistency of attitude but by the conventions and expectations of literary patronage at Rome; each poem is Statius' response to a particular patron's needs and desires in a given situation. It is apparent that modern standards of tact and discretion do not correspond precisely to Flavian conventions; the patron-client relationship, marked by inequality and reciprocity, may even require the poet to confront less savoury aspects of his patron's background and give them a positive interpretation (Nauta 2002). The patron, for his part, expects a rhetorical display, the more fantastically complimentary the better (Dewar 1994); and the poet is responding to the political and economic realities of a social hierarchy in which the buying power of the wealthy classes is topped by the absolute political power of the emperor (Römer 1994, Geyssen 1996). Minding the gap between poet and patron, even on such an ostensibly egalitarian occasion as the Saturnalia, is a delicate balance between humility and self-assertion (Damon 1992). Jocular respect is seen to be a suitable stance, all the more appropriate in proportion to the absolute authority of the supreme imperial patron (Newman 1987).

The paradox of publishing strictly 'occasional' poetry is a preoccupation of Statius' prefaces. A model for the circulation and distribution of topical verse has been deduced from the evidence of the *Silvae* and Martial's epigrams (White 1974 and 1978). The most obvious illustration of the chronological gap between composition and publication is the poem of thanks for the recovery of the prominent senator, Rutilius Gallicus, which was published after his relapse and death (*Silvae* 1.4); the memorial qualities of this poem strikingly complement the surviving epigraphic testimony to Gallicus' career (Henderson 1998). In tandem with the tension between topical composition and the posterity anticipated in publication, Statius' protestations of haste in versifying have to be reconciled with the extreme artifice of his poetry (Bright 1980, with significant modifications in the introductions to van Dam 1984, Laguna 1992, Coleman 1988). His choice of metre has been shown to be a subtle and sophisticated vehicle for conveying the theme of a poem (Morgan 2000), and the structuring of individual poems, and their grouping into books, is demonstrably crafted according to elaborate principles of arrangement (Newmyer 1979). Statius' learning, and his intertextual dialogue with his predecessors,

15

have been recorded in detail (Taisne 1994). The *Silvae*, in their turn, can be seen to have provided models for villa poetry in the Renaissance and beyond (Dewar 1990, Newlands 1988b), a measure of the intense interest that these poems generated once they had been rediscovered in the fifteenth century (Reeve 1977, Cesarini Martinelli 1978).

Most of the poems in the *Silvae* are too long to qualify for inclusion in modern anthologies. One exception is the short, emotionally charged address to Sleep (*Silvae* 5.4), which is generally the best-known piece in the collection today. Yet this poem seems to have hardly anything in common with the rest; even its stance of authorial subjectivity lacks the circumstantial detail that characterizes the poem addressed to Statius' wife (*Silvae* 3.5), or the laments for his deceased father and foster son (*Silvae* 5.3 and 5.5). But it is infused with the same sophisticated atmosphere of rhetorical allusion that permeates the rest of the collection, and the short compass of this poem belies the complexity of its response to Statius' Greek and Latin predecessors treating the same theme (Gibson 1996).

Indeed, the depth of Statius' learning, combined with the social and political climate of Domitian's Rome, may seem to pose the most formidable challenge to readers attempting to enter the world of the *Silvae*; their densely decorated style teases the reader at every turn, and their daring compliments strain credulity. But we have to contend with a difficulty even more fundamental than these, a difficulty that is disguised by the medium of translation and one that we have been eloquently cautioned not to forget (Willis 1966): when all is said and done, our appreciation of the *Silvae* and the world that they reveal depends

16

upon a single corrupt manuscript, and upon the skills and the learning—and indeed the scepticism—of its editors.

BIBLIOGRAPHY

Ahl 1984: Ahl, F. M. "The rider and the horse: politics and power in Roman poetry from Horace to Statius," with an appendix by J. Garthwaite: "Statius, *Silvae* 3.4," *Aufstieg und Niedergang der römischen Welt* II 32.1 (Berlin and New York, 1984), 40–124

Bergmann 1991: Bergmann, B. "Painted perspectives of a villa visit: landscape as status and metaphor," in: E. K. Gazda (ed.) *Roman Art in the Private Sphere* (Ann Arbor, 1991), 49–70

Bright 1980: Bright, D. F. *Elaborate Disarray: The Nature of Statius' Silvae* (Meisenheim am Glan, 1980)

Cancik 1965: Cancik, H. *Untersuchungen zur lyrischen Kunst des P. Papinius Statius* (Hildesheim, 1965)

Cancik 1986: Cancik, H. "Statius, 'Silvae'. Ein Bericht über die Forschung seit Friedrich Vollmer (1893) (Bibliographie unter Mitarbeit von H.-J. van Dam)," *Aufstieg und Niedergang der römischen Welt* II 32.5 (Berlin and New York, 1986), 2681–2726

Cesarini Martinelli 1978: Cesarini Martinelli, L. (ed.) *Commento inedito alle Selve di Stazio di Angelo Poliziano* (Florence, 1978)

Coleman 1986: Coleman, K. M. "The emperor Domitian and literature," *Aufstieg und Niedergang der römischen Welt* II 32.5 (Berlin and New York, 1986), 3087–3115

Coleman 1988: Coleman, K. M. *Statius Siluae* IV (Oxford, 1988; repr. London, 1998)

Coleman 1999: Coleman, K. "Mythological figures as

17

spokespersons in Statius' Silvae," in: F. de Angelis and S. Muth (eds), *Im Spiegel des Mythos. Bilderwelt und Lebenswelt—Lo specchio del mito. Immaginario e realtà* (Wiesbaden, 1999), 67–80

Coleman 2000: Coleman, K. M. "Latin literature after AD 96: change or continuity?" *American Journal of Ancient History* 15 (1990 [2000]), 19–39

Corti 1991a: Corti, R. "Commentare le *Silvae* di Stazio (a proposito di un'edizione e commento al IV libro)," *Maia* n.s. 43 (1991), 115–142

Corti 1991b: Corti, R. "La tematica dell'*otium* nelle *Silvae* di Stazio," in: M. Pani (ed.), *Continuità e Trasformazioni fra Repubblica e Principato: Istituzione, politica, società* (Bari, 1991), 189–224

Damon 1992: Damon, C. "Statius *Silvae* 4. 9: *Libertas Decembris*," *Illinois Classical Studies* 17 (1992), 301–308

D'Arms 1970: D'Arms, J. H. *Romans on the Bay of Naples* (Cambridge, Mass., 1970)

Darwall-Smith 1996: Darwall-Smith, R. H. *Emperors and Architecture: a Study of Flavian Rome* (Brussels, 1996)

Dewar 1990: Dewar, M. "Blosio Palladio and the *Silvae* of Statius," *Studi Umanistici Piceni* 10 (1990), 59–64

Dewar 1994: Dewar, M. "Laying it on with a trowel: the proem to Lucan and related texts," *Classical Quarterly* n.s. 44 (1994), 199–211

Geyssen 1996: Geyssen, J. W. *Imperial Panegyric in Statius. A Literary Commentary on Silvae* 1.1 (New York, 1996)

Gibson 1996: Gibson, B. J. "Statius and insomnia: allusion and meaning in *Silvae* 5.4," *Classical Quarterly* n.s. 46 (1996), 457–468

Hardie 1983: Hardie, A. *Status and the* Silvae: *Poets, Patrons and Epideixis in the Graeco-Roman World* (Liverpool, 1983)

Henderson 1998: Henderson, J. *A Roman Life: Rutilius Gallicus on Paper and in Stone* (Exeter, 1998)

Holford-Strevens 2000: Holford-Strevens, L. "In search of Poplios Papinios Statios," *Hermathena* 168 (2000), 39–54

Krüger 1998: Krüger, A. *Die lyrische Kunst des Publius Papinius Statius in Silve II 2: Villa Surrentina Pollii Felicis* (Frankfurt, 1998)

Laguna 1992: Laguna, G. *Estacio, Silvas III* (Madrid, 1992)

Laguna-Mariscal 1996: Laguna-Mariscal, G. "Philosophical topics in Statius' *Silvae*: sources and aims," in: F. Delarue, S. Georgacopoulou, P. Laurens, A.-M. Taisne (eds), *Epicedion. Hommages à P. Papinius Statius 96–1996* (Poitiers, 1996), 247–259

Malamud 1995: Malamud, M. A. "Happy birthday, dead Lucan: (P)raising the dead in *Silvae* 2.7," *Ramus* 24 (1995), 1–30

McNelis 2002: McNelis, C. "Greek grammarians and Roman society during the early Empire: Statius' father and some contemporaries," *Classical Antiquity* 21 (2002), 67–94

Morgan 2000: Morgan, L. "Metre matters: some higher-level metrical play in Latin poetry," *Proceedings of the Cambridge Philological Society* 46 (2000), 99–120

Myers 2000: Myers, K. S. "'Miranda fides': poets and patrons in paradoxographical landscapes in Statius' *Silvae*," *Materiali e discussioni per l'analisi dei testi classici* 44 (2000), 103–138

19

Nauta 2002: Nauta, R. R. *Poetry for Patrons. Literary Communication in the Age of Domitian* (Leiden, Boston and Cologne, 2002)

Newlands 1988a: Newlands, C. E. "Horace and Statius at Tibur: an interpretation of *Silvae* 1. 3," *Illinois Classical Studies* 13 (1988), 95–111

Newlands 1988b: Newlands, C. E. "Statius' villa poems and Ben Jonson's *To Penshurst:* the shaping of a tradition," *Classical and Modern Literature* 8 (1988), 291–300

Newlands 2002: Newlands, C. E. *Statius'* Silvae *and the Poetics of Empire* (Cambridge, 2002)

Newman 1987: Newman, J. K. "Domitian, Justinian and Peter the Great: the ambivalent iconography of the mounted king," *Illinois Classical Studies* 12 (1987), 315–335

Newmyer 1979: Newmyer, S. T. *The Silvae of Statius: Structure and Theme* (Leiden, 1979)

Nisbet 1978: Nisbet, R. G. M. "*Felicitas* at Surrentum (Statius, *Silvae* II.2)," *Journal of Roman Studies* 68 (1978), 12–21

Öberg 1978: Öberg, J. "Some notes on the marvels of civilisation in imperial Roman literature," *Eranos* 76 (1978), 145–155

Pavlovskis 1973: Pavlovskis, Z. *Man in an Artificial Landscape* (Leiden, 1973)

Reeve 1977: Reeve, M. D. "Statius' *Silvae* in the fifteenth century," *Classical Quarterly* n.s. 27 (1977), 202–225

Römer 1994: Römer, F. "Mode und Methode in der Deutung panegyrischer Dichtung der nachaugusteischen Zeit," *Hermes* 122 (1994), 95–113

Taisne 1994: Taisne, A.-M. *L'esthétique de Stace. La peinture des correspondances* (Paris, 1994)

van Dam 1984: van Dam, H.-J. *P. Papinius Statius, Silvae Book II: A Commentary* (Leiden, 1984)

van Dam 1986: van Dam, H.-J. "Statius, 'Silvae.' Forschungsbericht 1974–1984," *Aufstieg und Niedergang der römischen Welt* II 32.5 (Berlin and New York, 1986), 2727–2753

van Dam 1992: van Dam, H.-J. "Notes on Statius *Silvae* IV," *Mnemosyne* 45 (1992), 190–224

Vessey 1986: Vessey, D. W. T. "Transience preserved: style and theme in Statius' 'Silvae,'" *Aufstieg und Niedergang der römischen Welt* II 32.5 (Berlin and New York, 1986), 2754–2802

Wallace-Hadrill 1996: Wallace-Hadrill, A. "The imperial court," *Cambridge Ancient History*[2] 10 (Cambridge, 1996), 283–308

White 1974: White, P. "The presentation and dedication of the *Silvae* and the *Epigrams*," *Journal of Roman Studies* 64 (1974), 40–61

White 1975: White, P. "The friends of Martial, Statius, and Pliny, and the dispersal of patronage," *Harvard Studies in Classical Philology* 79 (1975), 265–300

White 1978: White, P. "*Amicitia* and the profession of poetry in early imperial Rome," *Journal of Roman Studies* 68 (1978), 74–92

Willis 1966: Willis, J. A. "The *Silvae* of Statius and their editors," *Phoenix* 20 (1966), 305–324

ABBREVIATIONS

Coleman	K. M. Coleman, *Statius Silvae IV* (Oxford 1988)
Håkanson	L. Håkanson, *Statius' Silvae* (Lund 1974)
Harvard Studies	D. R. Shackleton Bailey, *Harvard Studies in Classical Philology* 91 (1987) 273–82
Housman, *Cl. Papers*	A. E. Housman, *Classical Papers* (Cambridge 1972)
OLD	*Oxford Latin Dictionary*
RE	Pauly-Wissowa, *Realencyclopädie der classischen Altertumswissenschaft*
SCP	D. R. Shackleton Bailey, *Select Classical Papers* (Ann Arbor 1997)
TLL	*Thesaurus Linguae Latinae*
van Dam	H.-J. van Dam, *P. Papinius Statius, Silvae Book II* (*Mnemosyne* Suppl. 82: Leiden 1984)

Conventional abbreviations for classical authors and works are used in the Critical Notes and Appendix.

BOOK ONE

PREFATORY NOTES

1

Date: probably 91 or shortly after.

2

Date: after December 89. Martial 6.21, written shortly after the marriage, belongs to the latter half of 90. The bridegroom, L. Arruntius Stella, had held curule office and was a member of the prestigious College of Fifteen (vv. 176f.); he was to become Consul Suffect in 101 or 102. He had a reputation as author of love elegies addressed to or concerning his future wife Violentilla, a rich widow born in Naples, under the pseudonym Asteris (ἀστήρ, 'star,' = *Stella*). Both appear in a number of Martial's epigrams, she as Ianthis (ἴον, 'violet,' = *viola*); though her name is really diminutive of *violentus*.

3

Other than its presence in this Book, the poem offers no indication of date. The addressee is presented in the prefatory epistle and vv. 99–104 as a wealthy bachelor (no mention of a wife), no longer young, enjoying a life of literary leisure in his splendid villa or the Anio, a tributary of the Tiber. He was probably an Epicurean (v. 94).

4

Date: probably 89. Rutilius Gallicus was City Prefect in charge of Rome during Domitian's absence on his second Dacian campaign. The poem itself and a number of inscriptions give details of his long and distinguished career. Literary activity is attested in vv. 27–30. It does not appear that Statius had any personal relationship with him. He seems to write as a concerned citizen—no doubt in the hope of a quid pro quo of some kind.

5

Date: latter half of 90, probably contemporaneous with Martial 6.42 and 83 (the former on these same baths). On the recipient see III.3.

6

The month is December during the Saturnalia, the year uncertain.

LIBER PRIMUS

Diu multumque dubitavi, Stella, iuvenis optime et in studiis nostris eminentissime, qua parte [et] voluisti, an hos
libellos, qui mihi subito calore et quadam festinandi volup-
tate fluxerunt, cum singuli de sinu meo pro‹dierint›, con-
5   gregatos ipse dimitterem. quid enim ‹opus eo tempore
hos› quoque auctoritate editionis onerari, quo adhuc pro
Thebaide mea, quamvis me reliquerit, timeo? sed et Culi-
cem legimus et Batrachomachiam etiam agnoscimus, nec
quisquam est illustrium poetarum qui non aliquid operi-
10 bus suis stilo remissiore praeluserit. quid quod haec serum
erat continere, cum illa vos certe quorum honori data sunt
haberetis? sed apud ceteros necesse est multum illis
pereat ex venia, cum amiserint quam solam habuerunt gra-
tiam celeritatis. nullum enim ex illis biduo longius tractum,
quaedam et in singulis diebus effusa. quam timeo ne
15 verum istuc versus quoque ipsi de se probent!

De locis stellatis vide additamentum criticum, p. 383
2 *del.* Ç   4 *add. Saenger cum aliis: spat.* M
5 *item*   8 *et Heinsius:* haec M

---

[1] The apocryphal *Culex,* accepted as Virgil's also by Lucan and
Martial.

BOOK ONE

Much and long have I hesitated, my excellent Stella, distinguished as you are in your chosen area of our pursuits, whether I should assemble these little pieces, which streamed from my pen in the heat of the moment, a sort of pleasurable haste, emerging from my bosom one by one, and send them out myself. For why ‹should they too› be burdened with the authority of publication ‹at a time› when I am still anxious for my *Thebaid,* although it has left my hands? But we read *The Gnat*[1] and even recognize *The Battle of the Frogs;*[2] and none of our illustrious poets but has preluded his works with something in lighter vein. Moreover, it was too late to keep them back, since you at least and the others in whose honour they were produced already had them. But with the general public they must necessarily forfeit much of its indulgence since they have lost their only commendation, that of celerity. For none of them took longer than a couple of days to compose, some were turned out in a single day. How I fear that the verses themselves will testify on their own behalf to the truth of what I say!

[2] Properly *Batrachomyomachia, Battle of the Frogs and Mice,* a parody of epic attributed to Homer.

Primus libellus sacrosanctum habet testem: sumendum enim erat 'a Iove principium.' centum hos versus, quos in ecum maximum feci, indulgentissimo imperatori postero die quam dedicaverat opus, tradere ausus sum.

20 'potuisti illud'–dicet aliquis–'et ante vidisse.' respondebis illi tu, Stella carissime, qui epithalamium tuum, quod mihi iniunxeras, scis biduo scriptum: audacter mehercules, sed ter centum tamen hexametros habet et fortasse tu pro collega mentieris. Manilius certe Vopiscus, vir eruditissimus

25 et qui praecipue vindicat a situ litteras iam paene fugientes, solet ultro quoque nomine meo gloriari villam Tiburtinam suam descriptam a nobis uno die. sequitur libellus Rutilio Gallico convalescenti dedicatus, de quo nihil dico, ne videar defuncti testis occasione mentiri. nam Claudi

30 Etrusci testimonium donandum est, qui balneolum a me suum intra moram cenae recepit. in fine sunt kalendae Decembres, quibus utique credetur: noctem enim illam felicissimam et voluptatibus publicis inexpertam * * *

19 ausus sum *Sandstroem*: iussum M
22 ter centum *Elter*: tantum M   23 at *Bernartius*
28 convalescenti *Scriverius*: est valenti M
30 donandum* *scripsi*: domonnum M
32 credetur *Markland*: -ditur M

28

The first has a sacred witness. I had to follow the rule 'from Jove my beginning.'[3] I ventured to hand over these hundred lines on the Great Horse to our most indulgent Emperor the day after he dedicated the work. 'You might have seen it beforehand,' somebody will say. Dearest Stella, you will answer him; you know that your Wedding Ode, which you enjoined upon me, was written in a couple of days. A bold claim indeed—and after all it has three hundred hexameters, and maybe you will tell a fib for a colleague. To be sure, Manilius Vopiscus, a very learned gentleman and one who more than most others is rescuing our now almost vanishing literature from neglect, is by way of boasting in my name, and spontaneously, that my description of his villa at Tibur was done in one day. There follows a piece dedicated to Rutilius Gallicus on his recovery from illness. Of that I say nothing, for fear I may be thought to be taking advantage of the death of my witness to tell a falsehood. As for Claudius Etruscus' evidence, I must waive it:[4] he received his 'Bath' from me within the space of a dinner. Last come the 'Kalends of December.' They at least will be believed, for that happiest of nights, unprecedented among public pleasures * * *

3 Formulaic in hymns to the gods.
4 See Critical Appendix.

I.1

ECUS MAXIMUS DOMITIANI IMP.

Quae superimposito moles geminata colosso
stat Latium complexa forum? caelone peractum
fluxit opus? Siculis an conformata caminis
effigies lassum Steropen Brontenque reliquit?
5 an te Palladiae talem, Germanice, nobis
effinxere manus qualem modo frena tenentem
Rhenus et attoniti vidit domus ardua Daci?
    Nunc age fama prior notum per saecula nomen
Dardanii miretur equi, cui vertice sacro
10 Dindymon et caesis decrevit frondibus Ide.
hunc neque discissis cepissent Pergama muris,
nec grege permixto pueri innuptaeque puellae
ipse nec Aeneas nec magnus duceret Hector.
adde quod ille nocens saevosque amplexus Achivos,
15 hunc mitis commendat eques: iuvat ora tueri
mixta notis, bellum placidamque gerentia pacem.
nec veris maiora putes: par forma decorque,
par honor. exhaustis Martem non altius armis
Bistonius portat sonipes magnoque superbit
20 pondere nec tanto raptus prope flumina cursu

---

4 Steropen Brontenque *Bentley*: -em –emque M
6 effinxere ς: -igere M   16 bellum *Courtney*: belli M
20 tanto *Politianus*: tardo M

---

1 *Equus* = equestrian statue, as in Martial 8.44.6 and else-where.
2 On Mt Aetna, where Vulcan and the Cyclopes had their workshop.

30

I.1

THE GREAT EQUESTRIAN STATUE[1] OF EMPEROR DOMITIAN

What is this mass that stands embracing the Latian Forum, doubled by the colossus on its back? Did it glide from the sky, a finished work? Or did the effigy, moulded in Sicilian furnaces,[2] leave Steropes and Brontes weary? Or did Pallas fashion you for us, Germanicus, in such guise as the Rhine of late and the lofty home of the astounded Dacian saw you holding your reins?[3]

Come now, let an earlier fame wonder at the renown of the Dardanian horse, known through the ages, for whom Dindymon's sacred peak and Ida were diminished, their leafage felled. *This* horse Pergamus would not have contained, though her walls were riven asunder, nor would the mingled throng of boys and unwed girls have drawn him, nor yet Aeneas himself nor great Hector.[4] Besides, that horse was baneful, enfolding cruel Achaeans; this one his gentle rider commends, on whose face it is pleasant to gaze, where marks are mingled; war it bears and gentle peace. Nor think the work exaggerates: equal is his beauty and grace, equal his dignity. No more loftily does his Bistonian steed bear Mars, battles spent, and glories in the mighty weight; nor so great[5] his speed as he pelts steaming

[3] Domitian's German and Dacian wars are a long story. *Ardua* refers to the mountain stronghold mentioned in v. 80.

[4] As in the case of the Trojan Horse (*Aeneid* 2.234–40).

[5] So inferred from the statue's appearance? Careless writing perhaps but preferable to M's bathetic *nec tardo* (a slow-running horse of Mars would be a very rare animal).

fumat et ingenti propellit Strymona flatu.
    Par operi sedes. hinc obvia limina pandit
qui fessus bellis adscitae munere prolis
primus iter nostris ostendit in aethera divis;
25 discit et e vultu quantum tu mitior armis,
qui nec in externos facilis saevire furores
das Cattis Dacisque fidem: te signa ferente
et minor in leges gener et Cato Caesaris irent.
at laterum passus hinc Iulia tecta tuentur,
30 illinc belligeri sublimis regia Pauli,
terga pater blandoque videt Concordia vultu.
    Ipse autem puro celsum caput aëre saeptus
templa superfulges et prospectare videris,
an nova contemptis surgant Palatia flammis
35 pulchrius, an tacita vigilet face Troicus ignis
atque exploratas iam laudet Vesta ministras.
dextra vetat pugnas, laevam Tritonia virgo
non gravat et sectae praetendit colla Medusae,

22 huic *Laetus*: hinc M
28 gener et Cato Caesaris irent *Scriverius*: iret gener et cato castris M
35 tacita ⌐: tanta M: casta *Lenz*

---

6 Julius Caesar, to whom his adopted son (and great-nephew) Augustus dedicated a temple in 27 B.C. On the following topography see the plan of the imperial fora on page 236.

7 Trumping Caesar's vaunted clemency.

8 Pompey 'the Great' (Magnus)—but lesser than Caesar.

9 The statue is flanked by the Basilica Julia on one side and the Basilica Aemilia on the other. Statius unwarily credits the latter

along the river, urging Strymon forward with his prodigious blast.

The setting matches the work. Here opens wide his facing threshold he[6] that weary of wars first showed our divinities the way to heaven by the gift of his adopted son. From your countenance he learns how much gentler in arms are you,[7] that find it hard to rage even against foreign fury, giving quarter to Cattians and Dacians. Had you borne the standard, his lesser son-in-law[8] and Cato would have submitted to Caesar's ordinances. But the spread of the flanks is surveyed from one side by the Julian structure and from the other by the palace of martial Paullus.[9] The back your father beholds, and Concord with her smiling face.[10]

You yourself shine above the temples, your lofty head in the pure air. You seem to gaze before you—does the new palace[11] rise more beautiful than ever, despising the flames, does the secret band of the Trojan fire keep vigil, does Vesta now praise her servants well approved?[12] Your right hand bans battles; Tritonia is no burden to your left as she holds out severed Medusa's neck as though to spur

to L. Aemilius Paullus, victor in the second Macedonian War. Actually it originated with M. Aemilius Lepidus, Censor in 179, and was restored by L. Aemilius Paullus, Consul in 50, and again by his son Paullus Aemilius Lepidus, Consul-Suffect in 34.

[10] The temple of Vespasian (and Titus) and the temple of Concord.　　　　[11] On the Palatine, replacing one destroyed by fire. It was completed in 92 (cf. IV.2.18ff.).

[12] Domitian had punished a Vestal Virgin for unchastity in the ancient fashion (burial alive). The Vestals maintained the secret fire brought from Troy.

ceu stimulis accendit equum; nec dulcior usquam
40 lecta deae sedes, nec si pater ipse teneres.
pectora, quae mundi valeant evolvere curas
et quis se totis Temese dedit hausta metallis.
it tergo demissa chlamys, latus ense quieto
securum, magnus quanto mucrone minatur
45 noctibus hibernis et sidera terret Orion.

At sonipes habitus animosque imitatus eriles
acrius attollit vultus cursumque minatur,
cui rigidis stant colla iubis vivusque per armos
impetus et tantis calcaribus ilia late
50 suffectura patent. vacuae pro caespite terrae
aerea captivi crinem terit ungula Rheni.
hunc et Adrasteus visum extimuisset Arion
et pavet aspiciens Ledaeus ab aede propinqua
Cyllarus. hic domini numquam mutabit habenas,
55 perpetuus frenis, atque uni serviet astro.

Vix sola sufficiunt insessaque pondere tanto
subter anhelat humus; nec ferro aut aere, laborat
sub genio, teneat quamvis aeterna crepido
quae superingesti portaret culmina montis
60 caeliferique attrita genu durasset Atlantis.

Nec longae traxere morae. iuvat ipsa labores

---

43 it ⌐: et M   46 eriles *Markland*: equestres M
51 terit ⌐: tegit M

---

13 A statuette of Minerva, considered by Domitian as his
protectress, with her shield (aegis) on which was the Gorgon
Medusa's head. Since this should turn gazers to stone, something
seems askew in the poet's conception.

34

the horse forward;[13] nowhere did the goddess choose a sweeter resting place, not even, Father,[14] if yourself held her. Your breast is such as may suffice to unwind the cares of the universe; to make it, Temese has given her all, exhausting her mines. A cloak hangs down your back. A great sword protects your side, large as Orion's threatening blade on winter nights, affrighting the stars.

But the charger in counterfeit of his master's[15] mien and spirit sharply lifts his head and threatens gallop. His mane lies stiff on his neck, life thrills through his shoulders, his spreading flanks will suffice for the great spurs. Instead of a clod of empty earth, his brazen hoof chafes the hair of captive Rhine. Adrastus' Arion would have dreaded the sight of him, and Leda's Cyllarus trembles as he looks from his neighbouring shrine. This horse shall never change his master's reins, constant to his bit; he shall serve one star only.[16]

Scarce can the soil hold out, the ground pants beneath the pressure of such a weight. 'Tis not steel or bronze, 'tis your guardian spirit[17] that overloads it, even though an everlasting base support, one that might have carried a mountain peak piled on top, and held firm though rubbed by Atlas' knee.

No long delays drew out the time. The god's present

[14] Jupiter, Father of the gods, but also specially of this goddess, who was born from his head.

[15] *Equestris* is adjective from *eques,* not *equus;* not therefore 'equine.'   [16] Arion had several successive masters and Castor's horse Cyllarus might be ridden by Pollux, so Statius assumes. The two were stars—like Domitian!

[17] Genius, a mysterious sort of alter ego, accompanying the individual through life.

35

forma dei praesens, operique intenta iuventus
miratur plus posse manus. strepit ardua pulsa
machina; continuus septem per culmina Martis
65   it fragor et magnae vincit vaga murmura Romae.
      Ipse loci custos, cuius sacrata vorago
famosique lacus nomen memorabile servant,
innumeros aeris sonitus et verbere crudo
ut sensit mugire Forum, movet horrida sancto
70   ora situ meritaque caput venerabile quercu.
ac primum ingentes habitus lucemque coruscam
expavit maioris equi terque ardua mersit
colla lacu trepidans; laetus mox praeside viso:
'salve, magnorum proles genitorque deorum,
75   auditum longe numen mihi. nunc mea felix,
nunc veneranda palus, cum te prope nosse tuumque
immortale iubar vicina sede tueri
concessum. semel auctor ego inventorque salutis
Romuleae: tu bella Iovis, tu proelia Rheni,
80   tu civile nefas, tu tardum in foedera montem
longo Marte domas. quod si te nostra tulissent
saecula, temptasses me non audente profundo
ire lacu, sed Roma tuas tenuisset habenas.'
      Cedat equus Latiae qui contra templa Diones

---

[64] Martis *Gronovius*: montis M   [65] vincit *Heinsius*: fingit
M: frangit *Phillimore, fort. recte (cf. van Dam ad II.1.163)*

---

[18] The statue itself (not 'beauty'), or possibly the mould from
which it would be cast.   [19] Rather than 'crane.'
[20] The legendary M. Curtius, who plunged himself and his
horse into a chasm that had opened in the Forum, for country's
sake.

likeness[18] itself makes labour sweet and the men intent upon their task are surprised to find their hands more powerful. The lofty scaffolding[19] is loud with hammer strokes and an incessant din runs through Mars' seven hills, drowning the vagrant noises of great Rome.

The guardian of the place in person,[20] whose name the sacred chasm and the famous pool preserve in memory, hears the countless clashes of bronze and the Forum resounding with harsh blows. He raises a visage stark in holy squalor and a head sanctified by well-earned wreath of oak.[21] At first he took alarm at the huge accoutrements and flashing light of a mightier horse as thrice his lofty neck sank affrighted in the pool. Then, happy at sight of the ruler: 'Hail, offspring and begetter of great gods, deity known to me by distant report. Blessed is now my swamp, venerable now that it is vouchsafed me to know you close at hand and behold your immortal radiance. Once only did I make and find salvation for the people of Romulus; whereas you in length of fighting quell the wars of Jove,[22] the battles of the Rhine,[23] the civil outrage,[24] the mountain slow to treat.[25] But if our times had given you birth, you would have made to plunge into the deep pool, when I dared not venture, but Rome would have held your reins.'

Let that horse yield who stands in Caesar's Forum

---

[21] A military decoration bestowed for saving the life of a fellow soldier (*corona civica*).   [22] The fighting on the Capitol in 69 A.D. between partisans of Vitellius and Vespasian. Domitian was on the spot, but his contribution was minimal.

[23] Campaign against the German C(h)atti.

[24] The rebellion of Antonius Saturninus, governor of Upper Germany, in 89.   [25] See v. 7.

85 Caesarei stat sede Fori, quem traderis ausus
Pellaeo, Lysippe, duci (mox Caesaris ora
mirata cervice tulit); vix lumine fesso
explores quam longus in hunc despectus ab illo.
quis rudis usque adeo qui non, ut viderit ambos,
90 tantum dicat equos quantum distare regentes?
    Non hoc imbriferas hiemes opus aut Iovis ignem
tergeminum, Aeolii non agmina carceris horret
annorumve moras: stabit, dum terra polusque,
dum Romana dies. huc et sub nocte silenti,
95 cum superis terrena placent, tua turba relicto
labetur caelo miscebitque oscula iuxta.
ibit in amplexus natus fraterque paterque
et soror; una locum cervix dabit omnibus astris.
    Utere perpetuum populi magnique senatus
100 munere. Apelleae cuperent te scribere cerae,
optassetque novo similem te ponere templo
Atticus Elei senior Iovis, et tua mitis
ora Tarans, tua sidereas imitantia flammas
lumina contempto mallet Rhodos aspera Phoebo.
105 certus ames terras et quae tibi templa dicamus
ipse colas, nec te caeli iuvet aula, tuosque
laetus huïc dono videas dare tura nepotes.

94 huc ⊊: hoc M

26 A statue of Alexander the Great, whose head, after the deplorable practice of the time, had been replaced by Julius Caesar's. It stood in the Forum Julium opposite the temple of Venus Genetrix, mother of Aeneas and hence of the Julian clan and the Roman people.

opposite Latian Dione's temple, whom you, Lysippus (so
'tis said), dared make for Pella's captain.[26] Who so un-
schooled as, seeing both, not to declare the horses as far
apart as their riders?[27]

This work fears not rainy winters nor the troops of
Aeolus' dungeon nor the long-drawn years; it shall stand as
long as earth and heaven and Roman day. In the dead of
night, when earthly things please heavenly, your folk[28] will
glide from the sky and mingle kisses close. Son and brother
and father and sister will come to your arms. One neck
shall make room for every star.[29]

Enjoy for all time the gift of the people and the great
Senate. Apelles' wax would fain have inscribed you,[30] the
old Athenian[31] would have longed to set your likeness in a
new temple of Elean Jove, gentle Tarentum would have
preferred your countenance, fierce Rhodes your eyes like
starry flames, contemning Phoebus.[32] Steadfast may you
love earth and yourself frequent the temples we dedicate
to you. Let not heaven's palace delight you, and happily
may you see your grandsons give incense to this gift.

[27] *Regentes* could mean 'rulers,' but the other sense is determined by *equos*.

[28] Deified members of the imperial family.

[29] All the deified relatives.

[30] In encaustic painting.

[31] Phidias.

[32] Alluding to a colossal statue of Zeus (Jupiter) at Tarentum
('gentle' because of her reputation for soft living) by Lysippus and
to the Colossus of Rhodes, representing the Sun God (it was no
longer standing in Statius' time). Rhodes had a rugged terrain and
a martial history.

I.2

EPITHALAMION IN STELLAM ET VIOLENTILLAM

Unde sacro Latii sonuerunt carmine montes?
cui, Paean, nova plectra moves umeroque comanti
facundum suspendis ebur? procul ecce canoro
demigrant Helicone deae quatiuntque novena
5   lampade sollemnem thalamis coeuntibus ignem
et de Pieriis vocalem fontibus undam.
quas inter vultu petulans Elegea propinquat
celsior assueto divasque hortatur et ambit
alternum furata pedem, decimamque videri
10   se cupit et mediis fallit permixta sorores.
ipsa manu nuptam genetrix Aeneia duxit
lumina demissam et dulci probitate rubentem,
ipsa toros et sacra parat cultuque Latino
dissimulata deam crinem vultusque genasque
15   temperat atque nova gestit minor ire marita.
     Nosco diem causasque sacri: te concinit iste
(pande fores), te, Stella, chorus; tibi Phoebus et Euhan
et de Maenalia volucer Tegeaticus umbra
serta ferunt. nec blandus Amor nec Gratia cessat
20   amplexum niveos optatae coniugis artus
floribus innumeris et olenti spargere nimbo.
tu modo fronte rosas, violis modo lilia mixta
excipis et dominae nitidis a vultibus obstas.
     Ergo dies aderat Parcarum conditus albo

---

9 furata *Sandstroem*: futura M: suffulta *Leo*
10 mediis ⊊: -ias M   12 lumina ⊊: -ne M
13 cultu *T. Faber*: coctu M
23 nitidis* *scripsi*: niveis M

I.2

EPITHALAMIUM IN HONOUR OF STELLA AND VIOLENTILLA

Wherefore have Latium's hills resounded in sacred song? For whom, Paean, do you stir your quill and hang the eloquent ivory from your tressy shoulders? See, the goddesses afar come down from tuneful Helicon and with ninefold torch toss ritual fire of marriage union and vocal wave from Pieria's fount. Among them pert-faced Elegy draws near, taller than her wont; she urges the goddesses and courts them, concealing her alternate foot,[1] wanting to be seen as a tenth and mingling among the Sisters unnoticed. Aeneas' mother with her own hand led the bride, whose eyes are downcast as she blushes sweetly chaste. She herself prepares the bed and the rites, dissembling her deity with Latian attire, and tempers hair and face and eyes, anxious to walk less tall than the newly wed.

I learn the day and the reason for the ceremony. It is you, Stella, you that choir (fling wide the gates!) is singing. For you Phoebus and Euhan and the flying Tegean from Maenalus' shade bring garlands. Smiling Love and Grace ceaselessly scatter you with countless blossoms and fragrant shower as you embrace the snowy limbs of your longed-for bride. On your brow you receive now roses, now lilies mingled with violets, shielding your mistress' shining[2] face.

Here then was the day, hidden in the white wool of the

[1] The second line of an elegiac couplet (the pentameter) has five feet instead of six.

[2] See Critical Appendix.

25 vellere, quo Stellae Violentillaeque professus
   clamaretur hymen. cedant curaeque metusque,
   cessent mendaces obliqui carminis astus;
   Fama, tace. subiit leges et frena momordit
   ille solutus amor, consumpta est fabula vulgi
30 et narrata diu viderunt oscula cives.
   tu tamen attonitus, quamvis data copia tantae
   noctis, adhuc optas permissaque numine dextro
   vota paves. pone, o dulcis, suspiria vates,
   pone: tua est. licet expositum per limen aperto
35 ire redire gradu. iam nusquam ianitor aut lex
   aut pudor. amplexu tandem satiare petito
   (contigit) et duras pariter reminiscere noctes.
       Digna quidem merces, et si tibi Iuno labores
   Herculeos, Stygiis et si concurrere monstris
40 Fata darent, si Cyaneos raperere per aestus.
   hanc propter tanti Pisaea lege trementem
   currere et Oenomai fremitus audire sequentis.
   nec si Dardania pastor temerarius Ida
   sedisses, haec dona forent, nec si alma per auras
45 te potius prensum aveheret Tithonia biga.
       Sed quae causa toros inopinaque gaudia vati
   attulit? hic mecum, dum fervent agmine postes
   atriaque et multa pulsantur limina virga,
   hic, Erato iucunda, doce. vacat apta movere
50 colloquia et docti norunt audire penates.

32 permissa *Heinsius*: deprem- M
45 prensum (*Parrhasius*) aveheret *Baehrens*: -nsa veheret M
46 vati *Calderini*: -is M

Parcae, when the wedding of Stella and Violentilla was to be proclaimed and sung. Let cares and fears begone; a truce to lying wiles of hinting buzz; Rumour, hold your tongue. That footloose love has bowed to rules and bitten the bridle. Common tattle has run its course and the citizenry have seen the kisses so long retailed. But you[3] are nonplussed. Though the night of nights is yours to enjoy, you are still yearning and fear the prayers that kindly deity has granted. Sigh no more, sweet poet, sigh no more: she is yours. Open lies the entrance, you may come for all to see. No more janitor or rule or shyness! Take your fill at last of the embrace you sought, and as you do, remember the nights of discontent.

Worthy indeed were your reward had Juno assigned you Hercules' labours and the Fates made you clash with monsters or were you swept through Cyanean swell.[4] For her sake it were worth while to run trembling under Pisa's ordinance and hear Oenomaus bellowing in pursuit. If you had been the rash shepherd[5] on Dardanian Ida's judgment seat, such a gift would not be yours, nor yet if it was you[6] that gracious Tithonia took up in her chariot and carried away through the air.

But what was it that brought marriage and unlooked-for joys to our poet? Here with me, while entrances and halls seethe with the throng and doors are beaten with many a staff—here, delightful Erato, tell me true. Time serves to start apt converse and the poet's[7] home knows how to listen.

---

[3] Stella. [4] Like Jason and the Argonauts.
[5] Paris. [6] Instead of Tithonus.
[7] Stella's.

Forte, serenati qua stat plaga lactea caeli,
alma Venus thalamo pulsa modo nocte iacebat
amplexu duro Getici resoluta mariti.
fulcra torosque deae tenerum premit agmen Amorum.
55 signa petunt qua ferre faces, quae pectora figi
imperet; an terris saevire an malit in undis
an miscere deos an adhuc vexare Tonantem.
ipsi animus nondum nec cordi fixa voluntas;
fessa iacet stratis, ubi quondam conscia culpae
60 Lemnia deprenso repserunt vincula lecto.
hic puer e turba volucrum, cui plurimus ignis
torre manusque leves numquam frustrata sagitta,
agmine de medio tenera sic dulce profatur
voce (pharetrati pressere silentia fratres):
65 'Scis ut, mater,' ait 'nulla mihi dextera segnis
militia. quemcumque hominum divumque dedisti,
uritur. at quondam lacrimis et supplice dextra
et votis precibusque virum concede moveri,
o genetrix; duro nec enim ex adamante creati
70 sed tua turba sumus. clarus de gente Latina
est iuvenis, quem patriciis maioribus ortum
Nobilitas gavisa tulit praesagaque formae
protinus e nostro posuit cognomina caelo.
hunc egomet tota quondam (tibi dulce) pharetra
75 improbus et densa trepidantem cuspide fixi.
quamvis Ausoniis multum gener ille petitus
matribus, edomui <in>victum dominaeque potentis

55 qua *Jortin*: quas M: quis *Heinsius*
62 torre *Heinsius*: ore M   manusque (*Morel*) levis *Cruceus*
(*cf. Sen. Phaedr. 62*): manuque levi M
77 *add. Eden*

44

It chanced on a night just banished[8] that gracious Venus lay in her bower, where stands tranquil heaven's Milky Way, relaxed from her Getic husband's[9] rough embrace. A tender company of Loves presses the Goddess' couch and cushions. They seek her sign: where does she bid them carry their torches, what hearts are to be pierced? Would she rather they rage on land or in the waves? Should they confound the gods or go on tormenting the Thunderer? She herself has no mind as yet, no will fixed in her heart. Weary she lies on the draperies where once the Lemnian chains crept over the bed they had surprised, privy to the guilt.[10] Then a boy from out the winged multitude, whose brand had most of fire and whose light hands no shaft had ever failed, spoke up thus sweetly in his childish tone (his quivered brethren kept mum):

'Mother, you know' says he 'that my right hand is never slack in any service; whomsoever you give me, man or god, burns. But for once, mother mine, allow me to be moved by men's tears and suppliant hands, their vows and prayers; for we are not created from hard adamant, we are your children. There is a distinguished young man of Latian breed. Nobility produced him rejoicing, born of patrician forbears, and forthwith gave him a name from our heaven,[11] presage of beauty. Him I once pierced with all my quiver—it was your pleasure—as he trembled in a hail of darts, no mercy. Much was he sought by Ausonian dames for their daughters, but I conquered the unde-

---

[8] I.e. at dawn.   [9] Mars, by courtesy. Venus was married to Vulcan.   [10] See *Odyssey* 8.266ff. The chains were made by Hephaestus (Vulcan), who worked on his favourite island of Lemnos (as well as Aetna).   [11] Stella = 'Star.'

ferre iugum et longos iussi sperare per annos.
ast illam summa leviter (sic namque iubebas)
80 lampade parcentes et inerti strinximus arcu.
ex illo quantos iuvenis premat anxius ignes,
testis ego attonitus, quantum me nocte dieque
urguentem ferat: haud ulli vehementior umquam
incubui, genetrix, iterataque vulnera fodi.
85 vidi ego et immiti cupidum decurrere campo
Hippomenen, nec sic meta pallebat in ipsa.
vidi et Abydeni iuvenis certantia remis
bracchia laudavique manus et saepe natanti
praeluxi: minor ille calor, quo saeva tepebant
90 aequora: tu veteres, iuvenis, transgressus amores.
ipse ego te tantos stupui durasse per aestus
firmavique animos blandisque madentia plumis
lumina detersi. quotiens mihi questus Apollo
sic vatem maerere suum! iam, mater, amatos
95 indulge thalamos. noster comes ille piusque
signifer; armiferos poterat memorare labores
claraque facta virum et torrentes sanguine campos,
sed tibi plectra dedit mitisque incedere vates
maluit et nostra laurum subtexere myrto.
100 hic iuvenum lapsus suaque aut externa revolvit
vulnera. pro! quanta est Paphii reverentia, mater,
numinis! hic nostrae deflevit fata columbae.'
    Finierat: tenera matris cervice pependit
blandus et admotis tepefecit pectora pennis.

82 attonitus ⊊ (*cf.* 91): -ito M
98 sed *Politianus*: sic M
103 finierat ⊊: Emis (*i.e.* Finis) erat M

46

feated one, commanded him to bear the yoke of a potent mistress and hope through long years. As for her, I but lightly grazed her with the tip of my brand—for such was your command—and a flaccid bow. Ever since, I am witness in my wonderment to what fires the tormented youth keeps down, how night and day he bears my urging. None, mother, did I ever lean upon harder, thrusting wound on wound. I saw eager Hippomanes running down the cruel field, but even at the post he was never so pale; and I saw the arms of the youth of Abydos[12] rivalling oars, and praised his effort, and often lighted him as he swam; but his ardour that warmed the cruel sea was less. You, O youth, have surpassed the loves of old. I myself was amazed at your endurance through such fevers and strengthened your spirit, wiping your moist eyes with my balmy plumes. How often has Apollo complained to me of his poet's distress! Mother, grant him now the bridal of his desire. He is our companion, our loyal standard-bearer. He could have told of martial toils, famous deeds of heroes, fields streaming with gore; but he gave his quill to you, preferring to walk softly in his poesy and twine his bay in our myrtle. He tells of young folk's errors, of his own and others' wounds. How he reveres Paphos' deity, mother! He bewailed our dove's demise.'[13]

He ended. Hanging fondly on his mother's tender lap, he warmed her bosom with his covering pinions. She an-

[12] Leander.

[13] Doves were Venus' favourite birds. Stella had written a poem mourning Violentilla's black dove (Martial 7.14.6), following the precedent of Catullus for Lesbia's sparrow and Ovid for Corinna's parrot (cf. II.4, Melior's parrot).

105   illa refert, vultu non aspernata rogari:
       'grande quidem rarumque viris quos ipsa probavi,
       Pierius votum iuvenis cupit. hanc ego formae
       egregium mirata decus, cui gloria patrum
       et generis certabat honos, tellure cadentem
110   excepi fovique sinu. nec colla genasque
       comere nec pingui crinem deducere amomo
       cessavit mea, nate, manus. mihi dulcis imago
       prosiluit. celsae procul aspice frontis honores
       suggestumque comae. Latias metire quid ultra
115   emineat matres: quantum Latonia Nymphas
       virgo premit quantumque egomet Nereidas exsto.
       haec et caeruleis mecum consurgere digna
       fluctibus et nostra potuit considere concha,
       et, si flammigeras licuisset scandere sedes
120   hasque intrare domos, ipsi erraretis, Amores.
       huic quamvis census dederim largita beatos,
       vincit opes animo. querimur iam Seras avaros
       angustum spoliare nemus Clymenaeaque desse
       germina nec virides satis illacrimare sorores,
125   vellera Sidonio iam pauca rubescere tabo
       raraque longaevis nivibus crystalla gelari.
       huic Hermum fulvoque Tagum decurrere limo
       (nec satis ad cultus), huic Inda monilia Glaucum
       Proteaque atque omnem Nereida quaerere iussi.
130   hanc si Thessalicos vidisses, Phoebe, per agros,
       erraret secura Daphne; si in litore Naxi

        [118] *nihil mutandum*
        [119] licuisset *Eden*: potu- M
        [122] querimur *Peyrarède*: -itur M

swered with a look that scorned not his petition: 'Great indeed is the prize of the Pierian youth's desire, seldom granted to lovers by myself approved. Wondering at the matchless beauty of her person, rivalled by the glory of her forbears and her race's renown, I took her up as she fell to the ground and nursed her in my lap. Nor has my hand been slow, my son, to beautify her face and neck and comb her hair with rich balsam. She has shot up to be my sweet likeness. Look yonder at the dignity of her lofty brow, the pile of her tresses. Measure how far she tops Latium's matrons; by as much as Latona's maiden dwarfs her Nymphs and I myself stand out above the Nereids. She could worthily have risen with me from the cerulean waves and taken a seat in my shell. Had she been allowed to climb the flaming abodes and enter these dwellings, you yourselves, my Loves, could be deceived. Although I have lavished upon her the gift of ample wealth, her soul is greater than her riches. Already I complain that the greedy Seres[14] despoil too small a forest, that Clymene's gums are failing and the green sisters[15] weeping too little, that few fleeces now blush with Sidonian dye, that crystals too rare are frozen in long-lasting snows.[16] For her I have bidden Hermus and Tagus flow with tawny mud (there's not enough for her adornment), for her Glaucus and Proteus and every Nereid must search for necklaces of Ind.[17] If Phoebus had seen her in Thessaly's fields, Daphne had safely strayed.

[14] Producers of silk or cotton.   [15] Daughters of the Sun and Clymene (Heliades). Weeping for their brother Phaëthon, they were turned into poplars and their tears to amber.

[16] Crystals were believed to come from ice.

[17] Pearl.

Theseum iuxta foret haec conspecta cubile,
Cnosida desertam profugus liquisset et Euhan.
quod nisi me longis placasset Iuno querelis,
135 falsus huïc pennas et cornua sumeret aethrae
rector, in hanc ver⟨s⟩o cecidisset Iuppiter auro.
sed dabitur iuveni cui tu, mea summa potestas,
nate, cupis, thalami quamvis iuga ferre secundi
saepe neget maerens. ipsam iam cedere sensi
inque vicem tepuisse viro.'
140   Sic fata levavit
sidereos artus thalamique egressa superbum
limen Amyclaeos ad frena citavit olores.
iungit Amor laetamque vehens per nubila matrem
gemmato temone sedet. iam Thybris et arces
145 Iliacae: pandit nitidos domus alta penates
claraque gaudentes plauserunt limina cycni.
digna dea est sedes, nitidis nec sordet ab astris.
hic Libycus Phrygiusque silex, hic dura Laconum
saxa virent, hic flexus onyx et concolor alto
150 vena mari, rupesque nitent quis purpura saepe
Oebalis et Tyrii moderator livet aëni.
pendent innumeris fastigia nixa columnis,
robora Dalmatico lucent sociata metallo.
excludunt radios silvis demissa vetustis

---

136 verso *Herzog*: vero M   144 Thybris et *anon. ap. Hand*:
thybridis M   147 dea est *Saenger*: dea *coni. Courtney*
nitidis *Calderini*: viridis M   153 sociata *Lipsius*: sati- M

---

18 Ariadne.   19 Jupiter would have disguised himself as a
swan (as for Leda) or a bull (as for Europa) or a shower of gold (as
for Danaë), but for Violentilla the gold would be real (cf. Ovid,

If she had been spied beside Theseus' couch on Naxos'
beach, Euhan too would have fled and left the Cnosian
girl[18] forlorn. And if Juno had not appeased me with her
lengthy plaints, heaven's ruler would have donned disguise
of wings and horns for her sake, onto her would Jupiter
have fallen, in gold transformed.[19] Yet shall she be granted
to the young man you favour, my highest power, my sons,
though in her grief she often refuses to bear the yoke of a
second marriage. Already I have seen that she herself is
yielding, that she has warmed to him in her turn.'

Thus speaking, she raised her starry limbs and left the
proud threshold of her bower, summoning her Amyclaean
swans to the reins. Love yokes them and sits on the jewelled pole, wafting his happy mother through the clouds.
Here already are Tiber and the Ilian heights. A lofty mansion spreads open a shining home and the rejoicing swans
flap upon the famed entrance. The dwelling deserves the
goddess, nor seems it mean after the bright stars. Here
is Libyan stone and Phrygian, here hard Laconian rock
shows green, here are versatile alabaster and the vein
that matches the deep sea,[20] here marble oft envied by
Oebalian purple and the blender of the Tyrian cauldron.[21]
Airy gables rest on countless columns, beams glitter allied
with Dalmatian ore. Cool descends from ancient trees,

Metamorphoses 5.11 *falsum versus in aurum*), if *vero* is retained.
But this is a foolish conceit. Among the conjectures my choice is
verso: gold turned to Jupiter instead of Jupiter turned to gold, 'a
syntactical reversal of the main concepts,' to quote van Dam,
p. 243. Statius is notably fond of such inversions.

[20] Marble of Carystos, with wavy grey-green lines.

[21] Porphyry. Tyrian and Laconian purple dye were celebrated.

155 frigora, perspicui vivunt in marmore fontes.
  nec servat Natura vices: hic Sirius alget,
  bruma tepet, versumque domus sibi temperat annum.
    Exsultat visu tectisque potentis alumnae
  non secus alma Venus quam si Paphon aequore ab alto
160 Idaliasque domos Erycinaque templa subiret.
  tunc ipsam solo reclinem affata cubili:
    'Quonam hic usque sopor vacuique modestia lecti,
  o mihi Laurentes inter dilecta puellas?
  quis morum fideique modus? numquamne virili
165 summittere iugo? veniet iam tristior aetas.
  exerce formam et fugientibus utere donis.
  non ideo tibi tale decus vultusque superbos
  meque dedi viduos ut transmittare per annos
  ceu non cara mihi. satis o nimiumque priores
170 despexisse procos! at enim hic tibi sanguine toto
  deditus unam omnes inter miratur amatque,
  nec formae nec stirpis egens; nam docta per urbem
  carmina qui iuvenes, quae non didicere puellae?
  hunc et bis senos (sic indulgentia pergat
175 praesidis Ausonii) cernes attollere fasces
  ante diem; certe iam nunc Cybeleia movit
  limina et Euboicae carmen legit ille Sibyllae.
  iamque parens Latius, cuius praenoscere mentem
  fas mihi, purpureos habitus iuvenique curule
180 indulgebit ebur, Dacasque (et gloria maior)

<hr/>

176 novit ς

<hr/>

22 To her first husband's memory.   23 I.e. become Consul before the legal age (a Consul had twelve lictors).

24 As a member of the prestigious Board of Fifteen (Quindecimviri), charged with custody of the Sibylline Books and per-

shutting out the sunshine, translucent fountains live in
marble. Nor does Nature observe her order: here Sirius is
chill, midwinter warm. The house tempers the changing
year to its liking.

Fostering Venus exults at the sight, the dwelling of her
regal foster child, no less than if she were entering Paphos
from the deep sea or her Idalian home or Eryx' shrine.
Then she addressed the girl as she reclined upon her soli-
tary bed:

'How long this slumber, this modesty of empty couch,
O favourite mine among Laurentian girls? What limit to
propriety and loyalty?[22] Will you never submit to a husband's yoke? Soon a sadder time of life will come. Make the
most of beauty and use gifts that flee. I did not give you
such grace, such pride of countenance, and my own self to
let you pass through years of widowhood as though I loved
you not. Enough and overmuch to have scorned earlier
suitors. For truly this one is devoted to you with all his
manhood, loves and admires you among all; and he lacks
neither comeliness nor birth. As for his polished verses,
what youths, what girls in all Rome do not have them by
heart? Him shall you see raise the twice six rods before
the time[23]—so continue the favour of Ausonia's sovereign.
Even now to be sure he has opened Cybele's threshold and
reads the lays of the Euboean Sybil.[24] And presently the
Latian Father, whose mind I may lawfully know, shall
vouchsafe the young man purple robes and curule ivory[25]
and grant him to celebrate Dacian spoils and recent lau-

haps with supervision of foreign worships. For their connection
with Cybele cf. *RE* XI.2268.52, XXIV.55. Were the Books now
kept in her temple on the Palatine?

25 In which office is uncertain.

exuvias laurosque dabit celebrare recentes.
ergo age iunge toros atque otia deme iuventae.
quas ego non gentes, quae non face corda iugali

*   *   *   *   * ?

alituum pecudumque mihi durique ferarum
185 non renuere greges; ipsum in conubia terrae
aethera, cum pluviis rarescunt nubila, solvo.
sic rerum series mundique revertitur aetas.
unde novum Troiae decus ardentumque deorum
raptorem, Phrygio si non ego iuncta marito?
190 Lydius unde meos iterasset Thybris Iulos?
quis septemgeminae posuisset moenia Romae
imperii Latiale caput, ‹ni› Dardana furto
cepisset Martem, nec me prohibente, sacerdos?'
His mulcet dictis tacitaeque inspirat amorem
195 conubii. redeunt animo iam dona precesque
et lacrimae vigilesque viri prope limina questus
Asteris et vatis totam cantata per Urbem,
Asteris ante dapes, nocte Asteris, Asteris ortu,
quantum non clamatus Hylas. iamque aspera coepit
200 flectere corda libens et iam sibi dura videri.
Macte toris, Latios inter placitissime vates,
quod durum permensus iter coeptique labores
prendisti portus. nitidae sic transfuga Pisae
amnis in externos longe flammatus amores

183 mentes *Heinsius*   iugavi *Saenger*   *versum excidissse*
viderunt Postgate et Saenger
194 tacitae *Vollmer*: -to M (?): -te *fort.* M *primo, Otto*
amorem *Politianus*: honorem M
197 vati *Markland*   201 placitissime *scripsi**: -idissime M
202 labores *Markland*: -ris M

rels—a yet greater glory.[26] Up then, join beds and away
with youth's idleness! What races, what hearts has my nuptial torch * * * ? Neither birds nor cattle nor savage packs of
wild beasts have said me nay. I melt the very heaven into
marriage with earth when rains thin the clouds. So one
thing succeeds another and the world's youth returns.
Whence would have come Troy's new glory and the rescue of burning gods if I had not mated with a Phrygian
spouse?[27] Whence would Libyan Tiber have renewed my
Iuli? Who could have founded the walls of sevenfold
Rome, Latian imperial capital, if the Dardan princess[28]
had not taken Mars in secret dalliance—nor did I forbid.'

With these words she beguiles the silent girls, inspiring
love of wedlock. Now his gifts and prayers and wakeful
plaints at the doorway return to her mind, and the poet's
Asteris[29] chanted through all the city—Asteris before dinner, Asteris by night, Asteris at dawn; never was Hylas so
clamoured.[30] Now she began to bend her stern heart, not
loath, now to deem herself too hard.

Hail to your bridal bed, most favoured of Latian poets!
You have traversed your hard way, the toils of your enterprise; you have gained harbour. So the renegade river of
gleaming Pisa,[31] on fire for a distant, alien love, draws on

---

[26] Apparently Stella was to be in charge of games in honour of
Domitian's Dacian triumph at the end of 89.   [27] If Venus
and Anchises had not produced Aeneas, Troy would not have been
reborn as Rome nor would her household gods have been rescued
(by Aeneas) from the sack of the city.   [28] The Vestal Ilia,
mother of Romulus and Remus.   [29] Violentilla's pseudonym
in Stella's love elegies ('Ἀστήρ = 'Star').   [30] From Virgil, *Ec-
logues* 6.44 *ut litus 'Hyla, Hyla' omne sonaret.*   [31] Alpheus.
'Gleaming' refers to the oil used by athletes in the Olympic games.

205 flumina demerso trahit intemerata canali
donec Sicanios tandem prolatus anhelo
ore bibat fontes: miratur dulcia Nais
oscula nec credit pelago venisse maritum.
Quis tibi tunc alacri caelestum in munere claro,
210 Stella, dies! quanto salierunt pectora voto,
dulcia cum dominae dexter conubia vultus
annuit! ire polo nitidosque errare per astros
visus. Amyclaeis minus exsultavit harenis
pastor ad Idaeas Helena veniente carinas,
215 Thessala nec talem viderunt Pelea Tempe,
cum Thetin Haemoniis Chiron accedere terris
erecto prospexit equo. quam longa morantur
sidera! quam segnis votis Aurora mariti!
At procul ut Stellae thalamos sensere parari
220 Letous vatum pater et Semeleius Euhan,
hic movet Ortygia, ‹movet› hic rapida agmina Nysa.
huic Lycii montes gelidaeque umbracula Thymbrae
et, Parnase, sonas: illi Pangaea resultant
Ismaraque et quondam genialis litora Naxi.
225 tunc caras iniere fores comitique canoro
hic chelyn, hic flavam maculoso nebrida tergo,
hic thyrsos, hic plectra ferunt; hic enthea lauro
tempora, pampinea crinem premit ille corona.

223 Parnase sonas *D. Heinsius*: -sis honos M
228 pampinea *Eden*: minoa M

---

32 Arethusa.   33 Laconian. Amyclae itself lay inland.
34 Older name of Delos, Apollo's birthplace.

his inviolate stream in a sunken channel, until at last he comes to the surface and drinks the Sicilian fountain panting-mouthed. The Naiad[32] marvels at his sweet kisses, nor believes that her lover has come from the sea.

What a day for you, Stella, was that, as you sprang to the gods' splendid gift! How your heart leapt with desire when your mistress' favouring face assented to sweet wedlock! You thought you were in heaven, walking through the shining firmament. Less buoyant was the shepherd on Amyclaean[33] sands as Helen came to Ida's keels; nor did Thessalian Tempe see Peleus in such guise when Chiron from his upstanding horse beheld Thetis approach Haemonian land. How long the stars tarry! How slow is Aurora to hear a bridegroom's prayers!

But when the father of poets, Leto's son, and Euhan, son of Semele, perceived from far that Stella's wedding was preparing, they set their swift followings astir, the one from Ortygia,[34] the other from Nysa. For the one sound Lycia's mountains and the shades of chill Thymbra and Parnassus; for the other echo Pangaea and Ismara and the shores of once bridal Naxos. Then they enter the door they love. One brings to his songful friend a lyre, the other a yellow dappled fawn skin; one wands, the other quills. One covers his poetic temples with laurel, the other his hair with crown of vine leaves.[35]

---

[35] By one account, Bacchus took off his ivy crown and set it in the sky as the constellation Corona when Ariadne died. Hence if *Minoa* is right, the crown he normally wears is with questionable logic called Minoan = Cretan. But I have preferred Eden's conjecture; cf. Valerius Flaccus 5.79.

Vixdum emissa dies, et iam socialia praesto
230   omina, iam festa fervet domus utraque pompa.
fronde virent postes, effulgent compita flammis,
et pars immensae gaudet celeberrima Romae.
omnis honos, cuncti veniunt ad limina fasces,
omnis plebeio teritur praetexta tumultu;
235   hinc eques, hinc iuvenum coetu stola mixta laborat
felices utrosque vocant, sed in agmine plures
invidere viro. iamdudum poste reclinis
quaerit Hymen thalamis intactum dicere carmen
quo vatem mulcere queat, dat Iuno verenda
240   vincula, et insignit gemina Concordia taeda.
hic fuit ille dies: noctem canat ipse maritus,
quantum nosse licet. sic victa sopore doloso
Martia fluminea posuit latus Ilia ripa;
non talis niveos tinxit Lavinia vultus
245   cum Turno spectante rubet; non Claudia talis
respexit populos mota iam virgo carina.
      Nunc opus Aonidum comites tripodumque ministri
diversis certare modis. eat enthea vittis
atque hederis redimita cohors, ut pollet ovanti
250   quisque lyra; sed praecipue qui nobile gressu
extremo fraudatis epos date carmina festis
digna toris. hunc ipse Coo plaudente Philitas

231 effulgent *Markland*: et f- M
235 coetu *Perrotto*: questus hasta M *manus prima*
240 insignit gemina *Hopf*: -ni -nat M
244 tinxit ς: strin- M
251 epos *Heinsius*: opus M   faustis *Markland*

Scarce was day sent forth and already omens of union are to hand, both houses are alive with festal show. The doorposts are green with foliage, the crossroads ablaze, and the most crowded part of measureless Rome rejoices. Every office, all rods come to that threshold, every gown of state is jostled in commoners' turmoil. Knights mill on one side, on the other the matron's robe mingles with throng of youth. They call both the pair happy, but more in the assembly envy the groom. Hymen has been leaning against a doorpost, seeking to deliver a brand-new wedding song for beguiling of the poet. Juno gives the sacred bonds[36] and Concord marks with double torch. Such was that day; of the night let the bridegroom sing, so far as it be permitted to know. Thus Martian Ilia laid her down on the river bank, overborne by treacherous sleep; not so did Lavinia tinge her snow-white cheeks, blushing before Turnus' gaze, not so did Claudia look back at the crowd when the keel moved and made her virgin.[37]

Companions of the Aonian sisterhood and servants of the tripods,[38] now 'tis your work to vie in divers modes. Let the troop come forth wreathed in fillets and ivy, as each has skill with triumphant lyre. But you above all that cheat noble Epic of its final pace give songs worthy of the wedding feast: Philetas to Cos' applause and old Callimachus

36 Yellow ribbons (yellow being the nuptial colour), as it would seem from Tibullus 2.2.18.

37 Do these comparisons relate to how the bride looked when about to leave the company for the nuptial chamber? If so, that could have been made clearer, but Claudia (see Index) at least so indicates. She and Violentilla both looked triumphant, though for quite different reasons.

38 Of Apollo, therefore poets.

Callimachusque senex Umbroque Propertius antro
ambissent laudare diem nec tristis in ipsis
255 Naso Tomis divesque foco lucente Tibullus.
me certe non unus amor simplexque canendi
causa trahit. tecum similes iunctaeque Camenae,
Stella, mihi, multumque pares bacchamur ad aras
et sociam doctis haurimus ab amnibus undam.
260 at te nascentem gremio mea prima recepit
Parthenope, dulcisque solo tu gloria nostro
reptasti. nitidum consurgat ad aethera tellus
Eubois et pulchra tumeat Sebethos alumna,
nec sibi sulpureis Lucrinae Naides antris
265 nec Pompeiani placeant magis otia Sarni.
    Heia age praeclaros Latio properate nepotes,
qui leges, qui castra regant, qui carmina ludant.
acceleret partu decimum bona Cynthia mensem.
sed parcat Lucina precor, tuque ipse parenti
270 parce, puer, ne mollem uterum, ne stantia laedas
pectora; cumque tuos tacito Natura recessu
formarit vultus, multum de patre decoris,
plus de matre feras. at tu, pulcherrima forma
Italidum, tandem merito possessa marito,
275 vincla diu quaesita fove. sic damna decoris
nulla tibi, longae virides sic flore iuventae
perdurent vultus tardeque haec forma senescat.

---

276 longae ⛝: -ge M   virides *Politianus*: -dis M

---

39 Ovid's place of exile, where he wrote his *Tristia* (*Poems of Sadness*).
40 Writers of elegy, as was Stella. Tibullus 1.1.5f. *me mea*

and Propertius in his Umbrian dell would have competed
to praise this day, and Naso, not sad even though in Tomi,[39]
and Tibullus, rich in his blazing hearth.[40] As for me, for
sure no single love, no one cause for song leads me on.[41]
My Muses are like and linked to yours, Stella; at equal altars much we rave[42] and draw shared water from poetic
streams. But you, lady, did my Parthenope first take to her
bosom at your birth, on our soil you crawled, its sweet
glory. Let the Euboean land rise to the bright sky and
Sebethos swell with pride in his fair nurseling. Nor let the
Lucrine Naiads more plume themselves in their sulphur
caverns nor the quiet waters of Pompeian Sarnus.

To work! Hasten, splendid sons of Latium,[43] to rule
laws and armies, to sport with song. Let kind Cynthia
speed the tenth month for delivery, but let Lucina be merciful, I pray.[44] And you, boy, spare your mother, hurt not
her soft womb, her firm breasts. When Nature moulds
your face in her silent recess, may you take much beauty
from your father, more from your mother. But you, loveli-
est of Italy's daughters, at last in the keeping of a worthy
spouse, cherish the long-sought bonds. So may your
charms lose nothing, your face stay fresh in the flower of
enduring youth and this your beauty be slow to age.

*paupertas vita traducet inerti, / dum meus assiduo luceat igne
focus* is recalled.

[41] As he proceeds to explain, the groom is a fellow poet and the
bride a fellow Neapolitan.

[42] Poetic frenzy.

[43] Future children of the marriage.

[44] Cynthia (Diana) is the Moon, Lucina (sometimes conflated
with Juno) the goddess of childbirth. They are not to be identified.

I.3

VILLA TIBURTINA MANILI VOPISCI

Cernere facundi Tibur⟨s⟩ glaciale Vopisci
si quis et inserto geminos Aniene penates
aut potuit sociae commercia noscere ripae
certantesque sibi dominum defendere villas,
5   illum nec calido latravit Sirius astro
nec gravis aspexit Nemeae frondentis alumnus.
talis hiems tectis, frangunt sic improba solem
frigora, Pisaeumque domus non aestuat annum.
ipsa manu tenera tecum scripsisse Voluptas

        *   *   *   *   *

10   tunc Venus Idaliis unxit fastigia sucis
permulsitque comis blandumque reliquit honorem
sedibus et volucres vetuit discedere natos.
    O longum memoranda dies! quae mente reporto
gaudia, quam lassos per tot miracula visus!
15   ingenium quam mite solo, quae forma beatis
ante manus artemque locis! non largius usquam
indulsit Natura sibi. nemora alta citatis
incubuere vadis; fallax responsat imago
frondibus et longas eadem fugit umbra per undas.
20   ipse Anien (miranda fides!) infraque superque
saxeus, hic tumidam rabiem spumosaque ponit
murmura, ceu placidi veritus turbare Vopisci
Pieriosque dies et habentes carmina somnos.

¹ Tiburs *scripsi*: -ur M   *post* 9 *lac. agnovit Calderini*
²⁰ ipse Anien ⌐: ipsa autem M
²¹ spumeus . . . saxosaque *Lenz, ut vid., et Sandstroem*

I.3

THE VILLA OF MANILIUS VOPISCUS AT TIBUR

He that has had the chance to view the chill Tiburtine estate[1] of eloquent Vopiscus and the twin homes threaded by Anio or to acquaint himself with the intercourse of a common bank and the mansions that vie to keep their master each for herself, at him Sirius' hot star did not bark nor leafy Nemea's nurseling frown.[2] Such winter is in the edifice, unconscionable cools defeat the sun, the dwelling never swelters in a Pisaean season.[3] Pleasure herself <is said> with tender hand to have traced with you * * * Then Venus anointed the rooftops with Idalian juices, stroked them with her hair, and left gift of charm upon the residence, forbidding her winged children to depart therefrom.

Day long to be remembered! What joy does my mind bring back, what weariness of vision amid so many marvels! How gentle the nature of the ground! What beauty in the blessed spot before art's handiwork! Nowhere has Nature indulged herself more lavishly. Tall woods brooded over rapid waters. A deceptive image answers the foliage and the reflexion flows unchanging in the lengthening stream. Anio himself, wondrous to tell, full of rocks above and below, here rests his swollen rage and foamy din, as though loath to disturb Vopiscus' Pierian days and song-

---

[1] *Tiburtinum = villa Tiburtina.* The vulgate *Tibur* is a solecism; see my note on Martial 7.31.11 (Loeb edition).   [2] The Nemean lion killed by Hercules became the constellation Leo.

[3] Lit. 'year.' *Annum* stands for *tempus anni,* a bold internal accusative. The Olympian games were held in high summer.

SILVAE

litus utrumque domi, nec te mitissimus amnis
25 dividit; alternas servant praetoria ripas
non externa sibi fluviumve obstare queruntur:
Sestiacos nunc Fama sinus pelagusque natatum
iactet et audaci victos delphinas ephebo.
hic aeterna quies, nullis hic iura procellis,
30 numquam fervor aquis. datur hic transmittere visus
et voces et paene manus; nec Chalcida fluctus
expellunt reflui nec dissociata profundo
Bruttia Sicanium circumspicit ora Pelorum.
        Quid primum mediumque canam, quo fine quiescam?
35 auratasne trabes an Mauros undique postes
an picturata lucentia marmora vena
mirer an emissas per cuncta cubilia Nymphas?
huc oculis, huc mente trahor. venerabile dicam
lucorum senium? te, quae vada fluminis infra
40 cernis, an ad silvas quae respicis, aula, tacentes,
qua †tibi† tuta quies offensaque turbine nullo
nox silet aut pigros invitant murmura somnos?
an quae graminea suscepta crepidine fumant
balnea et impositum ripis algentibus ignem,
45 quaque vaporiferis iunctus fornacibus amnis
ridet anhelantes vicino flumine Nymphas?
        Vidi artes veterumque manus variisque metalla

---

²⁴ tectum mit- *Courtney*: nec clementissimus *Koch*
²⁶ fluviumve *Politianus*: fluviorum M   obstare *Calderini*:
opt- M   ³¹⁻² nec . . . nec* *scripsi*: sic . . . sic M
³² reflui ⊊: fluvii M
⁴¹ tuta *Politianus*: tota M
⁴² aut *scripsi*: et M   pigros *Heinsius*: ni- M   invitant
Peyrarède: mutantia *vel* imit- M

filled slumbers. Either shore is at home, nor does the gentle river divide you.[4] Stately mansions keep either bank, no strangers to each other, nor complain that the river blocks them: let Fame now boast of Sestos' bay and the sea a swimmer swam and dolphins outmatched by a bold stripling![5] Here is eternal quiet, storms have no jurisdiction, waters never boil. Here view and voice may be passed across, hands almost; neither do tidal waves drive Chalcis away nor does the Bruttian strand gaze on Sicanian Pelorus, sundered by the deep.[6]

What shall I sing to begin with or halfway, on what ending shall I fall silent? Shall I wonder at gilded beams or Moorish doorposts[7] everywhere or marble lucent with colours or water discharged through every bedchamber? Eyes draw me one way, mind another. Shall I tell of the venerable age of the groves? Of the courtyard that views the river's course below or that other looking back to the silent woods, where your rest is safe and night, impaired by no turbulence, is silent, or murmurs invite lazy slumber? Or of the steaming baths taken up by their grassy ledge and fire imposed on chilly banks, where the river linked to a vaporous furnace laughs at the Nymphs as they pant, though the stream be hard by?

Works of art I saw, creations of old masters, metals vari-

[4] Perhaps to be borne in mind is the use of *me* and *te* with prepositions for 'my (your) house,' e.g. in Terence, *Phormio* 795 *meum virum ex te exire video*.

[5] Leander, who swam the Hellespont (and drowned).

[6] See Critical Appendix.

[7] Of Mauritanian citrus wood.

viva modis. labor est auri memorare figuras
aut ebur aut dignas digitis contingere gemmas,
50 quicquid et argento primum vel in aere minori
lusit et enormes manus expertura colossos.
dum vagor aspectu visusque per omnia duco
calcabam necopinus opes. nam splendor ab alto
defluus et nitidum referentes aëra testae
55 monstravere solum, varias ubi picta per artes
gaudet humus superatque novis asarota figuris.
expavere gradus.

              Quid nunc iungentia mirer
aut quid partitis distantia tecta trichoris?
quid te, quae mediis servata penatibus arbor
60 tecta per et postes liquidas emergis in auras,
quo non sub domino saevas passura bipennes?
at nunc ignaro forsan vel lubrica Nais
vel non abruptos tibi debet Hamadryas annos.
    Quid referam alternas gemino super aggere mensas
65 algentesque lacus altosque in gurgite fontes,
teque, per obliquum penitus quae laberis amnem,
Marcia, et audaci transcurris flumina plumbo,
ne solum Ioniis sub fluctibus Elidis amnem
dulcis ad Aetnaeos deducat semita portus?
70 illic ipse antris Anien et fonte relicto
nocte sub arcana glaucos exutus amictus
huc illuc fragili praesternit pectora musco,

---

[57] iungentia *Calderini*: ing- M   *post* 57 *versum excidisse
putavit Otto*   [62] at *Gronovius*: et M
   [63] debet *Jortin*: demet M
   [65] algentesque *Heinsius*: albe- M   aliosque *Bernartius*
   [70] illic *Krohn*: illis M   [72] praesternit* *scripsi*: pros- M

66

ously alive. 'Tis labour to list the golden figures or the ivory or gems fit to adorn fingers or all that artist's imagination wrought, first in silver or bronze miniature, then to attempt huge colossi. As I wandered agaze and cast my eyes over it all, I suddenly found myself treading wealth. For radiance streaming from aloft and tiles reflecting the dazzle showed a bright floor where the ground rejoiced in painting's variety, with strange shapes surpassing the Unswept Pavement.[8] My steps were aghast.

Why now should I wonder at connecting structures or those distanced in separate stories?[9] Why at the tree preserved in the dwelling's midst, rising through ceilings and doorways to emerge in the open, sure to suffer the cruel axe under any other master? But now it may be that some little Nymph or Hamadryad owes you unbroken years, to you unknown.

Why should I relate the tables alternate on the double bank or cool pools and springs deep under water or you, Marcia, gliding far down athwart the river, your daring lead running across its flow? Or should only Elis' stream be led by a salt-free path below Ionian waters to Aetnaean haven? There Anio himself, leaving grotto and fount in the secrecy of night, stript of his grey-green garb moves this way and that, spreading his chest[10] with fragile moss; or his

[8] A celebrated mosaic floor in Pergamum representing scraps from a banquet (Pliny, *Natural History* 36.184).

[9] Text and interpretation doubtful.

[10] See Critical Appendix.

aut ingens in stagna cadit vitreasque natatu
plaudit aquas. illa recubat Tiburnus in umbra,
75   illic sulpureos cupit Albula mergere crines.
      Haec domus Egeriae nemoralem abiungere Phoeben
et Dryadum viduare choris algentia possit
Taygeta et silvis accersere Pana Lycaeis.
quod ni templa darent alias Tirynthia sortes,
80   et Praenestinae poterant migrare sorores.
quid bifera Alcinoi laudem pomaria vosque,
qui numquam vacui prodistis in aethera, rami?
cedant Telegoni, cedant Laurentia Turni
iugera Lucrinaeque domus litusque cruenti
85   Antiphatae, cedant vitreae iuga perfida Circes
Dulichiis ululata lupis, arcesque superbae
Anxuris et sedes Phrygio quas mitis alumno
debet anus, cedant quae te iam solibus artis
Antia nimbosa revocabunt litora bruma.
90   Scilicet hic illi meditantur pondera mores;
hic premitur fecunda quies, virtusque serena
fronte gravis sanusque nitor luxuque carentes
deliciae, quas ipse suis digressus Athenis
mallet deserto senior Gargettius horto.
95   haec per et Aegaeas hiemes Hyadumque nivosum

89 Antia *Politianus*: avia M
95 Hyadumque *Heinsius*: plia- M

---

11 I.e. take Egeria away from the Arician grove where she served Diana (not the other way round).

12 In the temple of Fortune at Praeneste lots were cast to foretell the future. The 'sisters' would be tempted to migrate to Tibur, were it not that a (presumably) oracular temple of Hercules

68

bulk plunges into the stream and splashes the glassy waters as he swims. In that shade reclines Tiburnus, there Albula would fain dip her sulphurous hair.

This house could part Phoebe from Egeria,[11] deprive chill Taygetus of his choirs of Dryads, and summon Pan from the woods of Lycaeus. And if the Tityrnthian shrine did not give other oracles, the sisters of Praeneste[12] could migrate. Why should I laud the twice-bearing orchards of Alcinous and the boughs that never stretched empty to the sky?[13] Let Telegonus' fields[14] and the Laurentian acres of Turnus yield, and the Lucrine dwellings and bloody Antiphates' shore; likewise the treacherous ridge of glassy Circe, where Dulichian wolves[15] howled, and Anxur's proud citadel and the home that the old dame owes to her Phrygian nurseling; likewise Antium's shores that will call you back when suns are narrowed in rainy midwinter.

Here for sure your way of life meditates weighty matters, here hides fertile repose and strenuous virtue with brow serene and sober elegance and enjoyment sans luxury, such as the old man of Gargettus would have preferred and left his Athens and forsaken the garden.[16] This to visit were worth a voyage through Aegean storms and the

---

was already there. Elsewhere we hear of only one Fortune at Praeneste, but there were two oracular Fortunes at Antium, the 'truth-telling sisters' of Martial 5.1.3.　　　[13] Pleonastic, but in the Latin the boughs are apostrophized.　　　[14] Tusculum. The other places indicated are: Ardea, Baiae, Circeii, Anxur (Tarracina), Caieta (where Aeneas' nurse was buried), and Antium.

[15] Ulysses' crew as transformed by Circe's magic.

[16] Epicurus established his philosophical school in his Athenian 'Garden.'

sidus et Oleniis dignum petiisse sub astris,
si Maleae credenda ratis Siculosque per aestus
sit via. cur oculis sordet vicina voluptas?
hic tua Tiburtes Faunos chelys et iuvat ipsum
100   Alciden dictumque lyra maiore Catillum,
seu tibi Pindaricis animus contendere plectris
sive chelyn tollas heroa ad robora sive
liventem saturam nigra rubigine vibres
seu tua non alia splendescat epistula cura.
105   Digne Midae Croesique bonis et Perside gaza,
macte bonis animi, cuius stagnantia rura
debuit et flavis Hermus transcurrere ripis
et limo splendente Tagus. sic docta frequentes
otia, sic omni detertus pectora nube
110   finem Nestoreae precor egrediare senectae.

I.4

SOTERIA RUTILI GALLICI

Estis, io, superi, nec inexorabile Clotho
volvit opus. videt alma pios Astraea Iovique
conciliata redit, dubitataque sidera cernit
Gallicus. es caelo, dive es Germanice cordi

---

¹⁰³ vibres *Scriverius*: turbes M   rivis *Bentley*
¹⁰⁹ detertus *Housman* (detersus *iam Heinsius*): detectus M
⁴ dive es *Politianus* (*cf. Ov. Trist. 3.1.78*): dives M: dis es ⊆

---

¹⁷ Known as Capella (Nanny Goat), rising in the rainy season.
The epithet 'Olenian' is variously explained; see J. G. Frazer, *The
Fasti of Ovid,* on *Fasti* 5.251.

snowy constellation of the Hyades under Olenian star,[17] though the ship must be trusted to Malea and the way lie through Sicily's surge.[18] Why do our eyes scorn pleasure near at hand? Here your lyre delights Tibur's Fauns and Alcides himself and Catillus, named by a greater harp,[19] whether you are minded to vie with Pindar's quill or lift your instrument to the doughty deeds of heroes or brandish satire, black with envy's venom,[20] or give no less care to your sparkling letters.[21]

O worthy of the wealth of Midas and Croesus and the treasure of Persia, hail to your soul's riches! Hermus should traverse your flooded fields with his yellow channel and Tagus with his shining silt. So may you cultivate learned leisure, I pray, so pass the limit of Nestor's age, and every cloud be wiped away from your heart.

I.4

TO RUTILIUS GALLICUS ON HIS RECOVERY

Hurrah! O High Ones, you exist and Clotho's spinning is not inexorable. Kindly Astraea[1] regards the pious and returns reconciled to Jove, and Gallicus sees the stars he despaired of. Heaven loves you, Germanicus, who would

---

[18] The dangerous Strait of Messina.

[19] Virgil's no doubt (*Aeneid* 7.672), though Horace also mentions him (*Odes* 1.18.2, *Cātili*).

[20] Lit. 'livid with black salt,' but *liventem* suggests *livor*, 'envy.'

[21] In verse presumably.

[1] Justice, who had left heaven in disgust; cf. V.3.90.

5 (quis neget?); erubuit tanto spoliare ministro
   imperium Fortuna tuum. stat proxima cervix

                    *   *   *   *   *

   ponderis immensi damnosaque fila senectae
   exuit atque alios melior revirescit in annos.
   ergo alacres quae signa colunt urbana cohortes
10 inque sinum quae saepe tuum fora turbida questum
   confugiunt leges urbesque ubicumque togatae
   quae tua longinquis implorant iura querelis
   certent laetitia, nostrique ex ordine colles
   confremite, et sileant peioris murmura famae.
15 quippe manet longumque aevo redeunte manebit
   quem penes intrepidae mitis custodia Romae,
   nec tantum induerint fatis nova saecula crimen
   aut instaurati peccaverit ara Tarenti.
       Ast ego nec Phoebum, quamquam mihi surda sine illo
20 plectra, nec Aonias decima cum Pallade divas
   aut mitem Tegeae Dircesve hortabor alumnum;
   ipse veni viresque novas animumque ministra
   qui caneris; docto nec enim sine numine nactus
   Ausoniae decora ampla togae centumque dedisti
25 iudicium mentemque viris. licet enthea vatis

       post 6 versum excidisse statuit Courtney
       10 questum *Markland*: -tu M   13 nostrique . . . colles
   Merrill: nosterque . . . collis M: septemplexque ordine collis *coni.*
   Courtney   14 confremite *Imhof*: -mat M
       23 nactus *Behotius*: tantus M

   _____

   2 Four Urban cohorts under Gallicus' command as City
   Prefect.
   3 Gallicus presided over the highest court of criminal jurisdiction, hearing cases from all over Italy.

deny it? Fortune thought shame to rob your rule of such a minister. The neck next to yours is upright * * * immeasurable weight, casting off old age's noxious thread, and grows young again for other years, better than ever. So let the smart cohorts[2] that worship our city standards, and the laws that ofttime flee to your bosom to complain of courts in turmoil, and gowned cities, wherever they be, that with distant plaints implore your justice,[3] vie in happiness; and Hills of Rome, in sequence raise a shout and let the murmurs of worser rumour be mum. For he stays and long shall stay in life returning, he with whom resides the gentle ward of fear-free Rome. With no such reproach shall our new era charge the Fates nor shall Tarentus'[4] altar now restored commit so grievous a fault.

But for my part I shall not call on Phoebus, though without him my lyre is dumb, nor the Aonian goddesses with Pallas as their tenth, nor the gentle nurseling of Tegea or of Dirce:[5] come in person and grant me new strength and spirit, you that are my theme. For not without divine power of eloquence did you attain the ample distinctions of Ausonia's gown and give judgment and wisdom to the Hundred.[6] Though inspired Pimplea shut out the poet's

---

[4] The Roman Tarentum was a depression in the Campus Martius associated with the celebration of Secular games, most recently by Domitian in 87. But as J. G. Frazer (*The Fasti of Ovid,* II, pp. 195f.) pointed out, Statius (also in IV.1.38) and Martial 4.1.8 'seem to have forgotten Tarentum as the name of the place where the games were held and to have converted it into a hero named Tarentus or Tarentos, in whose honour the festival was held.'   [5] I.e. Mercury or Bacchus.

[6] The court of the Centumviri with civil jurisdiction.

excludat Piplea sitim nec conscia detur
Pirene, largos potior mihi gurges in haustus
qui rapitur de fonte tuo, seu plana solutis
cum struis orsa modis seu cum tibi dulcis in artem
30   frangitur et nostras curat facundia leges.
quare age, si Cereri sua dona merumque Lyaeo
reddimus, et dives praedae tamen accipit omni
exuvias Diana tholo captivaque tela
Bellipotens, nec tu (quando tibi, Gallice, maius
35   eloquium fandique opibus sublimis abundas)
sperne coli tenviore lyra. vaga cingitur astris
luna et in Oceanum rivi cecidere minores.
      Quae tibi sollicitus persolvit praemia morum
Urbis amor! quae tum patrumque equitumque notavi
40   lumina et ignarae plebis lugere potentes!
non labente Numa timuit sic curia felix
Pompeio nec celsus eques nec femina Bruto.
hoc illud, tristes invitum audire catenas,
parcere verberibus nec qua iubet alta potestas
45   ire, sed armatas multum sibi demere vires
dignarique manus humilis et verba precantum,
reddere iura foro nec proturbare curules
et ferrum mulcere toga. sic itur in alta
pectora, sic mixto reverentia cedit amori.

---

[27] potior ⊊: -ius M   [29–30] artum *Barth* angitur *coni.*
Courtney   [34] quamquam *Heinsius*
[45] ultro sibi *O. Skutsch*   [49] cedit* *scripsi*: fidit M

---

[7] Grammatically with *lumina,* 'of the common folk.' But for
lumina another noun, as 'crowds,' is mentally substituted by
zeugma, a figure much favoured by Statius. *Ignarae* is not 'un-

thirst and Pirene's partnership be denied, better for my
deep draughts is the flood snatched from your fountain,
whether you compose plain prose in measures uncon-
strained or your sweet flow of words be broken into rule
and respect our laws. So to work! If we return her own gifts
to Ceres and wine to Lyaeus, if spoil-rich Diana accepts
trophies in every dome and the Lord of War our captured
weapons: Gallicus, do not scorn the tribute of a humbler
lyre because your voice is mightier and you abound sub-
limely in wealth of speech. The wandering moon is girt
with stars and lesser streams descend to Ocean.

What reward of virtue did Rome's anxious affection pay
you! What luminaries of Senate and Knights did I then
note, and the common folk[7] not wont to mourn the powerful! Not so afraid was the flourishing Senate House when
Numa was failing, nor the noble Knights for Pompey, nor
the women for Brutus.[8] And here is why: to hear unwilling
the clank of chains, to spare the lash nor go where height of
power commands but rather renounce much of one's own
armed might, to pay heed to humble pleas and the words of
petitioners, to give justice to the Forum and yet not push
aside the civil authorities—that is the way to go deep into
hearts, thus does reverence yield to[9] the love it mingles

known, obscure,' as Vollmer, but 'not knowing' (in the normal
course of things).   [8] Pompey's illness in 50 B.C. inspired
widespread demonstrations of concern among the Italian bour-
geoisie. Rome's married women mourned Brutus, the first Consul, for a year (another zeugma: *luxerunt occiso* mentally replaces
timuerunt labente). Numa was supposed to have died after a lingering illness (Plutarch, *Numa* 21).

   [9] See Critical Appendix.

50 ipsa etiam cunctos gravis inclementia Fati
    terruit et subiti praeceps iuvenile pericli
    nil cunctante malo. non illud culpa senectae
    (quippe ea bis senis vixdum orsa excedere lustris),
    sed labor intendens animique in membra vigentis
55 imperium vigilesque suo pro Caesare curae,
    dulce opus. hinc fessos penitus subrepsit in artus
    insidiosa quies et pigra oblivio vitae.
       Tunc deus, Alpini qui iuxta culmina dorsi
    signat Apollineos sancto cognomine lucos,
60 respicit heu tanti pridem securus alumni,
    praegressusque moras: 'hinc mecum, Epidauria proles,
    hinc' ait 'i gaudens. datur (aggredienda facultas)
    ingentem recreare virum. teneamus adorti
    tendentes iam fila colos. ne fulminis atri
65 sit metus: has ultro laudabit Iuppiter artes.
    nam neque plebeiam aut dextro sine numine cretam
    servo animam. atque adeo breviter, dum tecta subimus,
    expediam. genus ipse suis permissaque retro
    nobilitas; nec origo latet, sed luce sequente
70 vincitur et magno gaudet cessisse nepoti.
    prima togae virtus illi quoque: clarus et ingens
    eloquio; mox innumeris exercita castris
    occiduas primasque domos et sole sub omni

           *   *   *   *   *

    permeruit iurata manus, nec in otia pacis
75 permissum laxare animos ferrumque recingi.
    hunc Galatea vigens ausa est incessere bello

---

     61 praegressusque ⌐: prog- M: praecidensque *Housman*
hinc ⌐: hunc M   64 tendentis *Perrotto, Markland*: -datis M
post 73 *versum excidisse agnovit Housman*

76

with. The very cruelty of oppressive Fate terrified us all, the headlong thrust of sudden peril as the mischief made no pause. That was not the fault of his age, for scarce had it begun to pass twice six lustres, but stress of work, the rule of a strong mind over the body, cares vigilant for his Caesar, labour of love. Hence insidious rest crept deep into the weary limbs and sluggish oblivion of life.

Then the god that hard by the peaks of the Alpine ridge marks Apollonian groves with his sacred name[10] turns eyes too long alas! unregarding of such a favourite, and forestalling delay, 'Come with me now, my son of Epidaurus,'[11] he says, 'come in joy. The chance is offered, one to be seized, to restore a man of mighty mould. Let us go and grasp the distaff as it stretches the threads. Let there be no fear of the black thunderbolt:[12] Jove will be first to praise our skill. For 'tis no common life I save, born unblessed by deity. Himself he is pedigree for his own, he lets nobility go backward. Nor are his origins obscure, but eclipsed by brilliance to come they rejoice to yield to their great progeny. He too[13] first showed his mettle in the gown. Famous and mighty his eloquence. Then his hand sworn to service did duty in countless camps, east and west under every sun * * * , nor was he allowed to relax his energy in peaceful leisure and ungird his sword. Lusty Galatia dared assail

[10] These otherwise unknown woods were presumably near Turin, Gallicus' birthplace.

[11] Aesculapius (Asclepius).

[12] With which Jupiter had once destroyed Aesculapius as a punishment for bringing the dead Hippolytus back to life.

[13] Like his forbears.

(me quoque!) per⟨que⟩ novem timuit Pamphylia messes
Pannoniusque ferox arcuque horrenda fugaci
Armenia et patiens Latii iam pontis Araxes.

80   quid geminos fasces magnaeque iterata revolvam
iura Asiae? velit illa quidem ter habere quaterque
hunc sibi, sed revocant fasti maiorque curulis
nec promissa semel. Libyci quid mira tributi
obsequia et missum media de pace triumphum

85   laudem et opes quantas nec qui mandaverat ausus
exspectare fuit, [gaudet Trasimennus et Alpes]

86a   attollam cantu? gaudet Trasimennus et Alpes
Cannensesque animae; primusque insigne tributum
ipse palam laeta noscebat Regulus umbra.
non vacat Arctoas acies Rhenumque rebellem

90   captivaeque preces Veledae et, quae maxima nuper
gloria, depositam Dacis pereuntibus Urbem
pandere, cum tanti lectus rectoris habenas,
Gallice, Fortuna non admirante subisti.

        Hunc igitur, si digna loquor, rapiemus iniquo,

95   nate, Iovi. rogat hoc Latiae pater inclitus urbis
et meruit; neque enim frustra mihi nuper honora
carmina patricio, pueri, sonuistis in ostro.
si qua salutifero gemini Chironis in antro

---

83 permissa* ⌐   84 iustum *Markland*
85 quantas *Perrotto, Grotius*: ta- M
86 fuit ⟨laudatis impare factis⟩ *tempt. Postgate*
88 noscebat *Baehrens*: po- M

---

14 A host of Gauls attacked Delphi in 279 B.C. Gallicus' own
name is ignored.   15 The Praetorship (two lictors).
16 The Consulship.   17 See Critical Appendix.

him in war (me too),[14] and through nine harvests Pamphylia feared him, as did the bold Pannonian and Armenia, formidable with fleeing bow, and Araxes that now brooks a Latian bridge. Why tell of the double rods[15] and two terms as Asia's governor? She to be sure would wish for a third and fourth, but the Fasti and a greater curule chair,[16] promised[17] more than once, call him home. Why praise the wondrous compliance of Libya's tribute, triumph sent to Rome from the midst of peace, and exalt in song such wealth as not even he that commissioned you[18] had dared expect? * * * Trasimene and the Alps and the ghosts of Cannae rejoice, and first of all Regulus himself appeared, his happy shade taking note of the splendid tribute. Time lacks to set forth the armies of the north and rebel Rhine, the prayers of Veleda, and, greatest and latest glory, Rome placed in your charge as the Dacians were perishing, when you, Gallicus, were chosen to take the reins from so great a ruler,[19] to Fortune no surprise.

Him then, my son, if my words be meet, shall we snatch from the adverse Jove.[20] The renowned father of the Latian city demands it; for not for nothing, you boys, did you lately sound your song in my honour, clad in patrician purple.[21] If there be any herb in Chiron's health-giving

---

[18] Vespasian, who had put up taxes in certain provinces. Gallicus will have been sent to Africa to look after the business there.   [19] Domitian went to the campaign.

[20] Dis (Pluto) in the Underworld. Jupiter proper was benevolent (v. 65).   [21] At the Secular games in 87. At the previous celebration by Augustus, Horace's *Carmen Saeculare* was sung by a choir of boys and girls, so *pueri* will cover *puellae*. One wonders who wrote the hymn this time.

herba, tholo quodcumque tibi Troiana recondit
100 Pergamos aut medicis felix Epidaurus harenis
educat, Idaea profert quam Creta sub umbra
dictamni florentis opem, quoque anguis abundat
spumatu—iungam ipse manus atque omne benignum
virus odoriferis Arabum quod doctus in arvis
105 aut Amphrysiaco pastor de gramine carpsi.'
    Dixerat. inveniunt positos iam segniter artus
pugnantemque animam; ritu se cingit uterque
Paeonio monstrantque simul parentque volentes,
donec letiferas vario medicamine pestes
110 et suspecta mali ruperunt nubila somni.
adiuvat ipse deos morboque valentior omni
occupat auxilium. citius non arte refectus
Telephus Haemonia, nec quae metuentis Atridae
saeva Machaonio coierunt vulnera suco.
115   Quis mihi tot coetus inter populique patrumque
sit curae votique locus? tamen ardua testor
sidera teque, pater vatum Thymbraee, quis omni
luce mihi, quis nocte timor, dum postibus haerens
assiduus nunc aure vigil nunc lumine cuncta
120 aucupor; immensae veluti conexa carinae
cumba minor, cum saevit hiems, pro parte furentes
parva receptat aquas et eodem volvitur austro.
    Nectite nunc laetae candentia fila, sorores,
nectite, nemo modum transmissi computet aevi:

103 benignum *Lindenbrog*: -ne M
105 carpsi *Calderini* -sit M   118 haerens ⊊: -ret M
120 aucupor *Heinsius*: auguror M

cave, whatever Trojan Pergamus stores for you in your temple or fortunate Epidaurus raises in her healing sands, the virtue of flowering dittany that Crete brings forth under Ida's foliage, the foam in which your snake abounds—I myself shall join my hands, and every salutary juice that shepherd was taught to gather on Arabia's fragrant fields or I from Amphrysus' herbage.'[22]

He had spoken. They find the limbs lying in languor now, breath struggling. Both gird themselves Paeonian fashion[23] and together they readily give and take advice until with various medicine they have broken the banes and the sinister cloud of unwholesome sleep. He himself assists the gods; stronger than all his malady, he anticipates their aid. No more swiftly was Telephus cured by Haemonian skill nor fearful Atrides' cruel wounds closed by Machaon's balm.

Amid so many gatherings of Fathers and people what room for anxious prayers of mine? Yet I call the stars on high and you, Thymbraean, father of poets, to witness how I spent every day and night in terror, ever clinging to the doorway, watchful to pick up every hint now with eye, now with ear; as a little skiff attached to a great ship, when the storm blows high, takes in her small share of the raging waters and tosses in the same south wind.

Now, Sisters, merrily twine your white threads, twine them. Let none reckon the measure of life spent; this will

[22] Courtney retains *carpsit,* since Apollo is not recorded to have spent time in Arabia. Possibly careless writing, so to be expanded: *quod pastor doctus in Arabum arvis carpsit aut quod ego pastor Amphrysiaco de gramine carpsi* (cf. Virgil, *Georgics* 3.2 *pastor ab Amphryso*).

[23] Cf. *Aeneid* 12.400f.

125   hic vitae natalis erit. tu Troica dignus
saecula et Euboici transcendere pulveris annos
Nestoreique situs. qua nunc tibi pauper acerra
digna litem? nec si vacuet Mevania valles
aut praestent niveos Clitumna novalia tauros,
130   sufficiam. sed saepe deis hos inter honores
caespes et exiguo placuerunt farra salino.

I.5

BALNEUM CLAUDI ETRUSCI

Non Helicona gravi pulsat chelys enthea plectro
nec lassata voco totiens mihi numina Musas:
et te, Phoebe, choris et te, dimittimus, Euhan;
tu quoque muta ferae, volucer Tegeaee, sonorae
5   terga premas. alios poscunt mea carmina coetus.
Naidas, undarum dominas, regemque corusci
ignis adhuc fessum Siculaque incude rubentem
elicuisse satis. paulum arma nocentia, Thebae,
ponite; dilecto volo lascivire sodali.
10   iunge, puer, cyathos, sed ne numerare labora
cunctantemque intende chelyn; discede, Laborque
Curaque, dum nitidis canimus gemmantia saxis
balnea dumque procax vittis hederisque soluta

127 Nestoreique *Ker*: -osque M
10 sed ne num- *Scriverius*: et enum M
11 intende ⌐: ince- M

---

24 Priam's or Tithonus' (though the latter was immortal).
25 Apollo had granted the Sibyl of Cumae's wish for as many

be his life's birthday. Worthy are you to transcend Trojan centuries[24] and the years of Euboean dust[25] and Nestor's decay. Poor man that I am, how find a censer to make worthy offering on your behalf? Not though Mevania make void her vales or Clitumnus' acres supply their snowy bulls would I have enough. Yet often among such tributes has a sod of earth with meal and tiny saltcellar found favour with the gods.

I.5

THE BATHS OF CLAUDIUS ETRUSCUS

My frenzied lyre does not strike Helicon with weighty quill[1] nor do I invoke the Muses, the deities whom I have so often wearied. I dismiss you, Phoebus, from the choir, and you, Euhan. You too, winged one of Tegea, hide in silence the back of the tuneful beast.[2] My song calls on other assemblies. 'Tis enough to have drawn out the Naiads, mistresses of the waves, and the king of flashing fire,[3] still weary and ruddy with Sicilian anvil. Thebes, lay your guilty arms aside for a while.[4] I would frolic for a dear friend. Boy, pour cup on cup (but take no care to count them) and string the tarrying lyre. Begone Toil and Care, as I sing the Baths bejewelled with glistening marbles, and my Clio, wantoning in fillets and ivy and free of modest

years of life as there were grains in a sandheap (Ovid, *Metamorphoses* 14.136).

[1] As though knocking at the entrance.

[2] The tortoise shell from which Mercury invented the lyre.

[3] Vulcan.   [4] Work on the *Thebaid* is to be suspended.

fronde verecundo Clio mea ludit Etrusco.
15 ite, deae virides, liquidosque advertite vultus
et vitreum teneris crinem redimite corymbis
veste nihil tectae, quales emergitis altis
fontibus et visu Satyros torquetis amantes.
non vos quae culpa decus infamastis aquarum
20 sollicitare iuvat; procul hinc et fonte doloso
Salmacis et viduae Cebrenidos arida luctu
flumina et Herculei praedatrix cedat alumni.
vos mihi quae Latium septenaque culmina, Nymphae,
incolitis Thybrimque novis attollitis undis,
25 quas praeceps Anien atque exceptura natatus
Virgo iuvat Marsasque nives et frigora ducens
Marcia, praecelsis quarum vaga molibus unda
crescit et innumero pendens transmittitur arcu,
vestrum opus aggredimur, vestra est quam carmine molli
pando domus.
30   Non umquam aliis habitastis in antris
ditius. ipsa manus tenuit Cytherea mariti
monstravitque artes, neu vilis flamma caminos
ureret, ipsa faces volucrum succendit Amorum.
non huc admissae Thasos aut undosa Carystos;
35 maeret onyx longe queriturque exclusus ophites:
sola nitet flavis Nomadum decisa metallis
39 quoique Tyri livens fleat et Sidonia, rupes,
37 purpura, sola cavo Phrygiae quam Synnados antro
ipse cruentavit maculis lucentibus Attis.

    14 fronte ⊊   verecunda *Baehrens*
    29 molli ⊊: nulli M
    39 quoique *Housman, versu huc traiecto*: quoque M   livens
fleat *Courtney*: niveas secat M

leafage,[5] sports for Etruscus. Come, green goddesses, and
turn this way your liquid faces, bind your glossy hair with
tender clusters, as when you come out from your deep
springs and torment your Satyr lovers with the sight. But I
would not trouble those among you that have defamed the
waters' beauty by guilt. Far hence be Salmacis with her
treacherous fount and the stream of Cebron's deserted
daughter that grief made dry,[6] and she that ravished Hercules' favourite.[7] You Nymphs that dwell in Latium and the
Seven Hills and raise Tiber with fresh waters, you that fast
Anio delights and the Virgin who shall welcome swimmers,
and Marcia, bringer of Marsian snows and chills[8]—you
whose vagrant water multiplies on towering masses, trans-
mitted in the air by countless arches: yours is the work I
attempt, yours the mansion my soft song unfolds.

In no other grotto did you ever dwell in wealthier style.
Cytherea herself held her husband's hands and showed
them cunning; and lest a common flame burn the furnace,
she herself set alight the torches of her winged Loves. Not
Thasos or wavy Carystos are admitted here, alabaster sulks
afar, serpentine grumbles in exclusion; shines only stone
hewn from Numidia's yellow quarries and that other at
which Tyre's and Sidon's purple would weep for envy,[9]
only what Attis himself bloodied with gleaming flecks in

[5] The Muse (invoked or not) is to exchange Apollo's laurel and
white fillets for Bacchus' ivy and purple fillets; cf. II.7.9.

[6] See Index. The drying up seems not to be mentioned elsewhere.   [7] Hylas.

[8] Two famous aqueducts. The Marcia carried water for drink-
ing. Both contributed to Etruscus' baths; cf. Martial 6.42.18.

[9] Porphyry; cf. I.2.151, I.5.39.

85

40 vix locus Eurotae, viridis cum regula longo
Synnada distinctu variat. non limina cessant,
effulgent camerae, vario fastigia vitro
in species animata nitent. stupet ipse beatas
circumplexus opes et parcius imperat ignis.
45 multus ubique dies, radiis ubi culmina totis
perforat atque alio sol improbus uritur aestu.
nil ibi plebeium. nusquam Temesaea notabis
aera, sed argento felix propellitur unda
argentoque cadit, labrisque nitentibus instat
50 delicias mirata suas et abire recusat.
extra autem niveo qui margine caerulus amnis
vivit et in summum fundo patet omnis ab imo
cui non ire lacu pigrosque exsolvere amictus
suadeat? hoc mallet nasci Cytherea profundo,
55 hic te perspicuum melius, Narcisse, videres,
hic velox Hecate velit et deprensa lavari.
quid nunc strata solo referam tabulata crepantes
auditura pilas, ubi languidus ignis inerrat
aedibus et tenuem volvunt hypocausta vaporem?
60 nec si Baianis veniat novus hospes ab oris
talia despiciet (fas sit componere magnis
parva), Neronea nec qui modo lotus in unda
hic iterum sudare neget. macte, oro, nitenti
ingenio curaque, puer! tecum ista senescant
65 et tua iam melius discat fortuna renasci.

40 dum *coni. Courtney*
43 animata *Markland*: -moque M
52 summum fundo ⊊: fundum summo M

Synnas' hollow cave. Scarce is there space for Eurotas, whose long green streak picks out Synnas. The doorways are not behindhand, the ceilings are effulgent, the topmost parts are alive, shining with figures in vitreous variety. The very fire is amazed at the riches it surrounds and moderates its sway. Daylight everywhere abounds as the unconscionable sun penetrates the roof with all his rays, and is burned by a different heat. Nothing vulgar is here. Nowhere will you mark Temesean copper; by silver the happy flow is channelled and into silver falls, urging the bright brims, marvelling at its own charms and loath to leave. Outside a dark-blue river runs between snow-white banks in lively stream, clear from bed to surface; whom would it not persuade to fling off his sluggish clothes and plunge into the pool? From this deep would Cytherea rather have been born, herein, Narcissus, you would have seen yourself more clear, here swift Hecate would have been fain to bathe, even though surprised.[10] Why now should I relate the flooring strewn upon the ground to hear the sounding balls, where the fire strays faintly about the house and the furnaces roll up a mild warmth? Were a stranger to come from Baiae's shores, he would not scorn the like of this (lawful be it to compare great with small), nor would a bather fresh from Nero's water refuse to sweat here a second time. Hail, my boy, to your brilliant wit and care! Let all this grow old along with you and may your fortune now learn to be reborn better than before![11]

[10] As Hecate = Diana was by Actaeon.
[11] Etruscus' father had been in exile but the sentence had evidently just been lifted; cf. III.3.165–67.

I.6

KALENDAE DECEMBRES

    Et Phoebus pater et severa Pallas
et Musae procul ite feriatae:
Iani vos revocabimus kalendis.
Saturnus mihi compede exsoluta
5   et multo gravidus mero December
et ridens Iocus et Sales protervi
adsint, dum refero diem beatum
laeti Caesaris ebriamque aparchen.
    Vix Aurora novos movebat ortus,
10   iam bellaria linea pluebant:
hunc rorem veniens profudit Eurus.
quicquid nobile Ponticis nucetis
fecundis cadit aut iugis Idumes
quod ramis pia germinat Damascos
15   et quod percoquit Ebosea Caunos
largis gratuitum cadit rapinis,
molles gaïoli lucuntulique
et massis amerina non perustis
et mustaceus et latente palma
20   praegnantes caryotides cadebant.
non tantis Hyas inserena nimbis
terras obruit aut soluta Plias
qualis per cuneos hiems Latinos
plebem grandine contudit serena.
25   ducat nubila Iuppiter per orbem
et latis pluvias minetur agris
dum nostri Iovis hi ferantur imbres.

---

[8] aparchen *Phillimore, coll. Plut. Moral. 2.40B*: parcen M

I.6

THE KALENDS OF DECEMBER

Father Phoebus and stern Pallas and you Muses, away with you, take a holiday! We will call you back on Janus' Kalends. Let Saturn join me free of his chains[1] and wine-soaked December and laughing Jollity and wanton Jests, as I relate merry Caesar's joyous day and the tipsy feast.

Scarce was Aurora moving another dawn and already dainties were raining from the line—such the dew that rising East Wind poured down: the best that falls in Pontic nutteries or Idume's fertile hills,[2] what pious Damascus grows[3] upon her boughs and what Ebosean Caunus ripens[4]—free of charge descends the lavish loot. Mannikins[5] and pastries, Ameria's solidities unscorched,[6] must cakes and pregnant dates from an invisible palm[7]—down they fell. With no such showers does stormy Hyas deluge the earth as the tempest that pounded the Latian theatre with hail from a clear sky. Let Jupiter bring clouds throughout the world and threaten rains on the broad acres so long as our own Jove sends us downpours like these.

[1] Saturn was put in chains by his son Jupiter but freed to attend his annual festival.   [2] Dates.   [3] Plums. Many deities were worshipped there.   [4] Figs. See Critical Appendix.
[5] Gaïoli ('little Gaiuses'), pastries in the shape of a human figure.   [6] Apples and pears, picked in good time.
[7] Somehow different from ordinary dates mentioned in v. 13.

---

15 Ebosia* Vollmer: aeb- M   23 quali Markland
24 contudit ς: concu- M: concutit ς
26 laetis Morel, fort. recte

Ecce autem caveas subit per omnes
insignis specie, decora cultu
30   plebes altera non minor sedente.
hi panaria candidasque mappas
subvectant epulasque lautiores,
illi marcida vina largiuntur;
Idaeos totidem putes ministros.
35   orbem qua melior severiorque est
et gentes alis insemel togatas;
et cum tot populos, beate, pascas,
hunc Annona diem superba nescit.
i nunc, saecula compara, Vetustas,
40   antiqui Iovis aureumque tempus:
non sic libera vina tunc fluebant
nec tardum seges occupabat annum.
una vescitur omnis ordo mensa,
parvi, femina, plebs, eques, senatus:
45   libertas reverentiam remisit.
et tu quin etiam (quis hoc vocare,
quis promittere possit hoc deorum?)
nobiscum socias dapes inisti.
iam se, quisquis is est, inops beatus,
50   convivam ducis esse gloriatur.

      Hos inter fremitus novosque luxus
spectandi levis effugit voluptas.
stat sexus rudis insciusque ferri:
et pugnas capit improbus viriles.
55   credas ad Tanain ferumque Phasin
Thermodontiacas calere turmas.
hinc audax subit ordo pumilorum,

---

[37] beate *Hess*: -ta M   [38] nescis ⊊   [46] vocari *Ettig*

90

But look! Through all the aisles comes another crowd
no less in number than the seated throng, handsome and
smartly dressed. Some carry bread baskets and white nap-
kins and elegant eatables, others freely serve mellowing
wine. One could think them so many cupbearers from Ida.
At one and the same time you satisfy the Circle where it
is reformed and sobered[8] together with the peoples of
the gown; and since you feed so many folk, wealthy lord,
haughty Annona[9] knows not this day. Antiquity, compare if
you will the ages of ancient Jove[10] and the golden time: not
so freely did wine flow then, not thus would harvest forestall the tardy year. Every order eats at one table: children,
women, populace, Knights, Senate. Freedom has relaxed
reverence. Nay, you yourself (which of the gods could thus
invite, which accept invitation?)[11] entered the feast along
with us. Now everyone, be he rich or poor, boasts of dining
with the leader.

Amid such hubbub, such novel luxuries, the pleasure of
spectacle flits lightly by. The sex untrained and ignorant of
weaponry takes stand and dares engage in manly combat.
One would think them troops of Thermidon in battle heat
by Tanais or wild Phasis. Here comes a bold string of midg-

[8] The fourteen rows reserved for Knights in revival of earlier
practice. See Critical Appendix.

[9] The price of corn had become irrelevant.

[10] Saturn (*Saturnia saecla*).   [11] Domitian might be said to
have accepted his own invitation (*promittere,* 'promise [to come],'
is regular in this sense). *Hoc . . . hoc* are internal accusatives.

---

54 et ⊊: ut M   55 Phasin *coni. Courtney*: -im M
57 hinc ⊊: his *Barnartius*

quos Natura breves statim peracta
nodosum semel in globum ligavit.
60 edunt vulnera conseruntque dextras
et mortem sibi (qua manu!) minantur.
ridet Mars pater et cruenta Virtus
casuraeque vagis grues rapinis
mirantur †pumilos† ferociores.
65   Iam noctis proprioribus sub umbris
dives sparsio quos agit tumultus!
hic intrant faciles emi puellae,
hic agnoscitur omne quod theatris
aut forma placet aut probatur arte.
70 hoc plaudunt grege Lydiae tumentes,
illic cymbala tinnulaeque Gades,
illic agmina confremunt Syrorum.
hic plebs scenica quique comminutis
permutant vitreis gregale sulpur.
75   Inter quae subito cadunt volatu
immensae volucrum per astra nubes,
quas Nilus sacer horridusque Phasis,
quas udo Numidae legunt sub Austro.
desunt qui rapiant, sinusque pleni
80 gaudent dum nova lucra comparantur.
tollunt innumeras ad astra voces
Saturnalia principis sonantes
et dulci dominum favore clamant:
hoc solum vetuit licere Caesar.

64 pugiles *Friederich, vulg., perperam*: solito *conieci*
70 tumentes *neque damno neque intellego*

---

[12] Finding them fiercer than the Pygmies, whom they were

ets. Nature is cramped for them, finished in a trice, she
tied them once for all into knotted balls. They deal wounds
and mingle fists and threaten one another with death—by
what hands! Father Mars and bloody Valour laugh, and the
cranes, ready to swoop on their wandering prey, marvel at
their unusual (?) ferocity.[12]

Now as night's shades approach, a scattering of lar-
gesse[13] makes a fine commotion. Here enter girls[14] easily
bought; here is recognized whatever pleases the theatre
with comeliness or wins approval with skill. In one group
Lydian ladies[15] clap, elsewhere are cymbals and jingling
Gades, elsewhere again troops of Syrians make din. Here
is the mob of the stage and vendors of common sulphur[16]
for broken glass.

Meanwhile vast clouds of birds fall through the stars in
sudden flight such as holy Nile and rough Phasis and men
of Numidia[17] capture in a rainy South Wind. There are not
folk enough to snatch them all. Pockets fill gleefully as further gains are secured. They raise countless voices to the
stars, sounding the Emperor's Saturnalia, and acclaim him
Lord in loving favour. This licence only did Caesar ban.

accustomed to fight. *Pugiles* is generally read for *pŭmilos* (after
pūmilorum), but the Pygmies fought with weapons, not fists. I
have suggested *solito,* 'fiercer than usual,' regarding *pŭmilos* as a
marginal gloss that replaced it in the text.

[13] I.e. of vouchers (*tesserae*); cf. Martial 8.78.10.

[14] The vouchers would pay their fees.

[15] I have left *tumentes* untranslated, the most obvious meaning, 'pregnant,' seeming inappropriate.

[16] Matches; similarly Martial 1.41.4f. ('after considerable discussion the broken glass remains problematical').

[17] Flamingoes, pheasants, guinea fowl.

85 Vixdum caerula nox subibat orbem,
    escendit media nitens harena
    densas flammeus orbis inter umbras
    vincens Cnosiacae facem coronae.
    collucet polus ignibus nihilque
90 obscurae patitur licere nocti.
    fugit pigra Quies inersque Somnus
    haec cernens alias abit in urbes.
    quis spectacula, quis iocos licentes,
    quis convivia, quis dapes inemptas
95 largi flumina quis canat Lyaei?
    iamiam deficio tuoque Baccho
    in serum trahor ebrius soporem.
        Quos ibit procul hic dies per annos?
    quam nullo sacer exolescet aevo,
100 dum montes Latii paterque Thybris,
    dum stabit tua Roma dumque terris
    quod reddis Capitolium manebit!

⁸⁶ escendit* *Stange*: des- M
⁹⁶ tuoque ⊊: tuaque M   '*post* 96 *excidit versus huiusmodi,*
⟨fuso, dux bone, liberalitate⟩' *Courtney*
⁹⁹ *anne* quin?

Scarcely was dim night advancing upon the world when a flaming ball ascends from the centre of the arena shining in the dense gloom, surpassing the flare of the Cretan crown. The sky brightens with flames, allowing no license to night's obscurity. At the sight lazy Rest and Sleep must take off for other cities. Who should sing the shows, the unbridled jests, the banquets, the viands unbought,[18] the rivers of lavish Lyaeus? Now, now my strength fails and your Bacchus draws me tipsy into tardy slumber.

Through how many years shall this day travel? Sacred shall it endure throughout all time. So long as Latium's Hills and Father Tiber, so long as your Rome shall stand and the Capitol you restore to earth, it shall remain.

[18] See Critical Appendix.

BOOK TWO

PREFATORY NOTES

1

Martial's two epigrams on the same theme, 6.28 and 29, again point to late 90. Atedius Melior, recipient of Book II and two other of its constituents, was another wealthy patron (also of Martial), living in quiet elegance in his house on the Caelian hill. No mention of wife or family nor yet of literary or artistic pursuits.

2

Date: probably 90. Statius' visit to Pollius' villa in mid-August (vv. 6ff.) was in all probability the one mentioned in III.1.52ff., written about a year later. The proprietor of the villa, Pollius Felix, now apparently in his fifties, was born in Puteoli of a prominent local family and in his younger days took an active part in public life there and in Naples, of which he was also a citizen. In later years he devoted himself to poetry (vv. 112–15) and the philosophy of Epicurus (v. 113) along with building and improvements on his land, leaving financial management to his wife Polla (vv. 147–53). Other properties at Tibur, Limon near Puteoli, and Tarentum are mentioned (vv. 82,109–11).

From Statius' account the patron-client relationship had become a friendship, based on similarities of taste

and temperament. He was also on good terms with Polla
and Pollius' son-in-law Julius Menecrates, also of Naples
(IV.epist. and 8).

3

This birthday present to Melior (v. 62; 'Pollius' in Vollmer
is a slip) and the three following pieces offer no special
indication of date.

5

See on I.2.102. The theme of tame lion (and hare) is serial
in Martial's first Book.

LIBER SECUNDUS

Et familiaritas nostra qua gaudeo, Melior, vir optime nec
minus in iudicio litterarum quam in omni vitae colore
tersissime, et ipsa opusculorum quae tibi trado condicio
sic posita est ut totus hic ad te liber meus etiam sine epistu-
5 la spectet. primum enim habet Glauciam nostrum, cuius
gratissimam infantiam et qualem plerumque infelices
sortiuntur apud te complexus amabam, iam non tibi. huius
amissi recens vulnus, ut scis, epicedio prosecutus sum
adeo festinanter ut excusandam habuerim affectibus tuis
10 celeritatem. nec nunc eam apud te iacto qui nosti, sed et
ceteris indico, ne quis asperiore lima carmen examinet et a
confuso scriptum et dolenti datum, cum paene supervacua
sint tarda solacia. Polli mei villa Surrentina quae sequitur
debuit a me vel in honorem eloquentiae eius diligentius
15 dici, sed amicus ignovit. in arborem certe tuam, Melior, et
psittacum scis a me leves libellos quasi epigrammatis loco
scriptos. eandem exigebat stili facilitatem leo mansuetus,

---

4 ad te (*Baehrens*) . . . spectet *Vollmer*: altae . . . exp- M
5 gratissimam infantiam* *Calderini*: -ima -tia M

---

1 *Iam non tibi* has baffled interpreters; see van Dam and Critical Appendix.

BOOK TWO

Such is our friendship that is my joy, excellent Melior (elegant in your literary judgment no less than in the whole colour of your life), and such is the very nature of the little pieces which I am presenting to you that all this book of mine would look toward you even without a letter. For its first theme is our Glaucias, whose charming infancy (such as is so often the portion of the unfortunate) I took in my arms in your home and loved, no longer just for your sake.[1] As you know, I followed up the wound of his recent loss with a poem of consolation, in such haste that I thought I owed your feelings an apology for my promptitude. Nor do I now boast of that to you, who know, but point it out to others who might else criticize the piece with too sharp a file, coming as it did from a troubled writer to a grieving recipient, since tardy consolations are almost supererogatory. The Surrentine villa of my dear Pollius comes next; it deserved more careful composition if only in honour of his eloquence, but as a friend he forgave. You assuredly know, Melior, that I wrote the trifling items on your tree and your parrot like epigrams, as it were. The same facility of pen was required by the Tame Lion; if I had not presented him to our most sacred Emperor as he lay prostrate in the

quem in amphitheatro prostratum frigidum erat sacratissimo imperatori ni statim tradere. ad Ursum quoque nos-
20   trum, iuvenem candidissimum et sine iactura desidiae
doctissimum, scriptam de amisso puero consolationem super ea quae ipsi debeo huic libro libenter inserui, quia honorem eius tibi laturus accepto est. cludit volumen geneth-
liacon Lucani, quod Polla Argentaria, rarissima uxorum,
25   cum hunc diem forte †consuleremus†, imputari sibi voluit.
ego non potui maiorem tanti auctoris habere reverentiam
quam quod laudes eius dicturus hexametros meos timui.

     Haec, qualiacumque sunt, Melior carissime, si tibi non
displicuerint, a te publicum accipiant; si minus, ad me re-
30   vertantur.

II.1

GLAUCIAS ATEDI MELIORIS DELICATUS

Quod tibi praerepti, Melior, solamen alumni
improbus ante rogos et adhuc vivente favilla
ordiar? abruptis etiamnunc flebile venis
vulnus hiat magnaeque patet via lubrica plagae.
5   cum iam egomet cantus et verba medentia saevus
confero, tu planctus lamentaque fortia mavis
odistique chelyn surdaque averteris aure.
intempesta cano. citius me tigris abactis
fetibus orbatique velint audire leones.

    [19] tradere *Barth*: -rem M
    [23] est. cludit *Madvig*: excl- M
    [25] *anne* ⟨una⟩ consumeremus?
    [6] confero *ed.pr.*: consero M

amphitheatre, the piece would have fallen flat. I put into this book another consolation, addressed to our friend Ursus, a young man of sincere good will and literary culture, who loses none of his leisure. I did so gladly because, aside from what I owe himself, he will credit the compliment to you. A Birthday Ode to Lucan concludes the volume. Polla Argentaria, a pearl among wives, requested it as a favour when we chanced to be spending this day together (?). I could not show more reverence for so great an author than by distrusting my own hexameters[2] for a poem in his honour.

If you do not mislike these compositions, such as they are, my dearest Melior, let them receive their public from you. Otherwise, let them return to me.

II.1

GLAUCIAS, ATEDIUS MELIOR'S BOY FAVOURITE

How shall I begin, Melior, to console you for the foster child that Fate has snatched away from you, as I stand before the pyre and the embers still glow—'tis presumption. The pitiable wound still gapes with sundered veins and the perilous path of the gash lies open. While I cruelly weave song and words of healing, you prefer beating of breast and loud lament, hating the lyre and turning deaf ears away. Ill-timed my song. Sooner would a tigress robbed of her cubs or lions bereaved wish to listen. Not if threefold melody

---

[2] Lucan's poem on the Civil War being in hexameters, Statius says he chose not to invite comparisons. He was actually far the better versifier of the two.

10   nec si tergeminum Sicula de virgine carmen
affluat aut silvis chelys intellecta ferisque,
mulceat insanos gemitus. stat pectore demens
luctus et admoto latrant praecordia tactu.
      Nemo vetat; satiare malis aegrumque dolorem
15   libertate doma. iam flendi expleta voluptas,
iamque preces fessus non indignaris amicas?
iamne canam? lacrimis en et mea carmine in ipso
ora natant tristesque cadunt in verba liturae.
ipse etenim tecum nigrae sollemnia pompae
20   spectatumque Urbi (scelus heu!) puerile feretrum
produxi; saevos damnati turis acervos
plorantemque animam supra sua funera vidi,
teque patrum gemitus superantem et bracchia matrum
complexumque rogos ignemque haurire parantem
25   vix tenui similis comes offendique tenendo.
et nunc heu vittis et frontis honore soluto
infaustus vates versa mea pectora tecum
plango lyra. crudi comitem sociumque doloris,
si merui luctusque tui consortia sensi,
30   iam lenis patiare precor. me fulmine in ipso
audivere patres; ego iuxta busta profusis
matribus at⟨que⟩ piis cecini solacia natis,
et mihi, cum proprios gemerem defectus ad ignes
quem, Natura, patrem! nec te lugere severus
35   arceo; sed confer gemitus pariterque fleamus.

       17–8 carmine . . . ora *Friederich*: -na . . . ore M
       20 (scelus heu!) *Ker*: -us et M
       28 crudi *Housman*: et diu M
       30 me ⊊: iam M

floated here from Sicilian maid[1] or the lyre[2] that woods and wild beasts understood, would your mad moans be soothed. Frantic mourning stands in your heart, at a touch your breast barks.[3]

None forbids you. Take your fill of misery and tame bitter sorrow by giving it free course. Is the pleasure of weeping sated now? Are you now weary and no longer resentful of a friend's entreaties? Shall I sing now? See, my face too swims with tears even as my song proceeds and sad blots fall on the page. For I myself led forth the black-garbed funeral procession by your side, the childish bier (alas the crime!) watched by all Rome. I saw the cruel heaps of doomed incense and the soul weeping above its body. And as you outdid the groans of fathers and the arms of mothers, embracing the pyre and ready to swallow the flame, I could scarce restrain you, your companion in like case, and by restraining angered you. And now alas! a poet of ill omen, I cast off the fillets that dignify my brow, I turn my lyre over and with it beat my breast along with you. Be gentle now and suffer me as your fellow and partaker in raw grief, if I have so deserved and felt comradeship in your mourning. Fathers have listened to me in the very shock, I have sung solace to mothers prostrate by the pyre and loving children—and to myself, when at fires of my own I lamented fainting (O Nature!) what a father! I do not tell you sternly not to mourn; but mingle your groans and let us weep together.

[1] The three Sirens were sometimes located off Sicily, sometimes off Surrentum.   [2] Of Orpheus.

[3] A Homeric expression (*Odyssey* 20.13), borrowed by Ennius and others.

Iamdudum dignos aditus laudumque tuarum,
o merito dilecte puer, primordia quaerens
distrahor. hinc anni stantes in limine vitae,
hinc me forma rapit, rapit inde modestia praecox
40 et pudor et tenero probitas maturior aevo.
o ubi purpureo suffusus sanguine candor
sidereique orbes radiataque lumina caelo
et castigatae collecta modestia frontis
ingenuique super crines mollisque decorae
45 margo comae? blandis ubinam ora arguta querelis
osculaque impliciti vernos redolentia flores,
et mixtae risu lacrimae penitusque loquentis
Hyblaeis vox mulsa favis, cui sibila serpens
poneret et saevae vellent servire novercae?
50 nil veris affingo bonis. heu lactea colla,
bracchia quo numquam domini sine pondere cervix!
o ubi venturae spes non longinqua iuventae
atque genis optatus honos iurataque multum
barba tibi? cuncta in cineres gravis intulit hora
55 hostilisque dies; nobis meminisse relictum.
  Quis tua colloquiis hilaris mulcebit amatis
pectora, quis curas mentisque arcana remittet?
accensum quis bile fera famulisque tumentem
leniet ardentique in se deflectet ab ira?

---

39 hinc *Poggio* (*cf. TLL VI.2805 23*): hic M
48 mulsa *Housman*: mixta M: tincta *Markland*
51 quo *Saftien*: que M

---

4 The text may be corrupt. *Radiatus* does not occur elsewhere in the sense of *radians* ('radiant') and *caelo* is unclear.
5 'A small forehead could be the sign of a mobile mind' (van

For this long while, boy beloved as you deserved, I am torn as I seek a worthy approach, where to begin your praises. On this side your years standing on life's threshold clutch me, on that your beauty, on the other your precocious modesty, your sense of honour, your probity riper than your tender age. Oh where is that fair complexion, suffused with red of blood, those starry eyes radiant from heaven,[4] and the compact modesty of your smooth brow,[5] tresses untutored above, soft fringe of comely hair? Where that garrulous mouth with its winsome complaint, those lips redolent of spring flowers as you embraced him, those tears blended with laughter, those accents sweetened[6] through and through by Hybla's honeycombs, at which a serpent would cease from hissing and cruel stepmothers be fain to serve him? Truly those charms were his, nothing added by me. Alas! the milk-white throat, the arms ever weighing upon his master's neck![7] Where, oh where the not distant hope of coming manhood, the longed-for grace upon his cheeks, the beard you often swore by? A heavy hour, a hostile day has brought all to ashes: to us is left a memory.

Who shall soothe your breast with the merry talk you loved? Who relax your cares, your mind's secrets? Who shall calm you when angry bile inflames and you wax wroth with your servants, turning you from your hot choler to

Dam, quoting Pliny, *Natural History* 11.274, quoting Pompeius Trogus). It was also considered beautiful.

[6] Housman proposed *mulsa,* not *multa* (= *mulsa*), as represented by van Dam.   [7] Lit. 'without the weight of which his master never was' (van Dam after Saftien, rightly rejecting the popular *bracchiaque <et>*).

60 inceptas quis ab ore dapes libataque vina
auferet et dulci turbabit cuncta rapina?
quis matutinos abrumpet murmure somnos
impositus stratis, abitusque morabitur artis
nexibus aque ipso revocabit ad oscula poste?
65 obvius intranti rursus quis in ora manusque
prosiliet brevibusque umeros circumdabit ulnis?
muta domus, fateor, desolatique penates,
et situs in thalamis et maesta silentia mensis.
　　Quid mirum, tanto si te pius altor honorat
70 funere? tu domino requies portusque senectae,
tu modo deliciae, dulces modo pectore curae.
non te barbaricae versabat turbo catastae,
nec mixtus Phariis venalis mercibus infans
compositosque sales meditataque verba locutus
75 quaesisti lascivus erum tardeque parasti.
hic domus, hinc ortus, dominique penatibus olim
carus uterque parens atque in tua gaudia liber,
ne quererere genus. raptum sed protinus alvo
sustulit exsultans ac prima lucida voce
80 astra salutantem dominus sibi mente dicavit,
amplexusque sinu tulit et genuisse putavit.
fas mihi sanctorum venia dixisse parentum,
tuque oro, Natura, sinas, cui prima per orbem

64 aque ipso . . . poste ⊊: atque ipsos . . . postes M
67 fateor M: mussat *Housman*
71 dulcis . . . cura *Elter*
76 hic *Laetus*: hinc M

8 'The word suggests that Glaucias did not pass the night with Melior' (van Dam).

himself? Who shall steal from your lips the food you have begun to eat and the wine you have sipped, making general havoc with his sweet plunderings? Who jump on your bed-clothes and break your morning[8] slumbers, who hold up your departures with his clinging embraces and call you back from the very door for kisses? Who meet you as you come in again, leaping to your mouth and hands, ringing your shoulders with his tiny arms? Mute is the house, I don't deny,[9] desolate the hearth, neglect is in the bed-chambers, and silence at the board.

What wonder if your faithful foster father honour you with so grand a funeral? You were your master's rest, the haven of his old age, now his delight, now his heart's sweet care. You were not turned round on some foreigner's revolving platform,[10] you were no infant for sale among Pharian merchandise, retailing manufactured jests and words prepared, frolicking in quest of a master and slow to find one. Here your house, hence your origin. Both your parents have long been dear to your master's home and were freed to make you happy, lest you should complain of your birth. But no sooner were you taken from the womb than your master lifted you up exultantly as you greeted the shining stars with your first cry and in his mind he sealed you for his own, clasping you to his bosom and deeming you his begotten son. With sanction of venerated parents I may say it, and do you, Nature, whose province it is to lay down primal laws for man throughout the world,

[9] The parenthetic *fateor* ('I acknowledge') may perhaps be explained as implying 'yes, you may well be grief-stricken.'

[10] No other interpretation seems plausible, though independent evidence for such an apparatus in slave markets is to seek.

iura homini sancire datum: non omnia sanguis
85   proximus aut serie generis demissa propago
alligat; interius nova saepe ascitaque serpunt
pignora conexis. natos genuisse necesse est,
elegisse iuvat. tenero sic blandus Achilli
semifer Haemonium vincebat Pelea Chiron,
90   nec senior Peleus natum comitatus in arma
Troica, sed claro Phoenix haerebat alumno.
optabat longe reditus Pallantis ovantis
Evander, fidus pugnas spectabat Acoetes,
cumque procul nitidis genitor cessaret ab astris,
95   fluctivagus volucrem comebat Persea Dictys.
quid referam altricum victas pietate parentes?
quid te post cineres deceptaque funera matris
tutius Inoo reptantem pectore, Bacche?
se secura sati Tuscis regnabat in undis
100   Ilia, portantem lassabat Romulus Accam.
vidi ego transertos alieno in robore ramos
altius ire suis. et te iam fecerat illi
mens animusque patrem, necdum moresve decorve;
tu tamen et vinctas etiamnunc murmure voces
105   vagitumque rudem fletusque infantis amabas.
     Ille, velut primos exspiraturus ad austros
mollibus in pratis alte flos improbus exstat,
sic tener ante diem vultu gressuque superbo
vicerat aequales multumque reliquerat annos.
110   sive catenatis curvatus membra palaestris
staret, Amyclaea conceptum matre putares,

84 homini *scripsi*: animus M: -mis ⌐: hominum *van Dam*
97 fulmina *Markland*
99 se secura sati *Courtney*: iam s- patris M: iam s- parens *Eden*

110

give me leave, I beg: proximity of blood and offspring descending in lineal series is not the only bond; new children, adopted, often creep further in than our kindred. Sons begotten are a must, sons chosen a joy. So it was that kind half-beast Chiron meant more to Achilles than Haemonian Peleus. Nor did old Peleus go with his son to the Trojan War, but Phoenix stuck to his favourite pupil. From afar Evander prayed for Pallas' return in triumph: faithful Acoetes watched his combats. Up in the bright stars winged Perseus' father tarried: wave-wandering Dictys tended him. Why should I tell of mothers less loving than nurses? Why tell of you, Bacchus, creeping more safely in Ino's lap after your mother's ashes and duped death?[11] Ilia, careless of her son, reigned queen in the Tuscan waves: Acca was weary from carrying Romulus. I have seen branches grafted on an alien tree grow higher than its own.[12] And your mind and will had already made you his father, not yet his ways and beauty, but even then you loved his words cry-fettered, his innocent wails and infant weeping.

Like a flower destined to die at the first south winds, standing high, too high, in a soft meadow, so prematurely in countenance and proud step the child was surpassing his peers, leaving his years far behind. Did he stand fast in a wrestler's lock, you would think him born of Amyclaean

[11] Semele had been tricked by Juno into asking Jupiter to appear to her in all his splendour, whence her death by lightning.

[12] Usually taken as 'the branches of their own tree,' which is syntactically more of a stretch.

(Oebaliden illo praeceps mutaret Apollo,
Alciden pensaret Hylan); seu Graius amictu
Attica facundi decurreret orsa Menandri,
115 laudaret gavisa sonum crinemque decorum
fregisset rosea lasciva Thalia corona;
Maeonium sive ille senem Troiaeque labores
diceret aut casus tarde remeantis Ulixis,
ipse pater sensus, ipsi stupuere magistri.
120   Scilicet infausta Lachesis cunabula dextra
attigit et gremio puerum complexa fovebat
Invidia; illa genas et adultum comere crinem
haec monstrare artes et verba infigere quae nunc
plangimus. Herculeos annis aequare labores
125 coeperat assurgens, et adhuc infantia iuxta;
iam tamen et validi gressus mensuraque maior
cultibus et visae puero decrescere vestes,
cum tibi quas vestes, quae non gestamina mitis
festinabat erus? brevibus constringere laenis
130 pectora et angusta nolens artare lacerna,
enormes non ille sinus sed semper ad annos
texta legens, modo puniceo velabat amictu,
nunc herbas imitante sinu, nunc dulce rubenti
murice; nunc vivis digitos incendere gemmis
135 gaudebat. non turba comes, non munera cessant.
sola verecundo derat praetexta decori.
    Haec fortuna domus. subitas inimica levavit
Parca manus. quo, diva, feros gravis exseris ungues?

113 Graius ⚓: gratus M   123 haec *Baehrens*: et M
    125 et *Markland*: sed M   128 vestes M: telas *Sandstroem*:
lanas *Housman*   130 nolens *Courtney*: telas M: vitans *Watt*
    134 tum *Havet*   138 ungues *Scaliger*: an- M

mother; Apollo would have hurried to take him in exchange for Oebalus' son,[13] Alcides would have bartered Hylas. Or if in Grecian dress he ran through the Attic speech of eloquent Menander, wanton Thalia would have praised his accents in delight and ruffled his comely hair with a garland of roses. Or did he declaim the old Maeonian and Troy's labours or the adventures of laggard Ulysses, even his papa, even his teachers fell amazed at his intuition.

Methinks that Lachesis[14] touched the boy's cradle with her ill-omened hand and Envy fondled him on her lap; the one stroked his cheeks and abundant hair, the other showed him skills and instilled the words we now lament. Rising with the years, he bid fair to equal Hercules' labours—and infancy was still close. Yet already his steps were firm, his stature bigger than his wear, clothes seemed to shrink upon him—and what clothes, what trappings did your gentle master not hasten for you? Not wishing to constrain your chest with narrow mantles and cramp it in a tight cloak, not giving you folds too long, always choosing garments to suit your years, now he would cover you in scarlet habit, now in grass-green, now in sweet blush of purple, now rejoice to set your fingers afire with vivid jewels. Unceasing the throng of attendants, the gifts. Your modest finery lacked only the bordered gown.[15]

Such the fortune of the house. Suddenly the hostile Parca raised her hands. Whom, goddess, do you bare your

---

[13] Hyacinthus, favourite of Apollo (by whom he was accidentally killed).   [14] 'There are no distinct tasks for each of the Parcae' (van Dam).   [15] Toga with purple border (*praetexta*) worn by boys of free birth.

non te forma movet, non te lacrimabilis aetas?
140 hunc nec saeva viro potuisset carpere Procne
nec fera crudeles Colchis durasset in iras,
editus Aeolia nec si foret iste Creusa;
torvus ab hoc Athamas insanos flecteret arcus;
hunc, quamquam Hectoreos cineres Troiamque perosus,
145 turribus e Phrygiis flesset missurus Ulixes.
 Septima lux, et iam frigentia lumina torpent,
iam complexa manu crinem tenet infera Iuno.
ille tamen Parcis fragiles urgentibus annos
te vultu moriente videt linguaque cadente
150 murmurat; in te omnes vacui iam pectoris efflat
reliquias, solum meminit solumque vocantem
exaudit, tibique ora movet, tibi verba relinquit
et prohibet gemitus consolaturque dolentem.
gratum est, Fata, tamen quod non mors lenta iacentis
155 exedit puerile decus, manesque subibit
integer et nullo temeratus corpora damno,
qualis erat.
 Quid ego exsequias et prodiga flammis
dona loquar maestoque ardentia funera luxu,
quod tibi purpureo tristis rogus aggere crevit,
160 quod Cilicum flores, quod munera graminis Indi,
quodque Arabes Phariique Palaestinique liquores
arsuram lavere comam? cupit omnia ferre

155 subibit *van Dam*: subivit M
158 loquar *Calderini*: -uor M

---

16 Daughter of Creon, king of Corinth, and so descended from
Aeolus father of Sisyphus (to be distinguished from Aeolus, god of
the Winds).

savage claws to harm? Does not beauty move you or piteous youth? Fierce as she was to her husband, Procne could not have torn him, nor would the savage Colchian have steeled herself to ruthless wrath, not though he had been the son of Aeolian Creusa.[16] From him grim Athamas would have turned away his mad bow. Ulysses would have wept as he made to cast him from the Phrygian battlements, much as he hated Hector's ashes and Troy.

Comes the seventh dawn and already his cold eyes are dull, already nether Juno holds his hair in her clasp.[17] But even as the Parcae urge his frail years, his dying gaze sees you and his failing tongue murmurs your name. All that is left of his empty breast he breathes on you, you only he remembers, your call only he catches, for you moves his lips, for you leaves words, forbidding lament and comforting your grief. But we thank you, Fates, that no lingering death devoured his boyish beauty as he lay; he will go whole to the shades, nothing lost, body inviolate, just as he was.

Why should I tell of the obsequies, the lavish gifts bestowed upon the flames,[18] the corpse ablaze with lugubrious luxury? How the sad pyre rose high for you with purple mound, how Cilician flowers[19] and tribute of Indian herbage, and perfumes Arabian, Pharian, Palestinian washed the hair about to burn? Prodigal Melior is eager to bring all

---

[17] Proserpina is about to cut off a lock, as in *Aeneid* 4.698f. and elsewhere. The action 'seems to symbolize the release of the soul from the body' (van Dam, referring to Pease on *Aeneid* l.c.).

[18] Or, as van Dam, 'lavish with the flames,' i.e. needing much fire to burn them up.

[19] Saffron. The perfumes that follow are *costum* (see van Dam), myrrh, cinnamon (?), and balsam (*opobalsamum*).

prodigus et totos Melior succendere census
desertas exosus opes; sed non capit ignis
165   invidus atque artae desunt in munera flammae.
        Horror habet sensus. qualem te funere summo
atque rogum iuxta, Melior placidissime quondam,
extimui! tune ille hilaris comisque videri?
unde animi saevaeque manus et barbarus horror,
170   dum modo fusus humi lucem aversaris iniquam,
nunc torvus pariter vestes et pectora rumpis
dilectosque premis visus et frigida labris
oscula? erant illic genitor materque iacentis
maesta, sed attoniti te spectavere parentes.
175   quid mirum? plebs cuncta nefas et praevia flerunt
agmina, Flaminio quae limite Mulvius agger
transvehit, immeritus flammis dum tristibus infans
traditur et gemitum formaque aevoque meretur.
talis in Isthmiacos prolatus ab aequore portus
180   naufragus imposita iacuit sub matre Palaemon,
sic et in anguiferae ludentem gramine Lernae
rescissum squamis avidus bibit ignis Ophelten.
        Pone metus letique minas desiste vereri.
illum nec terno latrabit Cerberus ore,

        172 labris *Peerlkamp*: lambis M: libas *Bentley*
        178 aevoque *Gulielmius*: ac voce M   179 perlatus *Saenger,*
quod noluerat Otto   182 ignis *Koestlin*: anguis M

        20 Lit. 'lips (*labris*),' persuasively correcting *lambis* ('you lick').
        21 During the burning the crowd went ahead to the grave,
which was across the Tiber, presumably on the Via Flaminia, over
the Mulvian Bridge. The cremation will have taken place on the
south bank; perhaps Melior had a villa (*horti*) in the area.

he has, to put his entire fortune to the torch, hating his forsaken wealth. But the jealous fire does not take it, the flames are choked, unequal to the offerings.

A shudder seizes my senses. Melior, most equable of men, how I feared you at the final rite, hard by the pyre! Is this the cheerful, friendly face I know? Whence that passion, those cruel hands, that outlandish shaking? Now prostrate on the ground you shun the cruel daylight, now fiercely you tear your dress and breast alike, pressing with your mouth[20] the beloved eyes and the cold lips. The father and mother of the dead were present, but the parents gazed on you dumbfounded. No wonder! All the populace bewept the outrage, and the crowds ahead[21] that crossed the Mulvian bridge by the Flaminian road as the blameless child is surrendered to the sad flames, earning lamentation by beauty and by age. So shipwrecked Palaemon was carried by the sea to the Isthmian harbour and lay with his mother covering the body. So too the greedy fire consumed Opheltes, torn by scales as he played in snake-infested Lerna's grass.[22]

But put aside your fears and cease to dread Death's threats. Cerberus shall not bark at him with triple muz-

[22] As usually represented, Ino sprang into the sea with her son Melicertes to escape her mad husband Athamas; there they became sea deities, renamed Leucothea and Palaemon. There are variants, but this of Statius is found nowhere else. Presumably the two bodies were washed up together. The comparisons are stretched. Glaucias was on the verge of puberty, Melicertes (*Theb.* 4.563) and Opheltes babies; and the circumstances were quite dissimilar. But presumably Statius wanted mythological precedents and these were the best he could think of; cf. II.6.30ff., III.1.142ff. (much less forced). Lerna stands for nearby Nemea.

185 nulla Soror flammis, nulla assurgentibus hydris
  terrebit; quin ipse avidae trux navita cumbae
  interius steriles ripas et adusta subibit
  litora, ne puero dura ascendisse facultas.
   Quid mihi gaudenti proles Cyllenia virga
190 nuntiat? estne aliquid tam saevo in tempore laetum?
  noverat effigies generosique ardua Blaesi
  ora puer, dum saepe domi nova serta ligantem
  te videt et similes tergentem pectore ceras.
  hunc ubi Lethaei lustrantem gurgitis oras
195 Ausonios inter proceres seriemque Quirini
  agnovit, timide primum vestigia iungit
  accessu tacito summosque lacessit amictus,
  inde magis sequitur; neque enim magis ille trahentem
  spernit et ignota credit de stirpe nepotum.
200 mox ubi delicias et rari pignus amici
  sensit et amissi puerum solacia Blaesi,
  tollit humo magnaque ligat cervice diuque
  ipse manu gaudens vehit et, quae munera mollis
  Elysii, steriles ramos mutasque volucres
205 porgit et obtunso pallentes germine flores.
  nec prohibet meminisse tui, sed pectora blandus
  miscet et alternum pueri partitur amorem.

193 ceras *Sandstroem*: curas M
205 porgit *Barth, Grotius*: porsit M

---

23 *Adusta* relates to Phlegethon, the river of fire, though Charon's river is the Styx.

24 A special friend of Melior's, known only from this passage, II.3.77, and Martial 8.38.

25 Some kind of encaustic painting, as generally supposed

zle, no Sister shall frighten him with flames and rearing
snakes. Even the surly skipper of the greedy boat will steer
further into the barren banks and scorched[23] shore, lest
the boy have a hard time climbing aboard.

What does Cyllene's son announce to me with his joyous wand? In so cruel a time can anything be glad? The boy
knew noble Blaesus'[24] likenesses and lofty countenance,
for often had he seen you at home twining new garlands
and rubbing waxen portraits[25] with your heart. Recognizing him as he paced the banks of Lethe's flood among
Ausonian magnates and Quirinus' line, at first the boy
walks timidly by his side, approaching silently and plucking the hem of his robe, then rather follows[26] and tugs the
more. Nor does Blaesus put him off, thinking him a young
relative, how related he knows not. When presently he became aware[27] that this is the darling child of his special
friend, the boy who consoled him for lost Blaesus, he lifts
him up and winds him around his mighty neck, happily carrying him on his arm[28] as he proffers the gifts of soft Elysium—barren branches, silent birds, wan flowers nipped
in the bud. Neither does he forbid him to remember you,
but fondly mingles hearts, sharing the boy's affection for
you and yours for him.

(cf. I.1.100); or perhaps a wax image such as Laodicea made of
Protesilaus (II.2.63, II.7.125n).   26 Not getting Blaesus' notice, the boy falls behind, but goes on plucking more insistently
than ever. So I interpret the first *magis,* others otherwise.
Courtney obelizes.   27 'Presumably by addressing him' (van
Dam).   28 Perhaps with recollection of a father lifting a
newborn child from the ground in acknowledgment of parentage
(cf. v. 79); see van Dam.

Hic finis rapto. quin tu iam vulnera sedas
et tollis mersum luctu caput? omnia functa
210 aut moritura vides. obeunt noctesque diesque
astraque, nec solidis prodest sua machina terris.
nam populus mortale genus, plebisque caducae
quis fleat interitus? hos bella, hos aequora poscunt,
his amor exitio, furor his et saeva cupido,
215 ut sileam morbos; hos ora rigentia Brumae,
illos implacido letalis Sirius igni,
hos manet imbrifero pallens Autumnus hiatu.
quicquid init ortus, finem timet. ibimus omnes,
ibimus; immensis urnam quatit Aeacus umbris.
220 Ast hic quem gemimus, felix hominesque deosque
et dubios casus et caecae lubrica vitae
effugit, immunis Fatis. non ille rogavit,
non timuit meruitve mori. nos anxia plebes,
nos miseri, quibus unde dies suprema, quis aevi
225 exitus incertum, quibus instet fulmen ab astris,
quae nubes fatale sonet. nil flecteris istis?
sed flectere libens. ades huc emissus ab atro
limine, cui soli cuncta impetrare facultas,
Glaucia (nil sontes animas nec portitor arcet
230 nec durae comes ille serae): tu pectora mulce,
tu prohibe manare genas noctesque beatas
dulcibus alloquiis et vivis vultibus imple
et periisse nega, desolatamque sororem,
qui potes, et miseros perge insinuare parentes.

212 nos *Eden*
223 renuitve *Heinsius*
229 nil sontes *Saenger*: ins- M: non s- *Håkanson*
230 serae *Scaliger*: fe- M

120

He is taken: it is the end for him. So now soothe your wound and raise your grief-plunged head. All you see is dead or destined to die. Nights die and days and stars, and her structure does not avail the solid earth. As for people, they are of mortal race and who shall weep the passing of a transitory multitude?[29] Wars claim some, seas others, some love destroys, others madness and fierce greed, to say nothing of diseases. These Winter's frozen visage awaits, those deadly Sirius' implacable fire, others pale Autumn with her rainy jaws. Whatever had a beginning fears an end. We shall all go our way, ay, all. Aeacus shakes his urn for countless shades.

But he for whom we mourn is fortunate. He escapes men and gods and doubtful chances and the perils of blind life. The Fates cannot harm him. He did not ask for death or fear it or deserve it. We, anxious multitude, we are miserable, not knowing whence comes the final day, what shall be the manner of our going, from what stars looms the thunderbolt, what cloud booms our fate. Does all this not sway you? But swayed you shall be, and gladly. Come hither, dispatched from the dark threshold, you that alone can win all you ask, Glaucias (for neither the ferryman nor the companion of the inexorable bar[30] blocks guiltless souls), soothe his breast, forbid his eyes to flow. Fill nights of bliss with your secret comfortings and living countenance. Say you have not perished and then commend to him, as only you can, your bereaved sister and unhappy parents.

[29] As sometimes elsewhere, *populus* and *plebs* seem to be synonymous.

[30] Cerberus and the bar to which he is tied.

II.2

VILLA SURRENTINA POLLI FELICIS

Est inter notos Sirenum nomine muros
saxaque Tyrrhenae templis onerata Minervae
celsa Dicarchei speculatrix villa profundi,
qua Bromio dilectus ager collesque per altos
5 uritur et prelis non invidet uva Falernis.
huc me post patrii laetum quinquennia lustri,
cum stadio iam pigra quies canusque sederet
pulvis, ad Ambracias conversa gymnade frondes,
trans gentile fretum placidi facundia Polli
10 detulit et nitidae iuvenilis gratia Pollae,
flectere iam cupidum gressus qua limite noto
Appia longarum teritur regina viarum.
    Sed iuvere morae. placido lunata recessu
hinc atque hinc curvae perrumpunt aequora rupes.
15 dat Natura locum montique intervenit udum
litus et in terras scopulis pendentibus exit.
gratia prima loci, gemina testudine fumant
balnea, et e terris occurrit dulcis amaro
Nympha mari. levis hic Phorci chorus udaque crines
20 Cymodoce viridisque cupit Galatea lavari.

14 curvae* *scripsi*: -vas M
15 udum *Heinsius*: unum M

---

1 False etymology: Siren / Surrentum.

2 At Misenum, looking down on the Tyrrhene Sea from the summit of the headland.

3 The Augustalia at Naples with musical and literary and ath-

II.2

THE VILLA OF POLLIUS FELIX AT SURRENTUM

Between the walls well-known by the Sirens' name[1]
and the cliffs burdened with Tyrrhene Minerva's temple[2]
there is a lofty villa looking out upon the Dicarchean deep,
where the land is dear to Bromius and the grapes ripen on
the high hills nor envy Falernian presses. Hither I came
gladly across my native bay after the quinquennial festival
of my home,[3] when a lazy lull had settled on the stadium
and the dust lay white as the athletes turned to Ambracian
laurels. I was drawn by the eloquence of gentle Pollius and
elegant Polla's youthful[4] grace, though already eager to
bend my steps where Appia, queen of long highways, takes
the traveller along her familiar track.[5]

But the delay was worth while. Curving cliffs on either
side pierce crescent waters,[6] making a calm recess. Nature
provides space. The watery[7] beach interrupts the heights,
running inland between overhanging crags. The spot's first
grace is a steaming bathhouse with twin cupolas, and from
land a stream of fresh water meets the briny sea. Here
Phorcus' lightsome choir and Cymodoce with her dripping
locks and sea-green Galatea delight to bathe. Before his

letic contests, held every fourth year. It was followed by a festival
at Actium beginning on 2 September.   [4] Polla was far from
young (III.1.174f., IV.8.14f.) but she had not lost her youthful
charm.   [5] To Rome. Statius was still in Naples.
        [6] See Critical Appendix.   [7] *Udum* (cf. III.1.68) is sup-
pressed by Courtney. Defenders of the impossible *unum* labour
under the delusion that *uno* in Suetonius, *Tiberius* 40 *uno
parvoque litore* means 'uninterrupted.'

ante domum tumidae moderator caerulus undae
excubat, innocui custos laris; huius amico
spumant templa salo. felicia rura tuetur
Alcides. gaudet gemino sub numine portus:
25   hic servat terras, hic saevis fluctibus obstat.
mira quies pelagi. ponunt hic lassa furorem
aequora et insani spirant clementius austri.
hic praeceps minus audet hiems, nulloque tumultu
stagna modesta iacent dominique imitantia mores.
30   Inde per obliquas erepit porticus arces,
urbis opus, longoque domat saxa aspera dorso.
qua prius obscuro permixti pulvere soles
et feritas inamoena viae, nunc ire voluptas:
qualis, si subeas Ephyres Baccheidos altum
35   culmen, ab Inoo fert semita tecta Lechaeo.
     Non, mihi si cunctos Helicon indulgeat amnes
et superet Piplea sitim largeque volantis
ungula se det equi reseretque arcana pudicos
Phemonoe fontes vel quos meus auspice Phoebo
40   altius immersa turbavit Pollius urna,

25 *damn. Håkanson*
35 Lechaeo *cod. Vatic. 3283*: lyceo M: Lyaeo ⚒
38 se det *Gronovius*: sedet M

---

8 I.e. Neptune's temple (v. 23); his statue stood in front of it.
Others understand Pollius' villa or the bathhouse or Hercules'
shrine, against insuperable objections. But *innocui laris* (22) is the
villa (cf. II.3.15f. *Melioris . . . sine fraude lares*).
9 Perhaps, as elsewhere (107, 122), with a thought of Pollius'
name. Van Dam ad loc. has a list of such phenomena in the *Silvae*.
I usually leave them unnoticed.

house[8] the cerulean governor of the swelling wave keeps ward, guardian of the harmless home; his temple foams with the friendly surge. Alcides protects the happy[9] fields. The haven rejoices under its double deity. Wonderful is the calm of the sea; here the weary waters lay their rage aside and the wild south winds breathe more gently. Here the headlong tempest bates its daring; the pool lies modest and untroubled, imitating its master's manners.

From that point a colonnade creeps zigzag through the heights, a city's work,[10] mastering the rugged rocks with its lengthy spine. Where formerly sunshine mingled with foggy dust and the path was wild and ugly, 'tis pleasure now to go; like the covered way that leads from Ino's Lechaeum[11] if you climb the lofty height of Bacchis' Ephyre.

Not if Helicon were to grant me all his streams[12] or Piplea quench my thirst or the hoof of the flying horse[13] be generous to assuage it or sweet Phemonoë open her chaste springs[14] or those that my Pollius troubled when under

[10] Van Dam's parallels do indeed support his rendering 'vast as a city.' But how can that be said of a colonnade?

[11] Ino was worshipped in Corinth (Ephyre). Long walls ran from the port of Lechaeum to the city: 'but the walls were not covered, nor did they run up to Akrokorinth,' notes van Dam, who therefore prefers *Lyaeo* (read by Courtney), assumed to be an otherwise unknown temple of Dionysus (Bacchus). But temples are not usually called by the names or metonyms of their deities, and I think it far more likely that Statius was unaware of the discrepancies or did not trouble about them.

[12] There were two, Aganippe and Hippocrene.

[13] Priene in Corinth confused with Hippocrene, as elsewhere.

[14] Castalia.

innumeras valeam species cultusque locorum
Pieriis aequare modis. vix ordine longo
suffecere oculi, vix, dum per singula ducor,
suffecere gradus. quae rerum turba! locine
45 ingenium an domini mirer prius? haec domus ortus
aspicit et Phoebi tenerum iubar, illa cadentem
detinet exactamque negat dimittere lucem,
cum iam fessa dies et in aequora montis opaci
umbra cadit vitreoque natant praetoria ponto.
50 haec pelagi clamore fremunt, haec tecta sonoros
ignorant fluctus terraeque silentia malunt.
his favit Natura locis, hic victa colenti
cessit et ignotos docilis mansuevit in usus.
mons erat hic ubi plana vides, et lustra fuerunt
55 quae nunc tecta subis; ubi nunc nemora ardua cernis,
hic nec terra fuit: domuit possessor, et illum
formantem rupes expugnantemque secuta
gaudet humus. nunc cerne iugum discentia saxa
intrantesque domos iussumque recedere montem.
60 iam Methymnaei vatis manus et chelys una
Thebais et Getici cedat tibi gloria plectri;
et tu saxa moves, et te nemora alta sequuntur.
      Quid referam veteres ceraeque aerisque figuras,
si quid Apellei gaudent animasse colores,
65 si quid adhuc vacua tamen admirabile Pisa

59 intrantemque *Rothstein*

---

15 Pollius had his own poetic fountain.
16 *Domus,* a (flattering?) term for the buildings that made up

Phoebus' auspices he plunged deep his urn[15]—not so
could I match in Pierian strains the countless sights and
ornaments of the area. My eyes scarce held out in the long
procession, scarce my steps, as I was led from item to item.
What a multitude of objects! Should I marvel first at the
place's ingenuity or its master's? This mansion[16] faces sun-
rise and Phoebus' early ray; that detains him in his setting
and refuses to dismiss the light now spent, when the day is
weary and the dark mountain's shadow falls upon the sea
and the palace swims in its glassy water. Some buildings
are loud with the sea's clamour, others know nothing of the
sounding billows, preferring the silence of the land. Some
spots Nature has favoured, in others she has been overcome and yielded to the developer, letting herself be
taught new and gentler ways. Where you see level ground,
there used to be a hill; the building you now enter was wilderness; where now you see lofty woods, there was not
even land. The occupant has tamed it all; the soil rejoices
as he shapes rocks or expels them, following his lead. Now
behold the cliffs as they learn the yoke, and the dwellings
as they enter, and the mountain bidden to withdraw. Let
the hand of Methymna's bard and therewith the Theban
lyre and the glory of Getic quill give you best:[17] you too
move rocks and lofty forests follow you.

Why should I tell of ancient forms in wax[18] or bronze,
shapes animated by Apelles' gay colours or planed by

the villa (cf. I.3.58, II.2.50, III.1.79); not 'part of the house'
(Mozley).

[17] Arion, Amphion, Orpheus. The first, charmer of dolphins
but not of trees or rocks, does not tally as do the other two.

[18] See note on II.1.193.

Phidiacae rasere manus, quod ab arte Myronis
aut Polycliteo iussum est quod vivere caelo,
aeraque ab Isthmiacis auro potiora favillis,
ora ducum ac vatum sapientumque ora priorum,
70   quos tibi cura sequi, quos toto pectore sentis
expers curarum atque animum virtute quieta
compositus semperque tuus? quid mille revolvam
culmina visendique vices? sua cuique voluptas
atque omni proprium thalamo mare, transque iacentem
75   Nerea diversis servit sua terra fenestris.
haec videt Inarimen, illinc Prochyta aspera paret;
armiger hac magni patet Hectoris, inde malignum
aëra respirat pelago circumflua Nesis;
inde vagis omen felix Euploea carinis,
80   quaeque ferit curvos exserta Megalia fluctus,
angitur et domino contra recubante proculque
Surrentina tuus spectat praetoria Limon.
una tamen cunctis, procul eminet una diaetis
quae tibi Parthenopen directo limite ponti
ingerit.
85   Hic Grais penitus desecta metallis
saxa: quod Eoae respergit vena Syenes,
Synnade quod maesta Phrygiae fodere secures
per Cybeles lugentis agros, ubi marmore picto
candida purpureo distinguitur area gyro;
90   hic et Amyclaei caesum de monte Lycurgi
quod viret et molles imitatur rupibus herbas;

79 Euploea *Calderini*: euboea M   80 terit *Heinsius*
81 en *Saenger*   85 desecta *Avantius*: dele- M

---

19 Done prior to the famous statue of Zeus at Olympia.

Phidias' hands—wondrous work, though Pisa was still empty[19]—or bidden to live by Myron's or Polyclitus' chisel, bronzes from Isthmian ash more precious than gold,[20] faces of captains and poets, faces of olden sages, whom 'tis your study to follow, whom you feel in all your heart—free of cares as you are, mind composed in tranquil virtue, ever master of yourself? Why should I rehearse the thousand rooftops and the changing views? Every room has its own delight, each its peculiar sea; and beyond the expanse of Nereus each separate window commands its own landscape. One looks on Inarime, from another rugged Prochyta appears, this way great Hector's armour-bearer spreads, that way seagirt Nesis breathes her unwholesome air; yonder is Euploea[21] of happy omen for wandering keels and Megalia outthrust to strike the curving waves, and your own Limon is vexed that his lord rests opposite, as from afar he views your Surrentine palace. But one room stands far out, one room from all the rest, which over the sea's straight track presents you with Parthenope.

Here are marbles hewn from the depth of Grecian quarries: here vein-splashed product of eastern Syene, here what Phrygian axes hewed in mournful[22] Synnas amid the fields of wailing Cybele, where on painted stone the white space is picked out with purple circles. Here too is marble quarried from Amyclaean Lycurgus' mountain[23]— green, rocks mimicking soft grass—here glisten the yellow

[20] Corinthian bronze was supposed to have originated from metals melted together when the city was sacked in 146 B.C.

[21] 'Of fair sailing.' The temple of Aphrodite Euploea stood on a promontory (Pizzo Falcone) at the site of the old city of Naples.

[22] Mourning for Attis; cf. I.5.37f.

[23] Taygetus; see on IV.8.53.

hic Nomadum lucent flaventia saxa Thasosque
et Chios et gaudens fluctus aequare Carystos;
omnia Chalcidicas turres obversa salutant.
95   macte animo quod Graia probas, quod Graia frequentas
arva, nec invideant quae te genuere Dicarchi
moenia. nos docto melius potiemur alumno.
      Quid nunc ruris opes pontoque novalia dicam
iniecta et madidas Baccheo nectare rupes?
100   saepe per autumnum iam pubescente Lyaeo
conscendit scopulos noctisque occulta sub umbra
palmite maturo rorantia lumina tersit
Nereis et dulces rapuit de collibus uvas.
saepe et vicino sparsa est vindemia fluctu
105   et Satyri cecidere vadis nudamque per undas
Dorida montani cupierunt prendere Panes.
      Sis felix, tellus, dominis ambobus in annos
Mygdonii Pyliique senis nec nobile mutes
servitium, nec te cultu Tirynthia vincat
110   aula Dicarcheique sinus, nec saepius isti⟨s⟩
blanda Therapnaei placeant vineta Galaesi.
hic ubi Pierias exercet Pollius artes,
seu volvit monitus quos dat Gargettius auctor,
seu nostram quatit ille chelyn, seu dissona nectit

93 aequare *Salmasius*: spectare M
95 Graia (*bis*) *Gronovius*: grata (*bis*) M
110 istis *Avantius*: isti M

24 Cf. I.2.149.   25 Neapolitan. Naples originated from
Cumae, a colony of Chalcis.
26 Puteoli (Pozzuoli).
27 Naples being a centre of culture, Puteoli of trade.

stones of Numidia and Thasos and Chios and Carystos that joys to match the waves.[24] All face and salute the Chalcidian[25] towers. Bless your heart that you favour things Greek and spend your days in Grecian country! Nor let Dicarchus' city[26] that gave you birth be jealous. We shall more fitly possess our poet foster child.[27]

Why now should I tell of rural wealth, ploughlands cast upon the sea,[28] cliffs awash in Bacchus' nectar? Often in autumn, when Lyaeus is burgeoning, a Naiad has climbed the rocks and in night's secret shade wiped her dripping eyes with a ripened vine shoot[29] and snatched sweet grapes from the hills. Often the vintage is sprayed by the adjoining flood. Satyrs fell into the shallows and the mountain Pans lusted to catch Doris naked in the waves.

Be fruitful for your lord and lady, earth, unto the years of the Mygdonian ancient and the Pylian,[30] nor change your noble bondage! Let not the Tirynthian hall[31] be better appointed nor Dicarchus' bay nor the seductive vineyards of Therapnaean Galaesus more often please them. Here Pollius plies Pierian skills, whether meditating the precepts of the Gargettian teacher[32] or striking my lyre or

[28] Referred by Vollmer to a flat stretch fringing the water, still called Marina di Puolo.

[29] Perhaps 'a vine-shoot taken from a vine with grapes' (van Dam) or perhaps the Nymph is assumed to have eaten them. But I doubt if Statius gave the question a thought.

[30] Tithonus (rather than Priam; see van Dam) and Nestor.

[31] Probably an estate at Tibur, where Hercules had a famous temple.

[32] Epicurus. Pollius may have been writing on his philosophy in hexameters (Nisbet) or a translation or treatise in prose (van Dam). The former suits the context better.

115 carmina, sive minax ultorem stringit iambon,
hinc levis e scopulis meliora ad carmina Siren
advolat, hinc motis audit Tritonia cristis.
tunc rapidi ponunt flatus, maria ipsa vetantur
obstrepere, emergunt pelago doctamque trahuntur
120 ad chelyn et blandi scopulis delphines aderrant.
    Vive, Midae gazis et Lydo ditior auro,
Troica et Euphratae supra diademata felix,
quem non ambigui fasces, non mobile vulgus,
non leges, non castra terent, qui pectore magno
125 spemque metumque domas voto sublimior omni,
exemptus Fatis indignantemque refellens
Fortunam; dubio quem non in turbine rerum
deprendet suprema dies, sed abire paratum
ac plenum vita. nos, vilis turba, caducis
130 deservire bonis semperque optare parati,
spargimur in casus: celsa tu mentis ab arce
despicis errantes humanaque gaudia rides.
tempus erat cum te geminae suffragia terrae
diriperent celsusque duas veherere per urbes,
135 inde Dicarcheis multum venerande colonis,
hinc ascite meis, pariterque his largus et illis
ac iuvenile calens rectique errore superbus.
at nunc discussa rerum caligine verum

118 rabidi ⊊   124 tenent ⊊   125 voto *Waller*: tuto M
126 refellens *Markland*
137 recti *Courtney* (pulchri *iam Håkanson*): plectri M

---

[33] Writing epic or elegy or satire.   [34] Of Croesus.
[35] I.e. Persia.   [36] Fasces, emblems of magisterial power,
dubious because temporary and elective.

turning unequal verses or unsheathing the avenging iamb
in threatening vein.[33] From this side the Siren flits lightly
to better songs than hers, from that Tritonia hearkens,
nodding her crest. Then the swift winds subside, the very
seas are forbidden to roar, winsome dolphins emerge from
the water drawn to his accomplished harp, and wander by
the cliffs.

Long life to you, richer than Midas' treasures and Lydian gold,[34] fortunate beyond the diadems of Troy and Euphrates.[35] You shall not be chafed by the dubious rods,[36]
the fickle populace, the laws, the armies; for your great
soul masters hope and fear, loftier than any desire, im-
mune from the Fates and rebuffing indignant Fortune.
Your final day shall not find you caught in the doubtful
whirl of events, but ready to go, fed full with life. We,
worthless crew, ever ready to serve perishable blessings,
ever hoping for more, are scattered to the winds of chance;
whereas you from your mind's high citadel look down upon
our wanderings and laugh at human joys. Time was when
the suffrages of two lands tore you apart and you were
borne aloft through two cities, venerated on one hand by
the people of Dicarchus, on the other adopted by mine,
equally generous to both, in the fire of youth and proud in
your mistaken values.[37] But now the fog of things is shaken

[37] Lit. 'in error as to the right (good)'; cf. V.3.248 *amor recti*.
Håkanson saw the sense but left it to Courtney to supply the right
word. *Plectri* (did the 'p' come from *parites* in the line above?)
cannot refer to poetic contests here, even supposing that Pollius
went in for poetry at this early stage of his career. The following lines, especially 138, show that the 'error' was philosophical.
Pollio will have stood for office in both municipalities.

aspicis. illo alii rursus iactantur in alto,
140   sed tua securos portus placidamque quietem
intravit non quassa ratis. sic perge, nec umquam
emeritam in nostras puppem demitte procellas.
147   Tuque, nurus inter longe ‹praedocta Latinas
parque viro mentem, cui non› praecordia curae,
non frontem vertere minae, sed candida semper
150   gaudia et in vultu curarum ignara voluptas:
non tibi sepositas infelix strangulat arca
divitias avidique animum dispendia torquent
fenoris: expositi census et docta fruendi
temperies. non ulla deo meliore cohaerent
155   pectora, non alias docuit Concordia mentes

*   *   *   *   *

143   discite securi, quorum de pectore mixtae
in longum coiere faces sanctusque pudicae
servat amicitiae leges amor. ite per annos
146   saeculaque et priscae titulos praecedite famae.

II.3

ARBOR ATEDI MELIORIS

Stat quae perspicuas nitidi Melioris opacet
arbor aquas complexa lacus; quae robore ab imo

140 sed *Phillimore*: et M
142 demitte *Calderini*: dimittere M
147 *post* longae (-ge M) *lac. agnovit Calderini, ita supplevit Hardie*
143–46 *post 155 transt. Antonius Amiterninus et Gronovius, versum inter 155 et 143 excidisse vidit Housman*

apart and you see the truth. Others in their turn are tossed
upon that ocean, but your bark has made safe harbour and
tranquil rest, unshaken. So continue, nor ever send your
ship into our storms; her voyaging is over.

And you, ‹most accomplished› by far ‹among Latian
ladies, with mind to match your man›,[38] no cares have
changed your breast, no threats your brow; bright joy is
ever in your face and carefree pleasure. For you no sterile
strongbox strangles hoarded riches, nor do ramifications of
grasping usury[39] torment your soul: your wealth is plain to
view, and you enjoy it in educated temperance. No hearts
unite more blessed of heaven, no other minds has Concord
better taught ‹to love their bonds›. Learn untroubled ‹the
joys of life as it slips by unnoticed›.[40] Mingled flames from
your breasts coalesced for long time to come and hallowed
hope keeps chaste friendship's laws. Go through the years
and centuries, outdoing the glories of ancient fame.

II.3

THE TREE OF ATEDIUS MELIOR

There stands a tree, shading the limpid waters of elegant Melior, embracing a pool. Starting from the base of

---

[38] Hardie's supplement is excellent, *exempli causa.*

[39] *Dispendia faenoris,* as explained in *Harvard Studies.* Statius
lets it appear that Polla managed the finances, leaving her husband to higher avocations.   [40] Translating Housman's supplement *vincula amare magis fallentis gaudia vitae*: too long a
shot to be put in the text, but the case for a lacuna is strong.

<in>curvata vadis redit inde cacumine recto
ardua, ceu mediis iterum nascatur ab undis
5   atque habitet vitreum tacitis radicibus amnem.
     Quid Phoebum tam parva rogem? vos dicite causas,
Naides et faciles (satis est) date carmina, Fauni.
     Nympharum tenerae fugiebant Pana catervae.
ille quidem it cunctas tamquam velit, it tamen unam
10 in Pholoën. silvis haec fluminibusque sequentis
nunc hirtos gressus, nunc improba cornua vitat.
iamque et belligerum Iani nemus atraque Caci
rura Quirinalesque fuga suspensa per agros
Caelica tesca subit; ibi demum victa labore,
15 fessa metu, qua nunc placidi Melioris aperti
stant sine fraude lares, fluxos collegit amictus
artius et niveae posuit se margine ripae.
insequitur velox pecorum deus et sua credit
conubia; ardenti iamiam suspiria librat
20 pectore, iam praedae levis imminet. ecce citatos
advertit Diana gradus, dum per iuga septem
errat Aventinaeque legit vestigia cervae.
paenituit vidisse deam, conversaque fidas
ad comites: 'numquamne avidis arcebo rapinis

---

3 incurvata ⊊: cu- M: cur cur- *Havet*
9 it tamen ⊊: et t- M   14 tesca *Markland*: tecta M
16 fluxos *Scriverius*: flavos M

---

[1] *Causas* = αἴτια, the story behind the phenomenon.
[2] Because the doors of his temple were opened in wartime.
The grove, not elsewhere mentioned, is explained by van Dam as a
reminiscence of *Aeneid,* 8.345 *nemus Argileti.*
[3] His den on the Aventine. The Nymph's flight is erratic, as

the trunk, it bends into the pond and thence returns aloft, its top erect as though born anew from the midst of the waves and dwelling with hidden roots in the glassy stream.

Why ask Phoebus about such a trifle? Naiads, you tell the tale[1] and you, obliging Fauns (no more is needed), give me my poem.

The tender flock of Nymphs were fleeing Pan. On he comes as though he wants them all, but it is only Pholoë he is after. Through woods and streams she shies away, now from the shaggy legs, now from the shameless horns of her pursuer. Now she runs on tiptoe past Janus' martial[2] grove and Cacus' black country[3] and Quirinus' fields until she reaches the Caelian wilds. Then at last, overcome by the effort and weary with fright,[4] where now stands the open, innocuous dwelling of tranquil Melior, she gathered her flowing[5] garments about her and sank down on the verge of the snowy[6] bank. Swiftly the god of flocks follows, believing the nuptials his. Already his ardent breast moderates its panting, already he looms lightly over his prey. But see! Diana turns rapid steps that way as she roves through the Seven Hills, tracking the prints of a deer of the Aventine. The goddess was irked by what she saw, and turning back to her trusty companion: 'Shall I never fend off this bois-

though Statius was setting down the localities as they occurred to him.   [4] An inversion of the natural sequence *fessa labore, victa metu,* though Ovid too has *victa labore fugae* (*Metamorphoses* 1.544).   [5] *Flavos* ('yellow') in M seem to be corrupt; see van Dam. A Water Nymph would usually wear grey-green.

[6] I.e., perhaps, 'cool.' So Håkanson, taking *ripae* as the pond. Van Dam is 'not certain that the text is corrupt, but unable to explain it satisfactorily.'

25 hoc petulans foedumque pecus? semperque pudici
decrescet mihi turba chori?' sic deinde locuta
depromit pharetra telum breve, quod neque flexis
cornibus aut solito torquet stridore, sed una
emisit contenta manu laevamque soporae
30 Naidos aversa fertur tetigisse sagitta.
illa diem pariter surgens hostemque protervum
vidit et in fontem, niveos ne panderet artus,
sic tota cum veste ruit, stagnisque sub altis
Pana sequi credens ima latus implicat alga.
35 quid faceret subito deceptus praedo? nec altis
credere corpus aquis hirtae sibi conscius audet
pellis et a tenero nandi rudis. omnia questus
immitem Bromium, stagna invida et invida tela,
primaevam nisu platanum, cui longa propago
40 innumeraeque manus et iturus in aethera vertex,
deposuit iuxta vivamque aggessit harenam
optatisque aspergit aquis et talia mandat:
   'Vive diu nostri pignus memorabile voti,
arbor, et haec durae latebrosa cubilia Nymphae
45 tu saltem declinis ama, preme frondibus undam.
illa quidem meruit, sed ne, precor, igne superno
aestuet aut dura feriatur grandine; tantum
spargere tu laticem et foliis turbare memento.

---

29 laevamque soporae *Krohn*: levamque soporem M: laevum-
que soporem ⌐   33 sicut erat *Markland*
   38 Brimo *Scaliger*   stagna invia *Slater*
   39 nisu *Peyrarède*: visu M
   41 bibulamque *Watt*: flavamque *coni. Courtney*

138

terous, foul brood from their greedy raids, and shall the
number of my chaste company ever dwindle?' So speaking, she takes a short shaft from her quiver nor shoots it
with bent horns and the usual whiz, but despatches it content with one hand, and they say she touched[7] the sleeping
Naiad's left hand with the arrow reversed. Rising, with one
glance she saw the daylight and the wanton foe, and lest
she reveal her snow-white limbs, plunged as she was with
all her clothes into the spring; deep under water she thinks
Pan is following and wraps her flanks in the weeds at the
bottom. Suddenly foiled, what was the robber to do? He
dare not trust his body to the deep water, conscious of his
shaggy hide and from a boy untaught to swim. Of every-
thing he made complaint—cruel Bromius,[8] jealous pool,
jealous arrow. Then with an effort he set alongside a young
plane tree, with long stem, countless twigs, and a top that
would rise to heaven, and heaped up fresh sand around it
and sprinkled it with the longed-for water and thus gave
commission:

'Live long, tree, memorable token of my desire; and do
you at least stoop down and love this hidden couch of the
cruel Nymph, press the water with your foliage. She has indeed deserved it, but let her not pant, I pray, with the heat
above her or be struck by harsh hail; only be mindful to
scatter and ruffle the pool with your leaves. Then will I

[7] Note the meiosis: she had *thrown* the narrow (*emisit*).

[8] With van Dam I keep *Bromium* (= Dionysus); Pan was his
follower. *Brimo* = Hecate, hence Diana, widely accepted by editors including Courtney, is too recondite. And did Pan know that
Diana was involved? If he did, he would hardly blame the weapon
after blaming the one who threw it.

tunc ego teque diu recolam dominamque benignae
50 sedis et illaesa tutabor utramque senecta,
ut Iovis, ut Phoebi frondes, ut discolor umbra
populus et nostrae stupeant tua germina pinus.'
Sic ait. illa dei veteres animata calores
uberibus stagnis obliquo pendula trunco
55 incubat atque umbris scrutatur amantibus undas.
sperat et amplexus, sed aquarum spiritus arcet
nec patitur tactus. tandem eluctata sub auras
libratur fundo rursusque enode cacumen
ingeniosa levat, veluti descendat in imos
60 stirpe lacus alia. iam nec Phoebeia Nais
odit et exclusos invitat gurgite ramos.
Haec tibi parva quidem genitali luce paramus
dona, sed ingenti forsan victura sub aevo.
tu cuius placido posuere in pectore sedem
65 blandus honos hilarisque tamen cum pondere virtus,
cui nec pigra quies nec iniqua potentia nec spes
improba, sed medius per honesta et dulcia limes,
incorrupte fidem nullosque experte tumultus
et secrete, palam quod digeris ordine vitam,
70 idem auri facilis contemptor et optimus idem
promere divitias opibusque immittere lucem:

53 imitata *Markland*   57 sub undas* *debuit*
69 quo *Baehrens: anne* quom♀   71 promere *multi*: co- M

---

9 The Naiad's quarters (v. 44 *durae latebrosa cubilia Nym-phae*) have not so far deserved the epithet. Pan seems to be counting on better behaviour in the future (cf. 60f.).

10 *Animata* is difficult (see van Dam). Courtney and others read *imitata*.

long call you to mind, you and the mistress of the kindly dwelling,[9] and guard both in an inviolate old age, so that Jove's and Phoebus' leaves and the poplar of bicoloured foliage and my pines may marvel at your sprouting.'

So says he. The tree, alive with the god's ancient flame,[10] looms over the plenteous waters, hanging with trunk athwart and peering into them with loving shade. She hopes for an embrace, but the breath of the water fends her off nor suffers touch. At last she struggles down into the pool (?) and, balancing on the bottom, again cunningly raises her nodeless top as though descending into the bed of the pond from another root.[11] Now even Phoebe's[12] Naiad no longer hates her and invites the branches she had shut out from her water.

Such is the gift I make you on your birthday, small indeed but perhaps destined to live through vast stretch of time. In your calm bosom have made their dwelling a dignity that charms and virtue gay yet weighty. Not for you lazy repose or unjust power or vaulting ambition, but a middle way leading through the Good and the Pleasant.[13] Of stainless faith and a stranger to passion, private while ordering your life for all to see, a despiser too of gold yet none better at displaying your wealth to advantage and

[11] See Critical Appendix.

[12] Only here does *Phoebeius* refer to Diana (Phoebe), not Apollo (Phoebus).

[13] Perhaps an awkward amalgamation of two ideas: (a) 'between the Good (morally right) and the Pleasant'—but *per* is not *inter* and these are not two extremes. (b) The path leads through both—but *medius* belongs with (a).

hac longum florens animi morumque iuventa
Iliacos aequare senes et vincere persta
quos pater Elysio, genetrix quos detulit annos.
75 hoc illi duras exoravere Sorores,
hoc quae te sub teste situm fugitura tacentem
ardua magnamimi revirescet gloria Blaesi.

II.4

PSITTACUS EIUSDEM

Psittace, dux volucrum, domini facunda voluptas,
humanae sollers imitator, Psittace, linguae,
quis tua tam subito praeclusit murmura fato?
hesternas, miserande, dapes moriturus inisti
5 nobiscum, et gratae carpentem munera mensae
errantemque toris mediae plus tempore noctis
vidimus. affatus etiam meditataque verba
reddideras. at nunc aeterna silentia Lethes
ille canorus habes. cedat Phaëthontia vulgi
10 fabula: non soli celebrant sua funera cycni.
At tibi quanta domus rutila testudine fulgens
conexusque ebori virgarum argenteus ordo
argutumque tuo stridentia limina cornu
et querulae iam sponte fores! vacat ille beatus
15 carcer et angusti nusquam convicia tecti.
Huc doctae stipentur aves quis nobile fandi

77 revirescit ⊊

---

14 Priam and Tithonus.
1 Cycnus ('Swan'), Phaëthon's relative and friend, is in mind

letting the light in upon your riches, long flourishing in this youth of mind and conduct, go on to match Ilian ancients[14] and surpass the years your father and mother brought to Elysium. This have they begged from the harsh Sisters, this the high renown of great-souled Blaesus, which by your witness shall escape mute neglect and be green again.

II.4

THE PARROT OF THE SAME

Parrot, chief of birds, your master's eloquent delight, Parrot, skilled mimic of human tongue: who cut short your murmurs by so sudden a fate? Yesterday, poor bird, you joined our meal, about to die. We saw you sampling the grateful table's gifts, wandering from couch to couch, past midnight. And you had talked to us, given us your practised words. But now our tuneful one inherits Lethe's endless silence. No more of Phaëthon's common tale:[1] it is not only swans that celebrate their death.

But what a fine house was yours! Radiant the ruddy dome, married with ivory the range of silver bars, loud with your clattering beak the threshold and the doors, now alas! making their own complaint.[2] Empty is that happy prison, departed the clamour of the narrow dwelling.

Let scholar birds crowd hither, to whom Nature has

from Ovid, *Metamorphoses* 2.367ff. and possibly 2.252f. But the connection is loose, much looser than in Martial 4.32.1 and 6.15.1, compared by van Dam.

[2] The bird is no longer inside to rattle them, but they stand open and swing on their hinges (cf. II.5.11f.).

ius Natura dedit; plangat Phoebeius ales
auditasque memor penitus demittere voces
sturnus et Aonio versae certamine picae
20   quique refert iungens iterata vocabula perdix
et quae Bistonio queritur soror orba cubili.
ferte simul gemitus cognataque ducite flammis
funera, et hoc cunctae miserandum addiscite carmen:
    'Occidit aëriae celeberrima gloria gentis
25   Psittacus, ille plagae viridis regnator Eoae,
quem non gemmata volucris Iunonia cauda
vinceret aspectu, gelidi non Phasidis ales,
nec quas umenti Numidae rapuere sub Austro,
ille salutator regum nomenque locutus
30   Caesareum et queruli quondam vice functus amici,
nunc conviva levis monstrataque reddere verba
tam facilis, quo tu, Melior dilecte, recluso
numquam solus eras.
                At non inglorius umbris
mittitur: Assyrio cineres adolentur amomo
35   et tenues Arabum respirant gramine plumae
Sicaniisque crocis, senio nec fessus inerti
scandet odoratos phoenix felicior ignes.'

18 demittere ς: dim- M

144

granted the noble right of speech. Let Phoebus' fowl[3] beat his breast and the starling, whose memory faithfully releases the words he has heard, and magpies transformed[4] in Aonian contest and the partridge[5] that links words remembered and repeated and the desolate sister making moan in Bistonian bedchamber.[6] Together bring your lamentations, bearing your dead kinsman to the flames. And all learn this dirge:

'Dead the famed glory of the airy race, the Parrot, green sovereign of eastern clime, whose aspect not Juno's bird with her jewelled tail would have surpassed, nor the fowl of icy Phasis, nor they that Numidians capture under a rainy South Wind.[7] He, saluter of kings that spoke Caesar's name, would play the role of sympathizing friend or again be a lightsome dinner companion, so ready to return words shown. When he was released, dear Melior, you were never alone.

But not without glory is he sent to the shades. His ashes burn with Assyrian spice and his slender feathers are fragrant with Arabian incense and Sicanian saffron. Unwearied by sluggish age, he shall mount the perfumed pyre, a happier Phoenix.'

[3] The raven.

[4] The daughters of Pieros, who challenged the Muses to a singing match, were so metamorphosed (Ovid, *Metamorphoses* 5.254f.). *Picae* may be magpies or jays.

[5] Not a talker, but see van Dam.

[6] Philomela, the nightingale.

[7] Peacock, pheasant, guinea fowl; almost a repeat, probably inadvertent, of I.6.77f.

II.5

LEO MANSUETUS

Quid tibi constrata mansuescere profuit ira,
quid scelus humanasque animo dediscere caedes
imperiumque pati et domino parere minori?
quid quod abire domo rursusque in claustra reverti
5   suetus et a capta iam sponte recedere praeda
insertasque manus laxo dimittere morsu?
occidis, altarum vastator docte ferarum,
non grege Massylo curvaque indagine clausus,
non formidato supra venabula saltu
10 incitus aut caeco foveae deceptus hiatu,
sed victus fugiente fera. stat cardine aperto
infelix cavea et clausis circum undique portis
hoc licuisse nefas placidi tumuere leones.
tum cunctis cecidere iubae puduitque relatum
15 aspicere et totas duxere in lumina frontes.
at non te primo fusum novus obruit ictu
ille pudor: mansere animi virtusque cadenti
a media iam morte redit, nec protinus omnes
terga dedere minae. sicut sibi conscius alti
20 vulneris adversum moriens it miles in hostem
attollitque manum et ferro labente minatur,
sic piger ille gradu solitoque exutus honore
firmat hians oculos animumque hostemque requirit.
    Magna tamen subiti tecum solacia leti,
25 victe, feres, quod te maesti populusque patresque,

---

¹ constrata ⊊: mo- M   ¹² clausis . . . portis *Lipsius*: -sas
. . . portas M   ¹³ tumuere ⊊: tim- M
²³ animumque *Markland*: -mamque M

II.5

THE TAME LION

What has it availed you to smooth your rage and grow tame? To unlearn crime and human slaughter, to suffer command and obey a lesser master? To have grown used to leave your home and return again to prison, to retire of your own will from prey already captured, to loosen your jaws and let go the hand inside? You are slain, educated ravager of tall beasts. You were not hemmed in by a Massylian band and a cunning net nor plunging over hunting spears in a fearsom leap nor deceived by a pit's hidden cavity, but vanquished by a fleeing beast.[1] The luckless cage stands open on its hinges and all around behind their closed doors the placid lions are angry that such an outrage has been permitted. Then all drooped their manes to see him brought back and drew all their brows down upon their eyes. As for you, that sudden shame did not overwhelm you, laid low though you were at first blow. Your courage held, valour returned from the midst of death as you fell, nor did all your menace at once turn tail. As a dying soldier aware of his deep wound attacks the facing foe, lifting his hand and threatening with sagging sword: so he with sluggish step, stripped of his wonted dignity, steadies his eyes open-mouthed, seeking courage and the enemy.

Yet in defeat you will bear with you great comfort for your sudden death. For people and Fathers groaned at

[1] What beast? The Emperor would know, and Statius has not thought or not troubled to inform later readers.

ceu notus caderes tristi gladiator harena,
ingemuere mori, magni quod Caesaris ora
inter tot Scythicas Libycasque et litore Rheni
et Pharia de gente feras, quas perdere vile est,
30 unius amissi tetigit iactura leonis.

II.6

CONSOLATIO AD FLAVIUM URSUM DE AMISSIONE PUERI DELICATI

Saeve nimis, lacrimis quisquis discrimina ponis
lugendique modos! miserum est primaeva parenti
pignora surgentesque (nefas!) accendere natos,
durum et deserti praerepta coniuge partem
5 conclamare tori, maesta et lamenta sororum
et fratrum gemitus. alte tamen aut procul intrat
altius in sensus maioraque vulnera vincit
plaga minor. famulum (quia rerum nomina caeca
sic miscet Fortuna manu nec pectora novit),
10 sed famulum gemis, Urse, pium, sed amore fideque
has meritum lacrimas, cui maior stemmate iuncto
libertas ex mente fuit. ne comprime fletus,
ne pudeat; rumpat frenos dolor iste deisque,
si tam dura placent * * *
   * * * hominem gemis (ei mihi, subdo
15 ipse faces), hominem, Urse, tuum, cui dulce volenti
servitium, cui triste nihil, qui sponte sibique

28 et *Aldus*: in M
6 alte *Markland*: at te M   aut *scripsi*: at M: ac *Markland*
8 nomina *Leo*: omnia M

your fate, as though you were a famous gladiator falling on the cruel sand. And among so many beasts whose sacrifice is cheap, from Scythia and Libya and banks of the Rhine and the people of Pharos, the loss of one lion touched Caesar's countenance.

II.6

A CONSOLATION TO FLAVIUS URSUS ON THE DEATH OF A FAVOURITE SLAVE

Too cruel whoever sets grades to tears and limits to mourning! Sad it is for parents to put fire to young children and (outrage!) growing sons; hard too to bewail part of a forsaken bed when a wife is snatched away, and grievous the laments of sisters and the groans of brothers. Yet a lesser stroke enters the feelings as deep or far deeper, surpassing greater wounds. You mourn a slave, for so does Fortune blindly mingle names and knows not hearts—but a faithful slave, Ursus, who deserved those tears by love and loyalty, whose soul gave him a freedom beyond lineage. Suppress not your weeping, be not ashamed. Let your grief break the reins, and if such cruelty please the gods, * * * You mourn a human being (woe is me! I myself kindle the torch), *your* human being, Ursus, one that welcomed his sweet bondage, nothing resented, did every-

---

13 deisque *Calderini*: diesque M: decusque *Peyrarède*

14 *post* placent *duo hemisticha excidisse indicat Courtney, monente Leo*   ei ⌐: heu M

16 sibi ipse *Heinsius*

imperiosus erat. quisnam haec in funera missos
castiget luctus? gemit inter bella peremptum
Parthus equum fidosque canes flevere Molossi
20 et volucres habuere rogum cervusque Maronem.
    Quid si nec famulus? vidi ipse habitusque notavi
te tantum capientis erum; sed maior in ore
spiritus et tenero manifesti in sanguine mores.
optarent multum Graiae cuperentque Latinae
25 sic peperisse nurus. non talem Cressa superbum
callida sollicito revocavit Thesea filo,
nec Paris Oebalios talis visurus amores
rusticus invitas deiecit in aequora pinus.
non fallo aut cantus assueta licentia ducit:
30 vidi et adhuc video, qualem nec bella caventem
litore virgineo Thetis occultavit Achillem
nec circum saevi fugientem moenia Phoebi
Troilon Haemoniae deprendit lancea dextrae.
qualis eras, procul en cunctis puerisque virisque
35 pulchrior et tantum domino minor! illius unus
ante decor, quantum praecedit clara minores
luna faces quantumque alios premit Hesperos ignes.
non tibi femineum vultu decus oraque supra
mollis honos, quales dubiae quos crimina formae

22 capientis *Heinsius*: cup- M   spe maior *Housman*
39 quales *coni. Courtney*: -lis M   quos *Baehrens*: post M

1 Silvia's stag in *Aeneid* 7.475ff.
2 Than a slave's. The boy could accept Ursus as his master (no
one else), but he looked as though freeborn. *Spe* (Housman, read
by Courtney) for *sed* is not needed. The boy was evidently not

thing voluntarily, imperious to himself. Who would curb
tears shed for such a death? The Parthian bemoans his
horse slain in war, Molossians weep for their faithful
hounds, birds have had their pyres and a stag[1] his Maro.

How if he were not a slave? Myself have seen and noted
his courage; he stomachs you, only you, for his master, but
higher[2] the spirit in his face and manifest the character in
his young blood. Grecian and Latian brides would fondly
wish and pray for such a son. Not such was Theseus whom
the artful girl of Crete brought back with her anxious
thread, nor such was rustic Paris when he launched reluctant timber on the sea, soon to behold his Oebalian love. I
speak not false, nor does wonted licence lead my tongue: I
saw him and see him still. Such was not Achilles, whom
Thetis hid on a virginal shore as he sang of war, nor Troilus,
whom the lance of a Haemonian hand caught in flight
around cruel Phoebus' walls.[3] How fair you were! Fairer
by far than all other boys and men, yielding only to your
master. His comeliness alone surpassed yours, as the
bright moon outshines lesser beams and Hesperus dims
other flares. No womanish charm was in your face, no un-
manly grace, as with those whom reproach of ambiguous

home-bred and his origin left room for speculation; cf. v. 99.

[3] In Apollodorus (3.32) Achilles ambushes Troilus in the sanctuary of Thymbrean Apollo; and there are other variants. Statius
seems to be thinking of a death like Hector's, perhaps with *Aeneid*
1.474 as starting point; cf. V.2.121, where Troilus and his pursuer
are in chariots. But Ausonius (*Epitaphs* 18) implies that his body
like Hector's was dragged behind chariot wheels, pointing to an
independent version. Troy's walls were built by Apollo (Phoebus)
and Neptune.

40 de sexu transire iubent; torva ⟨at⟩que virilis
    gratia nec petulans acies blandique severo
    igne oculi, qualis bellus iam casside visu
    Parthenopaeus erat, simplexque horrore decoro
    crinis et obsessae nondum primoque micantes
45 flore genae; talem Ledaeo gurgite pubem
    educat Eurotas, teneri sic integer aevi
    Elin adit primosque Iovi puer approbat annos.
    nam pudor ingenuae mentis tranquillaque morum
    temperies teneroque animus maturior aevo
50 carmine quo patuisse queant? saepe ille volentem
    castigabat erum studioque altisque iuvabat
    consiliis, tecum tristisque hilarisque nec umquam
    ille suus, vultumque tuo sumebat ab ore,
    dignus et Haemonium Pyladen praecedere fama
55 Cecropiamque fidem. sed laudum terminus esto
    quem Fortuna sinit: non mente fidelior aegra
    speravit tardi reditus Eumaeus Ulixis.
        Quis deus aut quisnam tam tristia vulnera casus
    eligit? unde manus Fatis tam certa nocendi?
60 o quam divitiis censuque exutus opimo
    fortior, Urse, fores! si vel fumante ruina
    ructassent dites Vesuvina incendia Locroe

> [40] torva atque ⌐: -vaque M
> [42] bellus *Krohn*: bellis M: liber* *Baehrens pessime*
> [48] ingenuae *Heinsius*: unde notae M
> [50] patuisse *Unger*: potasse M   queant ⌐: queam M
> [58] casus ⌐: causas M
> [62] Locroe *Buecheler*: -ros M

---

[4] See Critical Appendix.   [5] I.e. Olympia.

beauty makes change their sex; your charm was stern and virile. Not impudent your look; your eyes were gentle with a spark of austerity, the like of Parthenopaeus now handsome in his helmet.[4] Your hair style simple and rough, yet becoming, your cheeks aflash with first down, but not yet smothered. Such youth Eurotas rears by Leda's stream, so comes a lad at the tender age of innocence to Elis,[5] approving his early years to Jove. As for modesty of a freeborn soul and calm temperance of manners and spirit riper than your tender age, what song could reveal them? Often he would chide his lord (and welcome!), aiding him with commitment and deep counsel. With you he was grave and gay, his mood never his own, from your face he took his his countenance. Worthy he to lead in fame the Haemonian Pylades[6] and Cecropian loyalty.[7] But let praises end where Fortune permits: no more faithful was Eumaeus, sadly hoping for tardy Ulysses' return.

What god or what chance chooses so grievous a wound? Whence did the Fates come by a harming hand so sure? Ah, how much braver, Ursus, would you be had you been stripped of your opulence and ample fortune! If wealthy Locri had belched Vesuvian fire in smoking avalanche, or

6 The Pylades of Thessaly, i.e. Patroclus; a portmanteau expression like *Ebusea Caunos* in I.6.15 or *Nasamonii Tonantis* in II.7.93 or *Gaetulum Ganymeden* in Juvenal 5.59. Van Dam takes as Achilles for the inconclusive reason that Patroclus is not called *Haemonius* elsewhere. Here it distinguishes him from the real Pylades, who came from Phocis. He and Patroclus were both junior partners in the relationships.

7 The friendship between Athenian Theseus and Pirithous, king of the Thessalian Lapithae.

seu Pollentinos mersissent flumina saltus
seu Lucanus Acir seu Thybridis impetus altas
65   in dextrum torsisset aquas, paterere serena
fronte deos, sive alma fidem messesque negasset
Cretaque Cyreneque et qua tibi cumque beato
larga redit Fortuna sinu. sed gnara dolorum
Invidia infelix animi vitalia vidit
70   laedendique vias. vitae modo margine adultae
nectere temptabat iuvenum pulcherrimus ille
cum tribus Eleis unam trieterida lustris:
attendit torvo tristis Rhamnusia vultu
ac primum implevitque toros oculisque nitorem
75   addidit ac solito sublimius ora levavit,
heu misero letale favens, seseque videndo
torsit et invidia, mortisque amplexa iacenti
iniecit nexus carpsitque immitis adunca
ora veranda manu. quinto vix Phosphoros ortu
80   rorantem sternebat equum: iam litora duri
saeva, Philete, senis dirumque Acheronta videbas,
quo domini clamate sono! non saevius atros
nigrasset planctu genetrix sibi salva lacertos,
nec pater; et certe qui vidit funera frater
erubuit vinci.
85   Sed nec servilis adempto
ignis. odoriferos exhausit flamma Sabaeos

---

[64] Acir *Madvig*: ager M   [70] margine *Håkanson ap. van Dam*: carmen M: cardine *Gronovius*
[77] invidit *Ellis*   mortisque *Baehrens*: -temque M
[79] quinto . . . ortu *Schrader*: -ta . . . hora M
[81] dirumque *Markland*: dur- M
[83] salva *Polster*: saeva M

rivers had submerged Pollentian glades, or Lucanian Acir[8] or Tiber's rush had turned deep waters to the right,[9] you would have endured the gods with unruffled brow; or if nurturing Crete and Cyrene had denied their pledged harvests or any place else where bounteous Fortune returns to you with plenteous bosom. But ill-omened Envy, connoisseuse of hurts, saw your soul's vital place, the path to injury. Fairest of youths, just at the threshold[10] of adult life, he was making to link three years with three Elean lustres. The gloomy dame of Rhamnus marked him frowning; and first she filled out his thews and gave his eyes new gleam, raising his head higher than of wont, deadly favours alas! to the hapless lad, torturing herself with malignant gaze; then embracing him as he lay, she cast upon him the chains of death, mercilessly plucking with her talons the face she should have revered. Scarce was Phosphorus at his fifth rising harnessing his dripping steed: already, Philetos,[11] you saw the cruel shores of the pitiless ancient[12] and dire Acheron. Ah, how your master cried your name! Not more cruelly would your mother, had she been preserved to you, have bruised her arms black with lamentation, nor your father; and 'tis sure your brother, who saw your funeral, blushed to be outdone.

But no slave's pyre for the taken one. The flame devoured sacred harvests of Sabaeans and Cilicians, cinna-

---

8 Aciris in Pliny, but the conjecture is dubious (see van Dam).

9 Ursus will have had a property (*horti*) on the north bank.

10 *Margine* seems much the most likely replacement for the senseless *carmen*, even though this metaphorical meaning is unattested. The literal sense, 'threshold,' is found only in Statius (twice; see van Dam).   11 'Beloved.'   12 Charon.

et Cilicum messes Phariaeque exempta volucri
cinnama et Assyrio manantes germine sucos,
et domini fletus; hos tantum hausere favillae,
90   hos bibit usque rogus. nec quod tibi Setia canos
restinxit cineres, gremio nec lubricus ossa
quod vallavit onyx, miseris acceptius umbris
quam gemitus. sed et ipse vetat. quid terga, dolori,
Urse, damus? quid damna foves et pectore iniquo
95   vulnus amas? ubi nota reis facundia raptis?
quid caram crucias tam saevis luctibus umbram?
eximius licet ille animi meritusque doleri,
solvisti. subit ille pios carpitque quietem
Elysiam clarosque illic fortasse parentes
100 invenit, aut illi per amoena silentia Lethes
forsan Avernales alludunt undique mixtae
Naides, obliquoque notat Proserpina vultu.
     Pone, precor, questus. alius tibi Fata Phileton,
forsan et ipse dabis, moresque habitusque decoros
105 monstrabis gaudens similemque docebis amorem.

II.7

GENETHLIACON LUCANI AD POLLAM

Lucani proprium diem frequentet
quisquis collibus Isthmiae Diones
docto pectora concitatus oestro

---

[88] germine *Heinsius*: gram- M   [93] vetat *Jortin*: iuvat M
    [104-05] dabis . . . monstrabis . . . docebis* *scripsi*: -it . . . -it . . .
-it M   [104] habitusque ⊊: -ture M   [105] amorem ⊊: -ri
M: amare ⊊   [3] concitatus ⊊: -avit LM

mon stolen from the Pharian fowl,[13] juices flowing from
Assyrian bud, and your master's tears; these only did the
embers consume, these the pyre drank and drank. Setine
wine quenched your grey ashes, smooth alabaster embos-
omed your bones; but to your poor shade more welcome
was the groaning. But he himself forbids. Ursus, why do we
yield to sorrow? Why nurse your loss and perversely love
the wound? Where is that eloquence well known to defendants hailed to judgment? Why do you torture the dear
shade with such savage mourning? Matchless though he
was and worthy to be grieved for: you have paid. He joins
the blessed, enjoys Elysium's peace, perchance finds illustrious parents there. Or in the pleasant silence of Lethe
perhaps Nymphs of Avernus mingle from all sides and play
with him, and Proserpine marks him with sidelong glance.

Put aside your plaints, I beg. Perhaps the Fates or you
yourself will give you another Philetos[14] and gladly you will
show him seemly ways and manners and teach him to love
you likewise.[15]

II.7

TO POLLA, AN ODE IN HONOUR OF LUCAN'S BIRTHDAY

Lucan's own day let him attend whosoever on the hill of
Isthmian Dione has quaffed the water of the flying hoof,[1]

---

[13] The phoenix.   [14] Who might be bought (so given by
the Fates) or home-bred.   [15] See Critical Appendix.

[1] Pirene on Acrocorinthos; cf. II.2.38. The mountain was sacred to Venus (Dione), whose temple was on the summit.

pendentis bibit ungulae liquorem.
5   ipsi quos penes est honor canendi,
vocalis citharae repertor Arcas
et tu, Bassaridum rotator Euhan,
et Paean et Hyantiae Sorores,
laetae purpureas novate vittas,
10   crinem comite candidamque vestem
perfundant hederae recentiores.
docti largius evagentur amnes
et plus, Aoniae, virete, silvae
et si qua patet aut diem recepit
15   sertis mollibus expleatur umbra.
centum Thespiacis odora lucis
stent altaria victimaeque centum
quas Dirce lavat aut alit Cithaeron.
Lucanum canimus, favete linguis;
20   vestra est ista dies, favete, Musae,
dum qui vos geminas tulit per artes,
et vinctae pede vocis et solutae,
Romani colitur chori sacerdos.

    Felix heu nimis et beata tellus,
25   quae pronos Hyperionis meatus
summis Oceani vides in undis
stridoremque rotae cadentis audis,
quae Tritonide fertiles Athenas
unctis, Baetica, provocas tapetis:
30   Lucanum potes imputare terris.
hoc plus quam Senecam dedisse mundo
aut dulcem generasse Gallionem.
attollat refluos in astra fontes
Graio nobilior Melete Baetis.
35   Baetim, Mantua, provocare noli.

heart stirred by poetic frenzy. You yourselves, to whom belongs the grace of poetic song, Arcadian finder of the vocal lyre, and Euhan, whirler of Bassarids, and Paean, and the Hyantian Sisters,[2] joyfully put on new purple[3] fillets, dress your hair, and let fresher ivy stream down your white robes. Let poetic rivers wander more copiously, and woods of Aonia be greener; if anywhere your shade opens letting in the sun, let soft garlands fill the gap. Let a hundred fragrant altars stand in Thespiae's groves, and a hundred victims that Dirce bathes or Cithaeron feeds: Lucan we sing. Be silent all. This is your day, Muses, be propitious while he is honoured that bore you through both arts,[4] of free speech and of fettered, priest of the Roman choir.

Happy, too happy alas, and blessed you land that see Hyperion's downward course on the surface of Ocean's waves and hear the hiss of his falling wheel, you that with your oily presses challenge Athens, fertile in Tritonis' olive![5] You can claim that the earth owes you Lucan. That is more than to have given Seneca to the world or produced honey-tongued Gallio. Let Baetis, more renowned than Grecian Meles, flow backwards, raising his waters to the stars.[6] Mantua, challenge not Baetis.

---

[2] The Muses. What follows applies to them, not the deities previously invoked. Saenger not unreasonably diagnosed a lacuna between *Paean* and *et,* changing the latter to *at.*

[3] Instead of white. Purple fillets and ivy are associated with Bacchus; cf. I.5.13.   [4] Verse and prose.

[5] Tritonis, signifying olive or olive oil as Lyaeus = Bacchus can signify wine. Pallas is sometimes so used.   [6] Flowing upward to the sky instead of downward to the sea, a proverbial impossibility (*adynaton*). The ideas of miracle and exaltation are combined.

          Natum protinus atque humum per ipsam
        primo murmure dulce vagientem
        blando Calliope sinu recepit.
        tum primum posito remissa luctu
40   longos Orpheos exuit dolores
        et dixit: 'puer o dicate Musis,
        longaevos cito transiture vates,
        non tu flumina nec greges ferarum
        nec plectro Geticas movebis ornos,
45   sed septem iuga Martiumque Thybrim
        et doctos equites et eloquente
        cantu purpureum trahes senatum.
        nocturnas alii Phrygum ruinas
        et tardi reduces vias Ulixis
50   et puppem temerariam Minervae
        trita vatibus orbita sequantur:
        tu cretus Latio memorque gentis
        carmen fortior exseres togatum.
          Ac primum teneris adhuc in annis
55   ludes Hectora Thessalosque currus
        et supplex Priami potentis aurum,
        et sedes reserabis inferorum;
        ingratus Nero dulcibus theatris
        et noster tibi proferetur Orpheus.
60   dices culminibus Remi vagantes
        infandos domini nocentis ignes.
        hinc castae titulum decusque Pollae
        iucunda dabis allocutione.
        mox coepta generosior iuventa
65   albos ossibus Italis Philippos

At first, down on the ground, as he sweetly wailed his earliest murmuring, Calliope took him onto her loving lap. Then easing for the first time, she set mourning aside, putting off her long grief for Orpheus, and spoke: 'Boy, dedicate to the Muses, soon to surpass immortal bards, not wild packs nor Getic ash trees shall you move with your quill; but the Seven Hills and Martian Tiber you shall draw with eloquent song, and cultured Knights and purple-clad Senate. Let others pursue the night of Phrygian downfall, the returning travels of tardy Ulysses, and Minerva's temerarious vessel:[7] born of Latium and mindful of your race,[8] you shall be bolder, unsheathing a song of Rome.[9]

And first, still in boyhood's years, you shall dally with Hector[10] and the Thessalian chariot and royal Priam's suppliant gold, and unbar the dwellings infernal. Ungrateful Nero and our Orpheus you shall recite to kindly theatres. You shall tell of the monstrous fires of a guilty ruler at large over the roofs of Remus. Next a charming address to chaste Polla, bestowing fame and ornament. Presently, nobler in early manhood, you shall thunder Philippi, white

[7] Argo.

[8] 'Your race,' not 'its race,' as van Dam. See Critical Appendix.

[9] Lit. 'a gowned song.'

[10] Regarding Lucan's juvenilia, from which hardly anything has survived, see e.g. H. J. Rose's *Handbook to Latin Literature*, 380f.

---

[52] cretus* *scripsi*: carus M
[53] exseres *Markland*: -ris LM   *post* 67 *versum excidisse statuit Saenger*

et Pharsalica bella detonabis,
quo fulmen ducis inter arma divi

    *   *   *   *   *

libertate gravem pia Catonem
et gratum popularitate Magnum.
70   tu Pelusiaci scelus Canopi
deflebis pius et Pharo cruenta
Pompeio dabis altius sepulchrum.
haec primo iuvenis canes sub aevo
ante annos Culicis Maroniani.
75   cedet Musa rudis ferocis Enni
et docti furor arduus Lucreti
et qui per freta duxit Argonautas
et qui corpora prima transfigurat.
quin maius loquar: ipsa te Latinis
80   Aeneis venerabitur canentem.
     Nec solum dabo carminum nitorem,
sed taedis genialibus dicabo

---

77 ducit *Markland*
79 quin ς: quid LM   loquar L: -uor M

---

11 Lucan's epic *On the Civil War,* still sometimes foolishly referred to as *Pharsalia,* breaks off with Caesar in Alexandria (48
B.C.). He probably intended to continue down to Philippi (42 B.C.)
or beyond, but I find it hard to believe that *Philippos* refers to
what was never written. Latin poets, taking their cue from Virgil
(*Georgics* I.490), imagine both battles, Pharsalia and Philippi, as
fought in the same place. Statius seems to extend this error to the
point of using both names for the same battle, but 'Pharsalian
wars' will include other fighting in the poem before and after it.

BOOK II.7

with bones,[11] and Pharsalian wars. The captain-thunder-
bolt[12] who became divine in warfare ∗ ∗ ∗ , Cato, hated for
his patriot assertion of independence, and Magnus, winning the favour he courted.[13] You shall shed pious tears for
the crime of Pelusian Canopus[14] and give Pompey a tomb
more lofty than bloody Pharos. All this you shall sing as a
young man in early life before the age of Maro's 'Gnat.'[15]
Bold Ennius' untutored Muse shall yield, and the high
frenzy of skilled[16] Lucretius, and he that led the Argonauts
through the seas,[17] and he that transforms bodies from
their first shapes.[18] Nay, a greater thing I shall utter:[19]
Aeneis herself shall do you reverence, as you sing to the
men of Latium.

Nor shall I give you the gleam of poetry alone, but with
the torches of wedlock bestow on you a mate, cultured to

He may even have made the modern mistake of relating *Pharsalia
nostra* in Lucan 9.985 to the poem instead of the battle.

[12] Caesar. For the genitive cf. V.1.133 *fulmen equi.*

[13] I believe vv. 69 and 70 have been misunderstood. They are
antithetical, *libertate gravem* in contrast to *gratum popularitate.*
For Cato's *libertas,* his assertion of independence and free speech
for the public good (*pia*), cf. Cicero, *Pro Sestio* 60 and my note in
SCP, 131. It made him *gravis* ('irksome') to some, whereas Pompey's popularity-mongering brought him favour: cf. Cicero, *Letters to Atticus* 1.20.2 *nihil non submissum atque populare* and
2.1.6 *populari levitate.*

[14] Pompey's murder in Egypt. The long passage on his burial is
indeed Lucan at his finest (Statius has nothing approaching it).

[15] See I.epist.7. [16] *Doctus* being a stock epithet for Hellenistic and Latin poets, though in Lucretius' case 'learned' would
be appropriate. [17] Varro Atacinus. [18] Ovid.

[19] See Critical Appendix.

doctam atque ingenio tuo decoram,
qualem blanda Venus daretque Iuno
85   forma, simplicitate, comitate,
censu, sanguine, gratia, decore,
et vestros hymenaeon ante postes
festis cantibus ipsa personabo.
        O saevae nimium gravesque Parcae!
90   o numquam data longa fata summis!
cur plus, ardua, casibus patetis?
cur saeva vice magna non senescunt?
sic natum Nasamonii Tonantis
post ortus obitusque fulminatos
95   angusto Babylon premit sepulchro;
sic fixum Paridis manu trementis
Peliden Thetis horruit cadentem;
sic ripis ego murmurantis Hebri
non mutum caput Orpheos sequebar;
100   sic et tu, rabidi nefas tyranni,
iussus praecipitem subire Lethen,
dum pugnas canis arduaque voce
das solacia grandibus sepulchris,
(o dirum scelus, o scelus!) tacebis.'
105   sic fata est leviterque decidentes
abrasit lacrimas nitente plectro.
        At tu, seu rapidum poli per axem
Famae curribus arduis levatus,
qua surgunt animae potentiores,
110   terras despicis et sepulchra rides,
seu pacis merito nemus reclusi
felix Elysii tenes in oris,
quo Pharsalica turba congregatur,
et te nobile carmen insonantem

grace your genius, one that a kindly Venus or Juno might grant for beauty, simplicity, graciousness, wealth, birth, charm, elegance; and myself shall sound the wedding song before your doors in festal chant.

Ah Parcae, too cruel, too harsh! Ah length of days never given to the highest! Why is eminence more open to mischance? Why the cruel lot of greatness, to die young? So does Babylon cover the Nasamonian Thunderer's son, whose lightning struck east and west, with a narrow tomb.[20] So Thetis shuddered to see the son of Peleus fall, pierced by the hand of trembling Paris. So once I followed Orpheus' vocal head on the banks of murmuring Hebrus. And so even you (outrage of a crazy tyrant!), bidden plunge into Lethe as you sang of battles and with lofty utterance gave solace to grand sepulchres (O foul crime, O crime!), shall be silent,' So she spoke and with her bright quill lightly brushed away her falling tears.

But you, whether soaring in Fame's lofty chariot through the rapid vault of heaven, where rise mighty souls, you look down on earth and laugh at tombs, or dwell happily in Elysium's retreat, the grove of peace you have deserved, where assembles the Pharsalian throng and the

[20] Alexander the Great, who claimed to be the son of Ammon (Jupiter), died in Babylon, but his tomb was in Alexandria.

115 Pompei comitantur et Catones,
seu magna sacer at superbus umbra
noscis Tartaron et procul nocentum
audis verbera pallidumque visa
matris lampade respicis Neronem:
120 adsis lucidus et vocante Polla
unum, quaeso, diem deos silentum
exores; solet hoc patere limen
ad nuptas redeuntibus maritis.
haec te non thiasis procax dolosis
125 falsi numinis induit figura,
ipsum sed colit et frequentat ipsum
imis altius insitum medullis;
nec solacia vana sumministrat
vultus, qui simili notatus auro
130 stratis praenitet incubatque somno
securae. procul hinc abite Mortes:
haec vitae genitalis est origo.
cedat luctus atrox genisque manent
iam dulces lacrimae dolorque festus
135 quicquid fleverat ante nunc adoret.

116 seu *Heinsius*: tu LM
117 noscis *Haupt*: nes- LM
128 nec *Schwarz*: ac M: ad L: at *Slater*
132 genialis *Markland*

Pompeys and Catos keep you company as you sound your noble lay; or, hallowed and proud, your great shade acquaints itself with Tartarus and hears from a distance the stripes of the guilty, regarding Nero as he pales at sight of his mother's torch:[21] come here in your splendour, Polla calls, and beg one day, pray you, of the gods of the silent ones. That door is apt to open for husbands returning to their brides. Not in the wantonness of a deceitful dance does Polla clothe you in the shape of a false deity,[22] but worships you as yourself and as yourself consorts with you, sunk deep in her inmost marrow. Nor idle the solace afforded by the face expressed in resembling gold that shines above her couch and hovers over her peaceful slumber.[23] Away with you, Deaths! This is life's birth and beginning. Let bitter mourning yield, let sweet tears flow and festal grief adore all that it wept aforetime!

[21] Nero put his mother to death. She is imagined as pursuing him like an avenging Fury; cf. III.3.15.

[22] Allusion to Laodicea, whose husband Protesilaus returned to her from death for one day. On this story was engrafted a rather murky legend of a wax image of him (cf. especially Ovid, *Heroides* 13.151–58) of which she made a cult. *Thiasis* refers to her worship of Bacchus; cf. III.5.49.

[23] Cf. III.3.196–202, where the spirit of the deceased is conceived of as really present in his images.

BOOK THREE

PREFATORY NOTES

1

Date: late summer of 91. For Pollius see on II.2.

2

The 'Send-off' has extant or partially extant precedents from Erinna to Ovid listed in Vollmer, pp. 394f. M. Maecius Celer is known only from Statius and the *Acts of the Arval Brethren,* which list him as Consul Suffect in 101.

3

The father of Claudius Etruscus was about ninety when he died in 92. Originally a slave, born in Smyrna, he spent most of his life in the service of successive emperors starting with Tiberius, who gave him his freedom. Hence the name Claudius; his slave name, which would have become his cognomen, is unknown. (His entry in the index in the first printing of my Loeb edition of Martial must be corrected on this point.) Nero made him head of the imperial treasury, and Vespasian made him a Knight. But under Domitian he fell into disgrace and exile (ca. 82), into which his son accompanied him. (Martial 6.83.8, *esse quod et comiti contigit et reduci*; the son will have returned to

Rome, and then, after the pardon, gone out to Arpi to bring the old man home again. Cf. 7.40, his epitaph.) Not long before his death the sentence had been lifted and he returned to Rome. His wife Etrusca, of distinguished family, gave him two sons, but died when they were very young. One of them, the recipient of the Consolation, bore her name. Claudius Etruscus' wealth, including the celebrated Baths of I.5 and Martial 6.42, derived from his father.

4

Following an ancient Greek custom, Domitian's boy eunuch Flavius Earinus sent the first clippings of his hair along with a mirror set in gold and gems to the temple of Asclepius in Pergamum, his birthplace. Martial has three related epigrams (9.16,17,36) and three others on the boy's unscannable name (from ἔαρ, spring): 9.11–13.

5

Statius is about to move from Rome to Naples, probably in 94.

LIBER TERTIUS

STATIUS POLLIO SUO SALUTEM

Tibi certe, Polli dulcissime et hac cui tam fideliter inhaeres
quiete dignissime, non habeo diu probandam libellorum
istorum temeritatem, cum scias multos ex illis in sinu tuo
subito natos et hanc audaciam stili nostri frequenter expa-
5   veris, quotiens in illius facundiae tuae penetrale seductus
altius litteras intro et in omnis a te studiorum sinus ducor.
securus itaque tertius hic Silvarum nostrarum liber ad te
mittitur. habuerat quidem et secundus ⟨te⟩ testem, sed hic
habet auctorem. nam primum limen eius Hercules Sur-
10   rentinus aperit, quem in litore tuo consecratum, statim ut
videram, his versibus adoravi. sequitur libellus quo splen-
didissimum et mihi iucundissimum iuvenem Maecium
Celerem, a sacratissimo imperatore missum ad legionem
Syriacam, quia sequi non poteram, sic prosecutus sum.
15   merebatur et Claudi Etrusci mei pietas aliquod ex studiis
nostris solacium, cum lugeret veris (quod iam rarissimum

---

5 penetrale *Politiano tributum 'errore felici (nam ita legendum
docent numeri' (Courtney)*: -li M

8 *add. Baehrens*

16 iam rarissimum *Baehrens, praeeunte Barth*: amariss- M:
rariss- ⊊

BOOK THREE

STATIUS TO HIS FRIEND POLLIUS GREETINGS

To you at least, dearest Pollius, most deserving of the tranquillity to which you so faithfully cling, I do not have to justify the temerity of these little pieces. For you know that many of them came suddenly to birth on your lap and you have often been alarmed by this audacity of my pen, when you take me aside into the sanctuary of your eloquence and I enter more deeply into letters, led by you into every cranny of study. So this third book of my Extempore Poems is sent to you without apprehension. The second had you as witness, but this one has you as sponsor. For its threshold is opened by Hercules of Surrentum; as soon as I saw him consecrated on your beach, I paid him homage with these verses. Follows a piece addressed to Maecius Celer, a young man of great distinction in whose friendship I take the greatest pleasure. He had been dispatched by our most sacred Emperor to a legion in Syria, and since I could not follow him, I sent it by way of escort. Then the filial devotion of my friend Claudius Etruscus deserved some solace from my pen as he mourned his father with unfeigned tears—something very unusual nowadays. Fur-

est) lacrimis senem patrem. Earinus praeterea, Germanici
nostri libertus, scit quam diu desiderium eius moratus sim,
cum petisset ut capillos suos, quos cum gemmata pyxide
20 et speculo ad Pergamenum Asclepium mittebat, versibus
dedicarem. summa est ecloga qua mecum secedere Neapolim Claudiam meam exhortor. hic, si verum dicimus,
sermo est, et quidem securus ut cum uxore et qui persua-
dere malit quam placere. huic praecipue libello favebis
25 cum scias hanc destinationem quietis meae tibi maxime in-
tendere meque non tam in patriam quam ad te secedere.
vale.

III.1

HERCULES SURRENTINUS POLLI FELICIS

Intermissa tibi renovat, Tirynthie, sacra
Pollius et causas designat desidis anni,
quod coleris maiore tholo nec litora pauper
nuda tenes tectumque vagis habitabile nautis,
5 sed nitidos postes Graisque effulta metallis
culmina, ceu taedis iterum lustratus honesti
ignis ab Oetaea conscenderis aethera flamma.
    Vix oculis animoque fides. tune ille reclusi
liminis et parvae custos inglorius arae?
10 unde haec aula recens fulgorque inopinus agresti

---

1 So in IV.epist.5. I do not think *nostri* is a familiarity ('our
friend') such as Statius would hardly have permitted himself, nor
yet analogous to *dominus noster* et sim., but used like *meus* (cf.
IV.1.30 *meus Caesar*), *suus*, *domesticus* as epithets of deities: see
A. D. Nock, *Essays on Religion and the Ancient World,* I, p. 41.

ther, Earinus, our Germanicus'[1] freedman, knows how
long I put off his request,[2] when he asked me to dedicate in
verse the hair that he was sending to Pergamene Asclepius
along with a jewelled box and mirror. Last comes a short
poem in which I urge my Claudia to retire with me to Naples. This, to tell the truth, is conversation, privileged conversation with my wife, aiming to persuade rather than
please. You will particularly favour this piece, knowing as
you do that in fixing on my place of retreat I had you most
of all in mind and that I was retiring not so much to my
country as to yourself.

III.1

THE HERCULES OF POLLIUS FELIX AT
SURRENTUM

Lord of Tiryns, Pollius renews your interrupted cult
and gives his reasons for a neglectful year. For you are worshipped under a larger dome, no pauper on a bare beach
with a shelter for stray sailors to lodge in, no, you have
shining doorposts and a roof supported by Grecian marbles, as though purified once again by brands of honouring
fire you have ascended to heaven from Oeta's flame.[1]

Eyes and mind scarce credit it. Are you that lowly warden of a doorless threshold and a petty altar? Where did
bumpkin Alcides find this new mansion, this unlooked-for

---

[2] I.e. how promptly I complied with it.
[1] In a second apotheosis.

Alcidae? sunt fata deum, sunt fata locorum.
o velox pietas! steriles hic nuper harenas
ac sparsum pelago montis latus hirtaque dumis
saxa nec ulla pati faciles vestigia terras
15 cernere erat. quaenam subito fortuna rigentes
ditavit scopulos? Tyrione haec moenia plectro
an Getica venere lyra? stupet ipse labores
annus et angusti bis seno limite menses
longaevum mirantur opus. deus attulit arces
20 erexitque suas atque obluctantia saxa
summovit nitens et magno pectore montem
reppulit; immitem credas iussisse novercam.
    Ergo age, seu patrios liber iam legibus Argos
incolis et mersum tumulis Eurysthea calcas,
25 sive tui solium Iovis et virtute parata
astra tenes haustumque tibi succincta beati
nectaris excluso melior Phryge porrigit Hebe,
huc ades et genium templis nascentibus infer.
non te Lerna nocens nec pauperis arva Molorchi
30 nec formidatus Nemees ager antraque poscunt
Thracia nec Pharii polluta altaria regis,
sed felix simplexque domus fraudumque malarum
inscia et hospitibus superis dignissima sedes.
pone truces arcus agmenque immite pharetrae
35 et regum multo perfusum sanguine robur
instratumque umeris dimitte rigentibus hostem.
hic tibi Sidonio celsum pulvinar acantho
texitur et signis crescit torus asper eburnis.

13 ac *Baehrens*: ad M
36 rigentibus *Gevartius*: geren- M: ingen- *Markland*

splendour? Gods have their destinies and places too. O
rapid piety! A little while ago all we could see here was barren sand and sea-splashed mountainside and rocks shaggy
with scrub and earth scarce willing to suffer print of foot.
What fortune has suddenly enriched these stark cliffs? Did
these walls arrive by Tyrian quill or Getic harp?[2] The year
itself is amazed at its labour, the twice six months, so nar-
rowly bounded, marvel at a work built to last. 'Tis the god
that brought and erected his towers, straining to dislodge
reluctant boulders and pushing back the mountain with his
great breast; one might suppose his harsh stepmother had
given the order.

Come then: whether free now of command you dwell in
your ancestral Argos and trample Eurystheus buried in his
grave or have your home by Jove your father's throne and
the stars your valour won, and Hebe, dress upgirt, proffers
you a draught of blessed nectar—better she than the banished Phrygian:[3] come hither and bring your guardian
spirit to your nascent shrine. Guilty Lerna is not inviting
you, nor the acres of pauper Molorchus, nor the feared
field of Nemea, nor Thracian caverns,[4] nor the polluted altar of the Pharian king,[5] but a happy, innocent house, ignorant of wicked guile, an abode most worthy of celestial
guests. Put by your fierce bow and your quiver's ungentle
host and your club, drenched in much blood of kings;
throw off the enemy[6] spread over your stiff shoulders.
Here are cushions piled high for you, embroidered with
Sidonian acanthus, and a couch rising rough with figures of

---

[2] Amphion's or Orpheus'.   [3] Ganymede.
[4] Of Diomedes.   [5] Busiris.
[6] The skin of the Nemean lion.

pacatus mitisque veni, nec turbidus ira
40 nec famulare timens, sed quem te Maenalis Auge
confectum thiasis et multo fratre madentem
detinuit qualemque vagae post crimina noctis
Thespius obstupuit totiens socer. hic tibi festa
gymnas et insontes iuvenum sine caestibus irae
45 annua veloci peragunt certamina lustro.
hic templis inscriptus avo gaudente sacerdos
parvus adhuc similisque tui cum prima novercae
monstra manu premeres atque exanimata doleres.

   Sed quaenam subiti, veneranda, exordia templi
50 dic age, Calliope. socius tibi grande sonabit
Alcides tensoque modos imitabitur arcu.

   Tempus erat caeli cum torrentissimus axis
incumbit terris ictusque Hyperione multo
acer anhelantes incendit Sirius agros.
55 iamque dies aderat profugis cum regibus aptum
fumat Aricinum Triviae nemus et face multa
conscius Hippolyti splendet lacus. ipsa coronat
emeritos Diana canes et spicula terget
et tutas sinit ire feras, omnisque pudicis
60 Itala terra focis Hecateidas excolit idus.
ast ego, Dardaniae quamvis sub collibus Albae
rus proprium magnique ducis mihi munere currens

---

7 Lit. 'with much of your brother.' Hercules and Bacchus were
sons of Jupiter.   8 The boxing glove of antiquity was a fear-
some affair, weighted with metal.

   9 Son of Julius Menecrates and Pollius' grandson; cf. IV.8.

   10 Diana's Arician wood by Lake Nemi, in which she concealed Hippolytus after Aesculapius had brought him back to life.
The priest of her shrine, called King of the Grove, was a runaway

ivory. Come in peace and gentleness, not in a storm of anger nor yet in slavish fear, but as Maenalian Auge had you to stay, o'erdone with revel and madid with abundance of your brother's gift,[7] or as Thespius saw you in amazement after your escapade of a roving night, so many times over the father of your bride. Here you have a holiday playground, where harmless angers of ungloved[8] youth go through annual contests as the lustre speeds. Here in your temple is your priest[9] inscribed to his grandfather's delight, still a child, such as you were when you strangled your stepmother's first monsters and were sorry they were dead.

But come, say, revered Calliope, how this sudden shrine came into being. Alcides will be your loud accompanist, making mock music with his sonorous bowstring.

It was the time when heaven's vault broods over the earth at its most torrid and fierce Sirius, hit by Hyperion's lavish rays, burns the panting fields. Now the day was nearly come when Trivia's Arician wood,[10] apt for runaway kings, makes smoke and the lake privy to Hippolytus shines with many a torch. Diana herself wreathes her veteran hounds and furbishes her darts and lets the wild beasts go in safety; all the land of Italy celebrates Hecate's Ides at its chaste hearths. As for me, although I had a property of my own beneath Dardan Alba's hills and a running stream by gift of our great leader,[11] enough to soothe

slave, due to be killed and succeeded by another such. On her festival day, 13 August, he and others ran about with smoking torches.

[11] The water may have come from the conduit that fed Domitian's own country seat at Alba. Cf. Martial 9.18.

unda domi curas mulcere aestusque levare
sufficerent, notas Sirenum nomine rupes
65 facundique larem Polli non hospes habebam,
assidue moresque viri pacemque novosque
Pieridum flores intactaque carmina discens.
forte diem Triviae dum litore ducimus udo
angustasque fores assuetaque tecta gravati
70 frondibus et patula defendimus arbore soles,
delituit caelum et subitis lux candida cessit
nubibus ac tenuis graviore Favonius Austro
immaduit, qualem Libyae Saturnia nimbum
attulit, Iliaco dum dives Elissa marito
75 donatur testesque ululant per devia Nymphae.
diffugimus, festasque dapes redimitaque vina
abripiunt famuli; nec quo convivia migrent,
quamvis innumerae gaudentia rura superne
insedere domus et multo culmine dives
80 mons nitet; instantes sed proxima quaerere nimbi
suadebant laesique fides reditura sereni.
stabat dicta sacri tenuis casa nomine templi
et magnum Alciden humili lare parva premebat,
fluctivagos nautas scrutatoresque profundi
85 vix operire capax. huc omnis turba coimus,
huc epulae ditesque tori coetusque ministrum
stipantur nitidaeque cohors gratissima Pollae.
nec cepere fores angustaque deficit aedes.
erubuit risitque deus dilectaque Polli
90 corda subit blandisque virum complectitur ulnis.
     'Tune,' inquit 'largitor opum, qui mente profusa

---

[12] Surrentum; cf. II.2.1.   [13] *Aeneid* IV.160ff.
[14] Parts of the villa; cf. on II.2.45.

my cares at home and alleviate the swelter, I was sojourning by the cliffs that bear the Sirens' name[12] at the hearth of eloquent Pollius, no stranger there, assiduously studying his peaceful way of life and new blossoms of the Pierides, virgin songs. It chanced that as we were spending Trivia's day on the watery beach, escaping from narrow doorways and the familiar house and warding off the sun with the foliage of a spreading tree, the sky went into hiding as bright daylight gave way to sudden clouds and Favonius' faint breeze grew wet with a heavy sirocco; such a downpour as Saturnia brought to Libya while wealthy Elissa was given to her Ilian bridegroom and witnessing Nymphs ululated in the wilds.[13] We scatter, and the servants snatch up the festal fare and garlanded wine. Our picnic has nowhere to go, though countless houses[14] sit above the smiling fields and the wealthy mountain shines with many a rooftop; but the urgent shower and assurance soon to return[15] of interrupted sunshine persuaded us to seek the nearest cover. There stood a little hut called by the name of a sacred temple, a tiny, humble home that cabined great Alcides, with scarce room enough to shelter sea-roving mariners and searchers of the deep. Hither all our number gather. Here are crowded the repast, the rich couches, the flock of servants, and elegant Polla's favourite band.[16] The doors did not hold them all, the narrow shrine could not cope. The god blushed and laughed and stole into the heart of his beloved Pollius, embracing him in loving arms.

'Are you,' he says, 'the lavish donor that in your youth

[15] *Reditura* instead of *redituri* (hypallage).
[16] Children and personal attendants.

181

tecta Dicaearchi pariter iuvenisque replesti
Parthenopen? nostro qui tot fastigia monti,
tot virides lucos, tot saxa imitantia vultus
95 aeraque, tot scripto viventes lumine ceras
fixisti? quid enim ista domus, quid terra, priusquam
te gauderet erum? longo tu tramite nudos
texisti scopulos, fueratque ubi semita tantum
nunc tibi distinctis stat porticus alta columnis
100 ne sorderet iter. curvi tu litoris ora
clausisti calidas gemina testudine Nymphas.
vix opera enumerem: mihi pauper et indigus uni
Pollius? et tales hilaris tamen intro penates
et litus quod pandis amo. sed proxima sedem
105 despicit et tacite ridet mea limina Iuno.
da templum dignasque tuis conatibus aras,
quas puppes velis nolint transire secundis,
quo pater aetherius mensisque accita deorum
turba et ab excelso veniat soror hospita templo.
110 nec te, quod solidus contra riget umbo maligni
montis et immenso non umquam exesus ab aevo,
terreat. ipse adero et conamina tanta iuvabo
asperaque invitae perfringam viscera terrae.
incipe et Herculeis fidens hortatibus aude.
115 non Amphioniae steterint velocius arces
Pergameusve labor.' dixit mentemque reliquit.
    Nec mora cum scripta formatur imagine tela.
innumerae coiere manus: his caedere silvas
et levare trabes, illis immergere curae

---

92 Dicaearchi *Krohn*: dicarchei M   iuvenisque* *Klotz*: -nem-
que M   97 erum *Håkanson, duce Baehrens* (ero): erant M:
erat *Aldus*   111 usquam *Baehrens*

filled alike the dwellings of Dicaearchus and Parthenope
with your prodigality, who on our mountain set so many
towers, so many green groves, so many images in stone and
bronze, so many lifelike waxen forms inscribed with colour? For what was that house, that land before it rejoiced
in you as its master? You covered the bare cliffs with a
lengthy road, and where there had been only a track now
stands your lofty arcade with its separate pillars, to give the
route some elegance. On the verge of the curving shore
you enclosed warm waters with twin cupolas (?). Scarce
could I number the works. Is Pollius a needy pauper just
for me? Even such a home I enter cheerfully and love the
shore you open up. But Juno nearby looks down on me and
silently laughs at my threshold. Give me a temple and an
altar worthy of your endeavours, one that ships under propitious sail would not wish to pass by, one to which my
heavenly father might come and a crowd of gods invited to
dine and my sister[17] from her lofty temple as my guest.
And be not daunted because a solid hump of unfriendly
mountain that measureless time has never consumed
stands stark in the way. I myself shall be there to assist so
great an enterprise, breaking through the rugged bowels
of the reluctant earth. Begin; trust Hercules' urging and
dare! Amphion's towers will not have sited themselves
more rapidly, nor the labour of Pergamus.' He spoke and
left his purpose behind him.[18]

Forthwith the model is drafted, sketched out the plan.
Innumerable hands assemble. Some take on the felling of
the woods and the smoothing of the beams, others the

17 Minerva.
18 Or, as usually understood, 'left his (Pollius') heart.'

SILVAE

120 fundamenta solo. coquitur pars umida terrae
protectura hiemes atque exclusura pruinas
indomitusque silex curva fornace liquescit.
praecipuus sed enim labor est exscindere dextra
oppositas rupes et saxa negantia ferro.
125 hic pater ipse loci positis Tirynthius armis
insudat validaque solum deforme bipenni,
cum grave nocturna caelum subtexitur umbra,
ipse fodit, ditesque Caprae viridesque resultant
Taurubulae et terris ingens redit aequoris echo.
130 non tam grande sonat motis incudibus Aetne
cum Brontes Steropesque ferit, nec maior ab antris
Lemniacis fragor est ubi flammeus aegida caelat
Mulciber et castis exornat Pallada donis.
decrescunt scopuli, et rosea sub luce reversi
135 artifices mirantur opus. vix annus anhelat
alter et ingenti dives Tirynthius arce
despectat fluctus et iunctae tecta novercae
provocat et dignis invitat Pallada templis.
    Iam placidae dant signa tubae, iam fortibus ardens
140 fumat harena sacris. hos nec Pisaeus honores
Iuppiter aut Cirrhae pater aspernetur opacae.
nil his triste locis; cedat lacrimabilis Isthmos,
cedat atrox Nemee: litat hic felicior infans.
ipsae pumiceis virides Nereides antris
145 exsiliunt ultro, scopulis umentibus haerent,
nec pudet occulte nudas spectare palaestras.
spectat et Icario nemorosus palmite Gaurus
silvaque quae fixam pelago Nesida coronat,

128 dites Capreae ς (*cf. III.2.23*)

184

sinking of foundations in the soil. Damp earth is baked to
fend off storms and shut out frosts and untamed stone
melts in the round furnace. But the chief labour is to hew
out by hand opposing crags and rocks that deny the steel.
Here the father of the place himself, the Tirynthian, lays
by his weapons and sweats at the work, himself digging the
unsightly ground with a stout pick, when the heavy sky is
veiled by the shades of night. Rich Capreae and verdant
Taurubulae reverberate and the sea's mighty echo returns
to the land. Not so loud does Aetna resound when the an-
vils shake at Brontes' and Steropes' blows, nor greater is
the din from Lemnos' caverns when fiery Mulciber em-
bosses an aegis, adorning Pallas with chaste gifts. The cliffs
diminish and the workmen returning at rosy dawn marvel
at the progress. Hardly is another year panting, and the
wealthy Tirynthian looks down from his great tower upon
the waves, challenging his stepmother's neighbouring edifice and inviting Pallas to a worthy temple.

Now the peaceful trumpets signal, now the hot sand
smokes with rites of strength.[19] Those honours Pisa's
Jupiter would not disdain nor the father of shady Cirrha.
Nothing sad is here. Let tearful Isthmus yield, and cruel
Nemea: here a happier child[20] makes offering. The green
Nereids themselves leap out unbidden from their pumice
grottoes. They cling to the wet rocks and are not ashamed
to watch the naked wrestlers from cover. Gaurus too
watches, wooded with Icarian vine, and the trees that
crown Nesis fixed fast in the sea,[21] and calm Limon, and

---

[19] An athletic contest *à la grecque.*
[20] Menecrates' son aforesaid.
[21] Pointing to νῆσος, 'island.'

et placidus Limon omenque Euploea carinis
150 et Lucrina Venus, Phrygioque e vertice Graias
addisces, Misene, tubas, ridetque benigna
Parthenope gentile sacrum nudosque virorum
certatus et parva suae simulacra coronae.
  Quin age et ipse libens proprii certaminis actus
155 invicta dignare manu. seu nubila disco
findere seu volucres zephyros praecedere telo
seu tibi dulce manu Libycas nodare palaestras,
indulge sacris et, si tibi poma supersunt
Hesperidum, gremio venerabilis ingere Pollae;
160 nam capit et tantum non degenerabit honorem.
quod si dulce decus viridesque resumeret annos
(da veniam, Alcide) fors huic et pensa tulisses.
  Haec ego nascentes laetus bacchatus ad aras
libamenta tuli. nunc ipsum in limine cerno
165 solventem voces et talia dicta ferentem:
  'Macte animis opibusque meos imitate labores,
qui rigidas rupes infecundaeque pudenda
Naturae deserta domas et vertis in usum
lustra habitata feris, foedeque latentia profers
170 numina! quae tibi nunc meritorum praemia solvam?
quas referam grates? Parcarum fila tenebo
extendamque colus (duram scio vincere Mortem),
avertam luctus et tristia damna vetabo
teque nihil laesum viridi renovabo senecta
175 concedamque diu iuvenes spectare nepotes
donec et hic sponsae maturus et illa marito,

157 dulce magis *Schrader*
162 huic ⊊: hic M
164 ipsum *Calderini*: ipse M

Euploea, omen for ships, and Lucrine Venus; and from your Phrygian height, Misenus, you shall learn Grecian trumpets, while Parthenope smiles benignly at the rites of her people, the contests of nude athletes and the small likeness of her watching crowd.

Nay, come and deign gladly to honour the course of your own contest with your invincible hand. Whether your pleasure is to split the clouds with discus or to outstrip the flying zephyrs with javelin or to tie Libyan wrestling knots with your arms,[22] do our rituals grace; and if you still have apples of the Hesperides, place them in the lap of venerable Polla, for she is worthy and will not demean so great an honour. But had she recovered the sweet beauty of her salad years, (by your leave, Alcides) haply you would have carried her spinning.[23]

These offerings I have brought to the nascent altars, a happy reveller. Now I see himself on the threshold, opening his mouth and speaking thus:

'Hail to your spirit and your wealth, imitator of my labours, tamer of stark rocks, barren Nature's disgrace, who turn the wilderness to use, haunt of wild beasts, and bring forth deities from shameful hiding! What rewards shall I now give your deserts, what thanks return? I shall grasp the threads of the Parcae and stretch their distaffs (I know how to best cruel Death).[24] I shall turn mourning away and forbid sad bereavements. I shall renew you scatheless in a green old age, letting you long watch your grandchildren grow to manhood, until he is ripe for a bride and she for a

---

[22] Alluding to Antaeus, the African giant outwrestled by Hercules.   [23] As he did for Omphale.

[24] He had brought Alcestis back from the Underworld.

rursus et ex illis suboles nova grexque protervus
nunc umeris irreptet avi, nunc agmine blando
certatim placidae concurrat ad oscula Pollae.
180 nam templis numquam statuetur terminus aevi
dum me flammigeri portabit machina caeli.
nec mihi plus Nemee priscumque habitabitur Argos
nec Tiburna domus solisque cubilia Gades.'
     Sic ait, et tangens surgentem altaribus ignem
185 populeaque movens albentia tempora silva
et Styga et aetherii iuravit fulmina patris.

III.2

PROPEMPTICON MAECIO CELERI

Di quibus audaces amor est servare carinas
saevaque ventosi mulcere pericula ponti,
sternite molle fretum placidumque advertite votis
concilium, et lenis non obstrepat unda precanti.
5   Grande tuo rarumque damus, Neptune, profundo
depositum: iuvenis dubio committitur alto
Maecius atque animae partem super aequora nostrae
maiorem transferre parat. proferte benigna
sidera et antemnae gemino considite cornu,
10   Oebalii fratres. vobis pontusque polusque
luceat; Iliacae longe nimbosa sororis
astra fugate, precor, totoque excludite caelo.
vos quoque, caeruleum Phorci, Nereides, agmen,
quis honor et regni cessit fortuna secundi,

4 lenis ς: levis M
13 Phorci *Krohn*: ponti M

188

husband, and from them in turn springs a new generation as the saucy brood now crawls on their grandfather's[25] shoulders, now runs together in affectionate rivalry to the knees of benignant Polla. As for the temple, no limit of age shall be set so long as the fabric of the fiery sky shall carry me. Nor shall Nemea or ancient Argos or my home in Tibur nor Gades, bedchamber of the sun, more often be my dwelling.'

So he speaks, and touching the fire that rises from his altar and nodding his temples white with poplar leaves, he swore by Styx and his heavenly father's thunderbolts.

III.2

SEND-OFF TO MAECIUS CELER

Gods whose joy it is to guard bold ships and allay the perils of the windy ocean, strew soft the waters and turn your counsel benignly to my entreaties. And let the waves be calm nor clamour against me as I pray:

Neptune, great and rare is the charge I give your deep. Young Maecius is committed to the uncertain main and makes ready to carry the greater part of my soul overseas. Bring forth your kind stars, Oebalian brethren,[1] and take seat upon the twin horns of the yardarm. Illumine sea and sky. Banish afar, I pray, your Ilian sister's stormy light, shut her out from all the heavens. You too, Nereids, cerulean host of Phorcus, to whom has fallen the honour and for-

---

[25] I.e. great-grandfather's (*proavi*).   [1] Castor and Pollux, brothers of Helen; her star was considered bad for shipping, theirs good when they appeared at the yardarm.

15 dicere quae magni fas sit mihi sidera ponti,
surgite de vitreis spumosae Doridos antris
Baianosque sinus et feta tepentibus undis
litora tranquillo certatim ambite natatu,
quaerentes ubi celsa ratis, quam scandere gaudet
20 nobilis Ausoniae Celer armipotentis alumnus.
nec quaerenda diu; modo nam trans aequora terris
prima Dicarcheis Pharium gravis intulit annum,
prima salutavit Capreas et margine dextro
sparsit Tyrrhenae Mareotica vina Minervae.
25 huius utrumque latus molli praecingite gyro
partitaeque vices vos stuppea tendite mali
vincula, vos summis annectite sipara velis,
vos zephyris aperite sinus. pars transtra reponat,
pars demittat aquis curvae moderamina puppis.
30 sint quibus explorent †primos gravis† arte molorchos,
quaeque secuturam religent post terga phaselon
uncaque summersae penitus retinacula vellant.
temperet haec aestus pelagusque inclinet ad ortus.
officio careat glaucarum nulla sororum.
35 hinc multo Proteus geminoque hinc corpore Triton
praenatet et subitis qui perdidit inguina monstris
Glaucus, adhuc patriis quotiens allabitur oris
litoream blanda feriens Anthedona cauda.
tu tamen ante omnes diva cum matre, Palaemon,
40 annue, si vestras amor est mihi pandere Thebas
nec cano degeneri Phoebeum Amphiona plectro.
et pater Aeolio frangit qui carcere ventos,
cui varii flatus omnisque per aequora mundi

---

19 quam *Barth, Heinsius*: qua M   30 *varia coniecta*
43 mundi M: ponti *Heinsius*

190

tune of the second realm (give me leave to call you stars of the great ocean), arise from foamy Doris' glassy grottoes and in tranquil rivalry swim round Baiae's bay and the shores pregnant with warm springs, seeking the tall ship that Celer, noble nurseling of Ausonia mighty in war, rejoices to board. She needs no lengthy search, for but lately was she the first to bring her cargo of Pharian harvest to Dicarchus' land, first to greet Capreae and scatter Mareotic wine from starboard in libation to Tyrrhene Minerva. Circle both her bows in a soft curve. Parcel out your duties: some brace the mast's hempen rigging, some attach the topsail to the mainsail, some spread canvas to the zephyrs; let others put back the thwarts, others let down into the water the rudder that guides the curving poop. There must be some to explore * * *, some to bind the skiff that will trail astern, some to dive deep and hoist the hooked anchor. One of you must control the tides and bend the sea eastwards. Let none of the sea-green sisters lack assignment. Let Proteus of many bodies swim ahead on one side and Triton with two[2] on the other, Glaucus too that lost his loins by sudden prodigy, still striking Anthedon's beach with fawning tail whenever he glides to his native shore. But above all do you grant your favour, Palaemon, with your goddess mother, if 'tis my desire to tell of your Thebes and I sing Phoebus' Amphion with no degenerate lyre. And may the father[3] who subdues the winds in Aeolian dungeon, whom the various breezes and

[2] Proteus could take any shape he wished (hence 'Protean'). Triton was half man, half fish.

[3] Aeolus.

spiritus at⟨que⟩ hiemes nimbosaque nubila parent,
45   artius obiecto Borean Eurumque Notumque
monte premat: soli Zephyro sit copia caeli,
solus agat puppes summasque supernatet undas
assiduus pelago, donec tua turbine nullo
laesa Paraetoniis assignet carbasa ripis.
50   Audimur. vocat ipse ratem nautasque morantes
increpat. ecce meum timido iam frigore pectus
labitur et nequeo, quamvis movet ominis horror,
claudere suspensos oculorum in margine fletus.
iamque ratem terris divisit fune soluto
55   navita et angustum deiecit in aequora pontem.
saevus ⟨et⟩ e puppi longo clamore magister
dissipat amplexus atque oscula fida revellit,
nec longum cara licet in cervice morari.
attamen in terras e plebe novissimus omni
60   ibo, nec egrediar nisi iam ⟨cedente⟩ carina.
   Quis rude et abscisum miseris animantibus aequor
fecit iter solidaeque pios telluris alumnos
expulit in fluctus pelagoque immisit hianti,
audax ingenii? nec enim temeraria virtus
65   illa magis, summae gelidum quae Pelion Ossae
iunxit anhelantemque iugis bis pressit Olympum.
usque adeone parum lentas transire paludes
stagnaque et angustos summittere pontibus amnes?
imus in abruptum gentilesque undique terras
70   fugimus exigua clausi trabe et aëre nudo.

49 laesa *Heinsius*: laeta M
56 *add.* ς   60 *add.* ς
70 exigua fugimus *Phillimore*

every breath upon the levels of all the firmament[4] and the rainy clouds obey, press down with his mountain more tightly upon Boreas and Eurus and Notus. Let only Zephyr have the freedom of the sky, him only drive vessels and skim the surface of the waves, never leaving the sea until he waft your sails to the Paraetonian shore by no tempest scathed.

I am heard. Himself[5] he calls the ship and scolds the tardy seamen. See, my heart now sinks in a chill of fear and though dread of the omen warns me, I cannot shut in the tears that hang on my eyelids. Now a sailor has slipped the cable and severed ship from land, letting a narrow gangway down into the water. From the stern the heartless skipper's long shout divides embraces and plucks back faithful lips, nor is it permitted to linger long on a beloved neck. But I shall be the last to go ashore, nor leave until the ship is under way.[6]

Who made the sea, untried and sundered, into a highway for hapless mankind, driving the loyal foster sons of solid earth into the waves, hurling them into the ocean's jaws? Bold of spirit was he! Not more venturesome the courage that joined snowy Pelion to Ossa and crushed panting Olympus under two mountains.[7] Was it not enough to cross sluggish swamps and meres and set straitened rivers under bridges? We go into the abyss, fleeing our native lands in all directions, confined by a small plank

---

[4] So Lucretius 6.108. But perhaps, as usually taken, 'the seas of all the world.'   [5] Zephyr.

[6] The scene is imaginary, as in vv. 78 ff.

[7] The intention or the fact attributed to the giants Otis and Ephialtes in their bid to storm heaven.

inde furor ventis indignataeque procellae
et caeli fremitus et fulmina plura Tonanti.
ante rates pigro torpebant aequora somno
nec spumare Thetis nec spargere nubila fluctus
75 ⟨g⟩audebant. visis tumuerunt puppibus undae,
inque hominem surrexit hiems. tunc nubila Plias
Oleniumque pecus, solito tunc peior Orion.
iusta queror.
　　　　　　Fugit ecce vagas ratis acta per undas
paulatim minor et longe servantia vincit
80 lumina, tot gracili ligno complexa timores,
teque super reliquos, te, nostri pignus amoris,
portatura, Celer. quo nunc ego pectore somnos
quove queam perferre dies? quis cuncta paventi
nuntius, an facili te praetermiserit unda
85 Lucani rabida ora maris, num torta Charybdis
fluctuat aut Siculi populatrix virgo profundi,
quos tibi currenti praeceps gerat Hadria mores.
quae pax Carpathio, quali te subvehat aura
Doris Agenorei furtis blandita iuvenci?
90 sed merui questus. quid enim te castra petente
non vel ad ignotos ibam comes impiger Indos
Cimmeriumque chaos? starem prope bellica regis
signa mei, seu tela manu seu frena teneres
armatis seu iura dares, operumque tuorum,
95 etsi non socius, certe mirator adessem.
si quondam magno Phoenix reverendus Achilli

75 gaudebant *Markland*: au- M
81 teque *Markland*: quaque M: quaeque *Politianus*
82–3 quo . . . quove *Rossberg*: quos . . . quosve M

194

and the open air. Hence raging winds and indignant tempests and a roaring sky and more lightning for the Thunderer. Before ships were, the sea lay plunged in torpid slumber, Thetis did not joy to foam nor billows to splash the clouds. Waves swelled at sight of ships and tempest rose against man. 'Twas then that Pleiad and Olenian Goat[8] were clouded and Orion worse than his wont. Just is my complaint.

See the vessel flies, driven over the wandering waves; gradually she dwindles, defeating the eyes that hold her from afar, clasping so many fears in her slender timbers. And you she shall carry, you above the rest, charge[9] of my love, Celer. With what heart can I now bear sleep or with what heart the days? Prey to every fear, who shall bring me word? Has the rabid coast of the Lucanian sea given you easy passage? Does whirling Charybdis eddy? Or the devouring virgin[10] of Sicily's deep? How does violent Hadria react to[11] your voyaging? Is the Carpathian calm? What kind of breeze wafts you over the waters that smiled on the dalliance of the Agenorean steer?[12] But I have deserved to complain. Why was I not your brisk companion as you went to war, were it even to India or Cimmerian darkness? I should be standing by my patron's martial standard, whether you held weapons or reins or gave judgment to men in arms, and if not as a partner in your works, I should at least be there to advise them. If Phoenix, honoured

---

[8] See on I.3.96. [9] *Pignus,* like *depositum* in v. 6.

[10] Scylla. [11] Just how this expression relates to the common *morem gerere alicui* ('humour somebody') let others determine. [12] The Cyprian Sea, through which Celer would sail on his voyage from Egypt to Palestine.

litus ad Iliacum Thymbraeaque Pergama venit
imbellis tumidoque nihil iuratus Atridae,
cur nobis ignavus amor? sed pectore fido
100   numquam abero longisque sequar tua carbasa votis.
     Isi, Phoroneis olim stabulata sub antris,
nunc regina Phari numenque Orientis anheli,
excipe multisono puppem Mareotida sistro,
ac iuvenem egregium, Latius cui ductor Eoa
105   signa Palaestinasque dedit frenare cohortes,
ipsa manu placida per limina festa sacrosque
duc portus urbesque tuas. te praeside noscat
unde paludosi fecunda licentia Nili,
cur vada desidant et ripa coerceat undas
110   Cecropio stagnata luto, cur invida Memphis,
curve Therapnaei lasciviat ora Canopi,
cur servet Pharias Lethaeus ianitor aras,
vilia cur magnos aequent animalia divos,
quae sibi praesternat vivax altaria phoenix,
115   quos dignetur agros aut quo se gurgite Nili
mergat adoratus trepidis pastoribus Apis.
duc et ad Emathios manes, ubi belliger urbis
conditor Hyblaeo perfusus nectare durat,
anguiferamque domum, blando qua mersa veneno

---

13 In Argos, when she was a cow (Io).

14 The sistrum, used in Isis' worship.

15 Celer's ship was bound for Alexandria. From Egypt, after
seeing the sights or at any rate being told about them, he would
take ship again for his destination in Syria.

16 Not that Statius himself would know the answers.

17 According to the elder Pliny (*Natural History* 10.94),

of great Achilles, once came to Ilium's shore and Thymbraean Pergamus, no warrior he nor sworn in fealty to the haughty son of Atreus, why is my affection slothful? But in my faithful heart I shall never be absent, following your sails with distant prayers.

Isis, once stalled in Phoroneus' caves,[13] now queen of Pharos and divinity of the panting east, receive the Mareotic vessel with your many-sounding rattle[14] and in person with kindly hand conduct the peerless young man to whom Latium's leader has given the standards of the east and command over the cohorts of Palestine through festal gates to your sacred harbour and city.[15] Under your protection let him learn[16] whence comes the fertile licence of marshy Nile, why the shallows sink and a bank flooded with Cecropian clay curbs the waters,[17] why Memphis[18] is jealous, or why wantons Therapnaean Canopus,[19] why Lethe's janitor[20] guards Pharian altars, why common beasts equal great gods, what altar the long-lived Phoenix strews for herself, what fields Apis thinks worthy of him or in what flood of Nile he bathes, worshipped by trembling hinds. Lead him also to the Emathian remains, where abides the warrior founder of the city steeped in Hybla's nectar, and the snake-haunted hall where Cleopatra of

swallows' nests on the banks of the Nile prevented flooding. 'Cecropian' because Procne, a princess of Athens, was turned into a swallow. *Stagnata,* properly of land under water, is here used of land covered by nest material (clay and straw).

[18] Linked with μέμφεσθαι, 'blame.'

[19] Spartan, called after Menelaus king of Sparta's helmsman, who was buried there. It was notorious for loose living.

[20] Cerberus, identified with the Egyptian dog deity Anubis.

120 Actias Ausonias fugit Cleopatra catenas.
usque et in Assyrias sedes mandataque castra
prosequere et Marti iuvenem, dea, trade Latino.
nec novus hospes erit: puer his sudavit in arvis
notus adhuc tantum maioris lumine clavi,
125 iam tamen et turmas facili praevertere gyro
fortis et Eoas iaculo damnare sagittas.
    Ergo erit illa dies qua te maiora daturus
Caesar ab emerito iubeat discedere bello.
at nos hoc iterum stantes in litore vastos
130 cernemus fluctus aliasque rogabimus auras.
o tum quantus ego aut quanta votiva movebo
plectra lyra, cum me magna cervice ligatum
attolles umeris atque in mea pectora primum
incumbes e puppe novus servataque reddes
135 colloquia inque vicem medios narrabimus annos!
tu rapidum Euphraten et regia Bactra sacrasque
antiquae Babylonis opes et Zeugma, Latinae
pacis iter, qua dulce nemus florentis Idumes,
quo pretiosa Tyros rubeat, quo purpura suco
140 Sidoniis iterata cadis, ubi germine primum
candida felices sudent opobalsama virgae:
ast ego devictis dederim quae busta Pelasgis
quaeve laboratas claudat mihi pagina Thebas.

> 124 lumine *Polster*: nu- M
> 129 at ⌐: ac M   138 quam *Baehrens*
> 139 quo . . . quo *Gronovius*: qua . . . qua M
> 140 cadis *Gronovius*: vadis M   opimo *Heinsius*

---

[21] Cleopatra committed suicide by the bite of an asp after her defeat at Actium to avoid being paraded at Octavian's triumph.

Actium, sunk in gentle poison, fled Ausonian chains.[21] And escort him on his way to the dwellings of Assyria and the camp of his charge, and hand him over, goddess, to Latian Mars. He will be no stranger guest; as a boy he laboured in those fields, known till then only for the gleam of the broader stripe,[22] but already strong to outstrip squadrons in agile wheel and put eastern arrows to shame with his javelin.

So the day will come when Caesar orders you to leave your war service in order to give you greater things. As for me, stationed once more upon this shore I shall view the vast waves and ask for other breezes. Oh, how tall shall I stand then, on how mighty a lyre shall I twang a votive quill! My arms about your stalwart neck, you shall raise me on your shoulders. Mine shall be the first breast on which you fall, fresh from board. You will give me the talk you have been hoarding up and we shall tell each other of the years between: you of swift Euphrates and royal Bactra and the sacred wealth of ancient Babylon and Zeugma, highway of Latian peace,[23] where the sweet woods of flowering Idume,[24] what the juice that makes costly Tyre to blush and the purple twice dipped in the vats of Sidon, where first[25] luxuriant branches sweat bright balsom from the bud: but my tale shall be of the tombs I have given to the vanquished Pelasgi and the page that closes my toil of Thebes.

[22] The tunic with broad purple stripe worn by Senators and their sons. Celer will have been a Military Tribune.

[23] Pax Romana.

[24] Producing dates.

[25] I.e., perhaps, before the gum was exported (Håkanson).

III.3

CONSOLATIO AD CLAUDIUM ETRUSCUM

Summa deum, Pietas, cuius gratissima caelo
rara profanatas inspectant numina terras,
huc vittata comam niveoque insignis amictu,
qualis adhuc praesens nullaque expulsa nocentum
5   fraude rudes populos atque aurea regna colebas,
mitibus exsequiis ades et lugentis Etrusci
cerne pios fletus laudataque lumina terge.
nam quis inexpleto rumpentem pectora questu
complexumque rogos incumbentemque favillis
10 aspiciens non aut primaevae funera plangi
coniugis aut nati modo pubescentia credat
ora rapi flammis? pater est qui fletur. adeste
dique hominesque sacris. procul hinc, procul ite nocentes,
si cui corde nefas tacitum fessique senectus
15 longa patris, si quis pulsatae conscius umquam
matris et inferna rigidum timet Aeacon urna.
insontes castosque voco. tenet ecce seniles
leniter implicitus vultus sanctamque parentis
canitiem spargit lacrimis animaeque supremum
20 frigus amat. celeres genitoris filius annos
(mira fides!) nigrasque putat properasse Sorores.
exsultent placidi Lethaea ad flumina manes,
Elysiae gaudete domus, date serta per aras,
festaque pallentes hilarent altaria lucos.

18 implicitus ς: -tor M: -tos ς

III.3

CONSOLATION ADDRESSED TO CLAUDIUS ETRUSCUS

Piety,[1] highest among deities, whose godhead beloved of heaven looks but rarely upon lacerated earth, come hither with fillets on your hair, shining in snow-white robe, as when present to aid nor yet expelled by sinners' wrong-doing, you cared for primitive peoples and a golden reign. Come to a gentle funeral[2] and behold the pious tears of sorrowing Etruscus, praise his eyes and wipe them. For who that saw him bursting his breast with insatiable lament and embracing the pyre and bending over the ashes but would think his mourning was for a young wife or that the flames were devouring the face of a son just growing to manhood? It is a father he weeps for. Gods and men, come to the rites. Far, far from hence you sinners, if any bear a crime unspoken in his heart and thinks his weary parent's old age too long, if any guilty wretch fear his beaten mother's snake[3] and stern Aeacus' infernal urn! I summon the innocent, the pure. See, in his arms he gently holds the age-worn countenance, bedewing his parent's revered white head with tears and loving his breath's final chill. A son thinks his father's years too swift (wonderful but true!), thinks the dark Sisters went too fast! Let ghosts benign exult by Lethe's stream; Elysian dwelling, rejoice. Strew garlands on the altars, let festal offerings cheer the dim

---

[1] Mingled by Statius with Astraea, but with particular reference to family duty and affection.   [2] The funeral of a gentle old man.   [3] As though the abused mother would herself become an avenging Fury with snakes for hair; cf. II.7.119.

25 felix heu, nimium felix plorataque nato
umbra venit. longe Furiarum sibila, longe
tergeminus custos, penitus via longa patescat
manibus egregiis. eat horrendumque silentis
accedat domini solium gratesque supremas
30 perferat et totidem iuveni roget anxius annos.
    Macte pio gemitu! dabimus solacia dignis
luctibus Aoniasque tuo sacrabimus ultro
inferias, Etrusce, seni. tu largus Eoa
germina, tu messes Cilicumque Arabumque superbas
35 merge rogis; ferat ignis opes heredis et alto
aggere missuri nitido pia nubila caelo
stipentur census: nos non arsura feremus
munera, venturosque tuus durabit in annos
me monstrante dolor. neque enim mihi flere parentem
40 ignotum; similis gemui proiectus ad ignem.
ille mihi tua damna dies compescere cantu
suadet: et ipse tuli quos nunc tibi confero questus.
    Non tibi clara quidem, senior placidissime, gentis
linea nec proavis demissum stemma, sed ingens
45 supplevit fortuna genus culpamque parentum
occuluit. nec enim dominos de plebe tulisti,
sed quibus occasus pariter famulantur et ortus.
nec pudor iste tibi: quid enim terrisque poloque
parendi sine lege manet? vice cuncta reguntur
50 alternisque premunt. propriis sub regibus omnis
terra; premit felix regum diademata Roma;

25 heu *Calderini*: et M: a *Baehrens*
34 superbis ⊊   37 census *Saenger*: cineres M
40 ignes *Markland*
49 reguntur *Meursius*: geru- M

202

groves. Happy, oh[4] too happy, comes the shade, mourned
by a son. Far be the hisses of the Furies, far the threefold
warden;[5] the long road lies open for choice spirits. Let him
go and approach the dread throne of the silent lord. Let
him bring last thanks and anxiously ask as many years for
his son.

Hail to your pious groans! I shall give consolation to
your worthy lament, Etruscus, and unasked consecrate
Aonian offerings to your aged parent. Lavishly plunge
Eastern gums into the flames, the proud harvests of Cilicia
and Arabia. Let the fire bear your inheritance and wealth
be piled on the tall mound to waft pious clouds to the wide
sky. I shall bear gifts that do not burn and your grief shall
endure through years to come as I portray it. For I too
know what it is to weep a father, like you I have groaned
prostrate at the pyre. That day moves me to assuage your
loss by song. I myself have borne the plaints I now offer
to you.

Gentlest of greybeards, no lustre of lineage was yours,
no pedigree handed down from forbears, but a splendid
career supplied the place of family, veiling your parents'
shortcomings. For the masters you served were no common folk; east and west alike are in thrall to them. No
shame to you in that. For what in earth or heaven stays
outside the law of obedience? All things are subject, and
rule in their turn. All earth is under particular kings. The
crowns of kings are pressed down by fortunate Rome.

---

[4] Håkanson favours *heu,* citing *Aeneid* 4.657 and other passages, and so Courtney reads; but in these there are tragic over-
tones, here *nimium* only emphasizes.

[5] Three-headed Cerberus.

hanc ducibus frenare datum; mox crescit in illos
imperium superis; sed habent et numina legem.
servit et astrorum velox chorus et vaga servit
55　luna, nec iniussae totiens redit orbita lucis.
et (modo si fas est aequare iacentia summis)
pertulit et saevi Tirynthius horrida regis
pacta, nec erubuit famulantis fistula Phoebi.
　　Sed neque barbaricis Latio transmissus ab oris.
60　Smyrna tibi gentile solum potusque verendo
fonte Meles Hermique vadum, quo Lydius intrat
Bacchus et aurato reficit sua cornua limo.
laeta dehinc series variisque ex ordine curis
auctus honos, semperque gradus prope numina, semper
65　Caesareum coluisse latus sacrisque deorum
arcanis haerere datum. Tibereia primum
aula tibi vixdum ora nova mutante iuventa
panditur (hic annis multum super indole victis
libertas oblata venit), nec proximus heres,
70　immitis quamquam Furiisque agitatus, abegit.
huic et in Arctoas tendis comes usque pruinas
terribilem affatu passus visuque tyrannum
immanemque suis, ut qui metuenda ferarum
corda domant mersasque iubent iam sanguine tacto

64 gradus *Gevartius*: -du M: -di *Meursius*
68 multum *Hoeufft*: -ta M
71 huic *Politianus*: hinc M　　　tendis *Phillimore*: tenuis M

6 Things human with things divine, Etruscus' father with Hercules and Phoebus; not, as Vollmer, Eurystheus and Admetus with
the Emperor.　　7 River near Smyrna, which city claimed the
honour of Homer's birthplace.

Rome's governance is given to her leaders. Over them
again rises the dominion of the High Ones. But even deities have their law. Serves the swift choir of stars, serves the
wandering moon, nor uncommanded does the light return
so often on its course, and (if only it be lawful to compare
the lowly with the highest)[6] the Tirynthian bore the harsh
covenant of a cruel king and Phoebus' flute did not blush
when he obeyed a master.

But neither were you transported to Latium from barbarian shores. Smyrna was your native soil and you drank
Meles' revered spring[7] and Hermus'[8] water, in which Lydian Bacchus bathes,[9] refurbishing his horns with golden
silt. Thence a happy sequence, your dignity increasing
with various successive charges; and always you were privileged to walk close to deity, always to attend Caesar's side
and be near the secrets of the gods. First Tiberius' palace
was opened to you when new manhood had hardly begun to change your cheeks. Here freedom came your way,
gifted as you were much beyond your years. Neither did
the next heir, cruel though he was and Fury-haunted, drive
you away. As his companion you travelled even to the Arctic frosts,[10] suffering a tyrant terrible in word and look and
savage to his own, like them that tame the fierce hearts of
wild beasts, ordering them when they have already tasted

---

[8] The gold-bearing river, perhaps with an eye to his future at
the imperial treasury (Vollmer).   [9] Cf. *Thebaid* 4.389. Otherwise Bacchus' association with Lydia has little support (see
Vollmer) and *Lydius* is not among his epithets. Perhaps a mis-
guided reminiscence of *Maeonii Bacchi* = Lydian wine, i.e. of
Tmolus, in Virgil, *Georgics* 4.380?   [10] On Caligula's German expedition (Suetonius, *Caligula* 43ff.).

75 reddere ab ore manus et nulla vivere praeda.
praecipuos sed enim merito subrexit in actus
nondum stelligerum senior dimissus in axem
Claudius et longo transmittit ab aere nepoti.
quis superos metuens pariter tot templa, tot aras
80 promeruisse datur? summi Iovis aliger Arcas
nuntius; imbrifera potitur Thaumantide Iuno;
stat celer obsequio iussa ad Neptunia Triton:
tu totiens mutata ducum iuga rite tulisti
integer inque omni felix tua cumba profundo.
85   Iamque piam lux alta domum praecelsaque toto
intravit Fortuna gradu; iam creditur uni
sanctarum digestus opum partaeque per omnes
divitiae populos magnique impendia mundi.
quicquid ab auriferis eiectat Hiberia fossis,
90 Dalmatico quod monte nitet, quod messibus Afris
verritur, aestiferi quicquid terit area Nili,
quodque legit mersus pelagi scrutator Eoi,
et Lacedaemonii pecuaria culta Galaesi
perspicuaeque nives Massylaque robora et Indi
95 dentis honos—uni parent commissa ministro
quae Boreas quaeque Eurus atrox, quae nubilus Auster
invehit: hibernos citius numeraveris imbres
silvarumque comas. vigil idem animique sagacis;

---

77 dimissus *Gronovius*: dem- M   78 longo* M: fratris *coni.*
Courtney   ab aere* *scripsi*: habere M   Neroni *Markland*
    98 idem *Koestlin*: ite M: iste *Puteolanus*   animique ς: -mae-
que M

blood to return hands plunged in and live without prey. But 'twas Claudius in his old age, not yet dispatched to the starry vault, that raised you to the highest office as you deserved and handed you over after your long service[11] to his grandson. Who that fears the gods is said to have served equally so many temples, so many altars? The winged Arcadian is the messenger of highest Jove, Juno is mistress of the rain-bearing daughter of Thaumas; prompt to obey stands Triton at Naptune's orders. You duly bore the yoke of leaders, so often changed, without mishap, your boat was fortunate on every sea.

Now a light from on high shone on the loyal house, and towering Fortune entered at full stride. Now to one alone was entrusted the distribution of the sacred treasure, riches garnered among all peoples, the outgoings of the great world.[12] All that Iberia ejects from her goldmines, that shines in Dalmatian mountains, that is swept up in Africa's harvests, whatever sultry Nile threshes on his floor, what the sunken searcher of eastern sea picks up, cherished sheepfolds of Lacedaemonian Galaesus, transparent snow,[13] Massylian timber, the beauty of Indian tusk: all that the North Wind and fierce East and cloudy South brings in, is entrusted to one minister and does his bidding. Sooner would you number winter's rains or the leaves of the forest. Watchful was that same and shrewd and promptly does he calculate expenditures: how much for

[11] On the conjecture *longo . . . ab aere* see Critical Appendix.
[12] I.e. commodities paid as tribute to the central government.
[13] Crystal, followed by citrus wood and ivory.

et citus evolvit quantum Romana sub omni
100 pila die quantumque tribus, quid templa, quid alti
undarum cursus, quid propugnacula poscant
aequoris aut longe series porrecta viarum,
quod domini celsis niteat laquearibus aurum,
quae divum in vultus igni formanda liquescat
105 massa, quid Ausoniae scriptum crepet igne Monetae.
hinc tibi rara quies animoque exclusa voluptas
exiguaeque dapes et numquam laesa profundo
cura mero. sed iura tamen genialia cordi
et mentem vincire toris ac iungere festa
110 conubia et fidos domino genuisse clientes.
        Quis sublime genus formamque insignis Etruscae
nesciat? haudquaquam proprio mihi cognita visu,
sed decus eximium famae par reddit imago,
vultibus et similis natorum gratia monstrat.
115 nec vulgare genus: fasces summamque curulem
frater et Ausonios enses mandataque fidus
signa tulit, cum prima truces amentia Dacos
impulit et magno gens est damnata triumpho.
sic quicquid patrio cessatum a sanguine, mater
120 reddidit, obscurumque latus clarescere vidit
conubio gavisa domus. nec pignora longe:
quippe bis ad partus venit Lucina manuque
ipsa levi gravidos tetigit fecunda labores.
felix a! si longa dies, si cernere vultus

99 et citus *Salmasius*: exitus M: exci- *edit. pr.*   evolvis
Salmasius
114 similis *Phillimore*: sibimet similis M *et sic Krohn, om.*
vultibus

Roman arms in every clime, how much for the tribes[14] and the temples, how much for watercourses aloft,[15] how much for bulwarks against the sea[16] or the far-stretched chain of roads; the gold that shines in our lord's lofty ceilings, the ore that is melted to shape the faces of gods or clinks stamped by the fire of Ausonia's mint. Hence rest was rare for you, pleasure excluded from your thoughts, meagre your repasts, your care never dulled by deep draughts of wine; but you favoured the claims of wedlock, willing to bind your mind with nuptial ties, make festal marriage, and beget faithful retainers for your lord.

Who but knows noble Etrusca's exalted birth and beauty? Although I never saw her with my own eyes, her portrait, equal to her fame, renders her surpassing loveliness, and the charm and resemblance of her children displays it in their faces. Nor common was her race: her brother bore the rods and the highest curule chair, faithfully commanding Ausonian swords and entrusted standards, what time madness first pushed the fierce Dacians and doomed their race to a grand triumph.[17] So whatever fell short in the father's blood the mother made good, and rejoicing in the marriage the house saw its dim side brighten. Nor was offspring far away, for fruitful Lucina came twice for a delivery and herself lightly touched the pangs of labour. Happy, ah, if length of days and just

[14] Electoral bodies through which free or subsidized corn was distributed to the people.   [15] Aqueducts.

[16] Probably breakwaters, but implying (*pars pro toto*) maintenance and improvement of harbours, especially Ostia.

[17] I.e. he had held a Consulship and then a command in Domitian's first Dacian War. The triumph was in 85.

125 natorum viridesque genas tibi iusta dedissent
stamina. sed media cecidere abrupta iuventa
gaudia florentesque manu scidit Atropos annos,
qualia pallentes declinant lilia culmos
pubentesque rosae primos moriuntur ad austros,
130 aut ubi verna novis exspirat purpura pratis.
illa, sagittiferi, circum volitastis, Amores,
funera maternoque rogos unxistis amomo.
nec modus aut pennis laceris aut crinibus ignem
spargere, collectaeque pyram struxere pharetrae.
135 quas tunc inferias aut quae lamenta dedisses
maternis, Etrusce, rogis, qui funera patris
haud matura putas atque hos pius ingemis annos!
    Illum et qui nutu superas nunc temperat arces,
progeniem claram terris partitus et astris,
140 laetus Idumaei donavit honore triumphi
dignatusque loco victricis et ordine pompae
non vetuit tenuesque nihil minuere parentes.
atque idem in cuneos populo deduxit equestres
mutavitque genus laevaeque ignobile ferrum
145 exuit et celso natorum aequavit honori.
    Dextra bis octonis fluxerunt saecula lustris
atque aevi sine nube tenor. quam dives in usus
natorum totoque volens excedere censu
testis adhuc largi nitor indesuetus Etrusci,
150 cui tua non humiles dedit indulgentia mores,

141 in *Baehrens*   145 honori *Salmasius*: -re M
149 indesuetus *Reeve*: inde ads- M

---

18 Hyacinth.
19 If you had been old enough.

threads had vouchsafed you to see your children's faces, their youthful cheeks! But your joys fell earthwards, broken off in mid youth, and Atropos' hand severed your blooming years, as lilies droop their paling stems and roses die at the first sirocco or as when vernal purple[18] expires in fresh meadows. Archer Loves, you fluttered around those obsequies and annointed the pyre with your mother's perfume. You spared not to strew the fire with your feathers or torn hair, and your heaped quivers built the pile. What offerings or what lamentations would you have given then to your mother's burning,[19] Etruscus, who think your father's death untimely and in piety mourn those years!

He[20] that now governs heaven's heights with his nod and has divided his progeny between earth and stars gladly granted him the honour of the Idumaean triumph,[21] deeming him worthy of a place in the order of the victory procession and not gainsaying. His humble parentage was no detraction. The same led him down from the people to the benches of the Knights, changed the family, stripped the base iron[22] from his hand and levelled him with the high station of his sons.[23]

Through twice eight lustres the generations of prosperity flowed by, the tenor of his life was unclouded. How rich he was for his sons' behoof, how ready to step away from his entire fortune, the unchanging elegance of lavish Etruscus still stands witness; 'twas your love that gave him

---

[20] Vespasian.

[21] He allowed Claudius to take part in Titus' triumph over the Jews in 81.

[22] Worn by freedmen. Knights wore gold rings.

[23] They were already Knights.

SILVAE

hunc siquidem amplexu semper revocante tenebas
blandus et imperio numquam pater; huius honori
pronior ipse etiam gaudebat cedere frater.
    Quas tibi devoti iuvenes pro patre renato,
155 summe ducum, grates aut quae pia vota rependant?
tu, seu tarda situ rebusque exhausta senectus
erravit, seu blanda diu Fortuna regressum
maluit, attonitum et venturi fulminis ictus
horrentem tonitru tantum lenique procella
160 contentus monuisse senem, cumque horrida supra
aequora curarum socius procul Itala rura
linqueret, hic molles Campani litoris oras
et Diomedeas concedere iussus in arces,
atque hospes, non exsul erat. nec longa moratus
165 Romuleum reseras iterum, Germanice, limen
maerentemque foves inclinatosque penates
erigis. haud mirum, ductor placidissime, quando
haec est quae victis parcentia foedera Cattis
quaeque suum Dacis donat clementia montem,
170 quae modo Marcomanos post horrida bella vagosque
Sauromatas Latio non est dignata triumpho.
    Iamque in fine dies et inexorabile pensum
deficit. hic maesti pietas me poscit Etrusci
qualia nec Siculae modulantur carmina rupes
175 nec fati iam certus olor saevique marita

155 rependant ⊊ (?), *Calderini*: -dunt M
174 modulantur *Bentley, Schrader*: moderantur M

24 Otherwise unknown, presumably a subordinate.
25 Arpi in Apulia, evidently by a second order removing him
further away from Rome.

212

his high style. For you held him in an embrace that ever called him back, a father in affection, never in authority. Even his brother too was glad to give him precedence, more eager for his advancement than for his own.

Highest of leaders, what thanks do the young men, devoted to you as they are, give you for father reborn! What pious vows discharge! Was it age that erred, grown slow with decay and worn out with affairs, or did Fortune so long indulgent choose to withdraw? The old man stood dumbfounded, trembling before the coming lightning stroke: you were content to warn him with mere thunder and lenient storm. While the partner of his care[24] was crossing rough seas and leaving Italy's fields far behind him, *he* was told to retire to the soft shores of Campania and the towers of Diomede.[25] He was a guest, not an exile. And after no long delay,[26] Germanicus, you once again unbar the gates of Romulus, soothing his grief and raising up the fallen house. No wonder, most merciful of rulers! For this is the clemency that grants mild terms to the vanquished Catti and their mountain to the Dacians, that lately after rough warfare did not deem the Marcomani and the nomad Sarmatians worthy of a Latian triumph.[27]

Now the day is ending and the inexorable thread runs out. Here sad Etruscus' piety asks of me such a song as the rocks of Sicily[28] do not modulate, nor the swan now sure of his fate, nor the bride of savage Tereus.[29] Alas! with what

[26] The data point to a period of about eight years.

[27] Cf. Martial 8.15. The Sarmatian campaign was in 92.

[28] I.e. the Sirens.

[29] Philomela the nightingale, actually Tereus' sister-in-law and rape victim.

Tereos. heu quantis lassantem bracchia vidi
planctibus et prono fusum super oscula vultu!
vix famuli comitesque tenent, vix arduus ignis
summovet. haud aliter gemuit per Sunia Theseus
180　litora quem falsis deceperat Aegea velis.
nunc immane gemens foedatusque ora tepentes
affatur cineres:

'Cur nos, fidissime, linquis
Fortuna redeunte, pater? modo numina magni
praesidis atque breves superum placavimus iras
185　nec frueris, tantique orbatus muneris usu
ad manes, ingrate, fugis. nec flectere Parcas
aut placare malae datur aspera numina Lethes.
felix cui magna patrem cervice vehenti
sacra Mycenaeae patuit reverentia flammae,
190　quique tener saevis genitorem Scipio Poenis
abstulit, et Lydi pietas temeraria Lausi!
ergo et Thessalici coniunx pensare mariti
funus et immitem potuit Styga vincere supplex
Thracius? hoc quanto melius pro patre liceret!
195　　Non totus rapiere tamen, nec funera mittam
longius. hic manes, hic intra tecta tenebo.
tu custos dominusque laris, tibi cuncta tuorum
parebunt: ego rite minor semperque secundus
assiduas libabo dapes et pocula sacris
200　manibus effigiesque colam; te lucida saxa,
te similem doctae referet modo linea cerae,
nunc ebur et fulvum vultus imitabitur aurum.
inde viam morum longaeque examina vitae

179 per Sunia *Polster*: periuria M　　　quem* *scripsi*: qui M
201 modo *coni. Courtney*: mihi M

214

blows of lamentation did I see him wearying his arms, spread out with face prone to kiss! Not otherwise by Sunium's shore did Theseus mourn for Aegeus whom his false sails had deceived.[30] Then with dreadful outcry and countenance befouled he speaks to the warm ashes:

'Why do you leave us, truest one, when Fortune is coming back? We have just appeased the godhead of our great ruler and the brief anger of the High Ones, and you profit not; robbed of the benefit of so great a boon, you flee to the Underworld, ingrate! Nor may we move the Parcae or appease the harsh deities of baneful Lethe. Happy he[31] that bore his father on his mighty neck while Mycenaean flames opened him passage in holy reverence! Happy young Scipio, who rescued his father from the cruel Poeni, and the rash piety of Lydian[32] Lausus! Could a wife then balance the death of her Thessalian husband with her own and the suppliant Thracian vanquish pitiless Styx?[33] How much better such a licence on a father's behalf!

But you shall not wholly be snatched away, nor shall I send your ashes far. Here I shall keep your spirit, within these walls. You shall be guardian and master of the hearth, all your folk shall obey you. Rightfully beneath you, always in second place, I shall offer meat and drink to your sacred spirit and worship your images. Now shining stone and line of cunning wax shall bring you back in semblance; now ivory and tawny gold shall imitate your countenance. From them I shall ask rule of conduct, the judgments of a

[30] See Critical Appendix.
[31] Aeneas. The Greek commander-in-chief Agamemnon was king of Mycenae.
[32] Etruscan.   [33] Alcestis and Orpheus.

affatusque pios monituraque somnia poscam.'
205   Talia dicentem genitor dulcedine laeta
audit, et immites lente descendit ad umbras
verbaque dilectae fert narraturus Etruscae.
    Salve supremum, senior, mitissime patrum,
supremumque vale! qui numquam sospite nato
210   triste chaos maestique situs patiere sepulchri.
semper odoratis spirabunt floribus arae,
semper et Assyrios felix bibet urna liquores
et lacrimas, qui maior honos. hic sacra litabit
manibus eque tua tumulum tellure levabit.
215   nostra quoque, exemplo meritus, tibi carmina sancit,
hoc etiam gaudens cinerem donasse sepulchro.

III.4

CAPILLI FLAVI EARINI

Ite, comae, facilemque, precor, transcurrite pontum,
ite coronato recubantes molliter auro,
ite; dabit cursus mitis Cytherea secundos
placabitque notos, fors et de puppe timenda
5   transferet inque sua ducet super aequora concha.
    Accipe laudatos, iuvenis Phoebeie, crines
quos tibi Caesareus donat puer, accipe laetus
intonsoque ostende patri. sine dulce nitentes
comparet atque diu fratris putet esse Lyaei.
10   forsan et ipse comae numquam labentis honorem
praemetet atque alio clusum tibi ponet in auro.

---

[8] sibe (sibi) *coni. Courtney, argute*

long life, words of love and counselling dreams.'

So he spoke, and sweet were his words to the happy father's ear. Slowly he descended to the pitiless shades, there to tell them to his beloved Etrusca.

Hail for the last time, old sir, gentlest of fathers, and for the last time farewell! While your son lives, you shall never suffer dismal chaos or the sadness of a neglected tomb. Always the altar shall breathe with fragrant flowers and your happy urn drink Assyrian perfumes and, greater tribute, tears. Here he shall make sacrifice to your spirit and raise a monument from your own soil.[34] My song too that he has earned by his example he dedicates to you, happy to have given this sepulchre also to your ashes.

III.4

THE HAIR OF FLAVIUS EARINUS

Go, locks, and speed, I pray, across a favouring sea, go, lying softly on garlanded gold, go! Gentle Cytherea shall give you fair voyage and calm the south winds. Perhaps she will take you from the perilous craft and lead you over the waters in her own shell.

Accept, son of Phoebus,[1] the lauded tresses that Caesar's lad presents to you; accept them gladly and show them to your unshorn father. Let him compare them how they shine, and long think they are from his brother Lyaeus. Perhaps he in turn will sever the beauty of his own unfailing hair and place it for you enclosed in other gold.

[34] The property at Alba.
[1] Aesculapius.

Pergame, pinifera multum felicior Ida,
illa licet sacrae placeat sibi nube rapinae
(nempe dedit superis illum quem turbida semper
15   Iuno videt refugitque manum nectarque recusat),
at tu grata deis pulchroque insignis alumno
misisti Latio placida quem fronte ministrum
Iuppiter Ausonius pariter Romanaque Iuno
aspiciunt et uterque probant, nec tanta potenti
20   terrarum domino divum sine mente voluptas.
     Dicitur Idalios Erycis de vertice lucos
dum petit et molles agitat Venus aurea cycnos
Pergameas intrasse domos, ubi maximus aegris
auxiliator adest et festinantia sistens
25   Fata salutifero mitis deus incubat angui.
hic puerum egregiae praeclarum sidere formae
ipsius ante dei ludentem conspicit aras.
ac primum subita paulum decepta figura
natorum de plebe putat; sed non erat illi
30   arcus et ex umeris nullae fulgentibus umbrae.
miratur puerile decus, vultumque comasque
aspiciens 'tune Ausonias' ait 'ibis ad arces
neglectus Veneri? tu sordida tecta iugumque
servitii vulgare feres? procul absit. ego isti
35   quem meruit formae dominum dabo. vade age mecum,
vade, puer. ducam volucri per sidera curru
donum immane duci, nec te plebeia manebunt
iura: Palatino famulus deberis honori.
nil ego, nil, fateor, toto tam dulce sub orbe
40   aut vidi aut genui. cedet tibi Latmius ultro

38 honori *Rothstein*: amori M

Pergamus, more fortunate by far than pine-clad Ida,
though Ida pride herself on the cloud of a holy rape—
for surely she gave the High Ones him[2] at whom Juno
ever looks askance, recoiling from his hand and refusing
the nectar: but *you* have the gods' favour, specially commended by your fair nurseling. You sent to Latium a
servant whom Ausonian Jupiter and Roman Juno[3] alike
regard with kindly brow, both approving; and not without
the will of the gods is the lord of earth so well pleased.

'Tis said that as golden Venus was driving her soft swans
on her way from Eryx' height to the Idalian groves, she entered the Pergamene dwelling where the gentle god is
present to aid the sick, their greatest helper, staying the
hastening Fates and brooding over his health-giving serpent. She sees a boy, shining with star of peerless beauty, as
he plays before the altar of the very god. Deceived at first
for a little while by the sudden apparition, she fancies him
one of her many sons; but he had no bow and no shades
springing from his radiant shoulders. She wonders at his
boyish grace, gazing at his face and hair, and 'Shall you go,'
she says, 'to the Ausonian towers neglected of Venus? Shall
you bear a mean dwelling and common yoke of servitude?
Far be it! I shall give this beauty the master it deserves.
Come now with me, boy, come! I shall fly you through
the stars in my winged chariot to the leader, a gift of gifts.
No common bondage shall await you: you are destined to
serve dignity in the Palace. Nothing so sweet in all the
world have I seen or given birth to, I own it. The boys of

2 Ganymede.
3 The Emperor and his wife Domitia Longina.

219

Sangariusque puer, quemque irrita fontis imago
et sterilis consumpsit amor. te caerula Nais
mallet et apprensa traxisset fortius urna.
tu, puer, ante omnes; solus formosior ille
cui daberis.'

45   Sic orsa leves secum ipsa per auras
tollit olorinaque iubet considere biga.
nec mora, iam Latii montes veterisque penates
Evandri, quos mole nova pater inclitus orbis
excolit et summis aequat Germanicus astris.

50 tunc propior iam cura deae, quae forma capillis
optima, quae vestis roseos accendere vultus
apta, quod in digitis, collo quod dignius aurum.
norat caelestes oculos ducis ipsaque taedas
iunxerat et plena dederat conubia dextra.

55 sic ornat crines, Tyrios sic fundit amictus,
dat radios ignemque suum. cessere priores
deliciae famulumque greges; hic pocula magno
prima duci murrasque graves crystallaque portat
candidiore manu; crescit nova gratia Baccho.

60   Care puer superis, qui praelibare verendum
nectar et ingentem totiens contingere dextram
electus, quam nosse Getae, quam tangere Persae
Armeniique Indique petunt! o sidere dextro
edite, multa tibi divum indulgentia favit.

65 olim etiam, ne prima genas lanugo nitentes
carperet et pulchrae fuscaret gaudia formae,
ipse deus patriae celsam trans aequora liquit

      47 veterisque *Barth*: -resque M
      66 gaudia *Gronovius*: gratia M

Latmos and Sangaris[4] shall freely yield to you, and he that a vain image in a fountain and a barren love consumed. The cerulean Naiad would have preferred you and seized your urn in a stronger grip to drag you down. Boy, you are beyond them all; more beautiful he only to whom you shall be given.'

So saying, she lifts him by her side through the light air and tells him to take a seat in the swan-drawn car. In a trice, there are the Latian Hills and the home of ancient Evander,[5] that Germanicus, renowned father of the world, adorns with new masonry and levels with the topmost stars. Then it becomes the goddess' closer care how best to arrange his locks, what dress is meet to kindle his rosy countenance, what gold is worthiest on his fingers, what on his neck. Well she knew the leader's celestial eyes; she herself had joined the marriage torches and given him his bride with bounteous hand. So she decks the hair, so drapes him with Tyrian raiment, gives him beams of her own fire. Former favourites retire, the flocks of servitors; *he* bears first cups to the great leader, weighty murrhine and crystal, with a hand more fair. New grace enhances the wine.

Boy dear to the High Ones, chosen to sip first the reverenced nectar and touch so often that mighty hand, the hand the Getae seek to know, and Persians, Armenians, Indians to touch! O born under a lucky star, greatly have the gods favoured you. Once too your country's god himself left lofty Pergamus to cross the sea, lest the first down mar your shining cheeks and darken your beauty's joys. None

---

[4] Endymion and Attis, followed by Narcissus and Hylas.
[5] The Palatine with Domitian's magnificent new palace.

Pergamon. haud ulli puerum mollire potestas
credita, sed tacita iuvenis Phoebeius arte
70　leniter haud ullo concussum vulnere corpus
de sexu transire iubet. tamen anxia curis
mordetur puerique timet Cytherea dolores.
nondum pulchra ducis clementia coeperat ortu
intactos servare mares; nunc frangere sexum
75　atque hominem mutare nefas, gavisaque solos
quos genuit Natura videt, nec lege sinistra
ferre timent famulae natorum pondera matres.
　　Tu quoque nunc iuvenis genitus si tardius esses
umbratusque genas et adultos fortior artus
80　non unum gaudens Phoebea ad limina munus
misisses. patrias nunc solus crinis ad oras
naviget. hunc multo Paphie saturabat amomo,
hunc bona tergemina pectebat Gratia dextra.
huic et purpurei cedet coma saucia Nisi
85　et quam Sperchio tumidus servabat Achilles.
ipsi, cum primum niveam praecerpere frontem
decretum est umerosque manu nudare nitentes,
accurrunt teneri Paphia cum matre volucres
expediuntque comas et Serica pectore ponunt
90　pallia. tunc iunctis crinem incidere sagittis
atque auro gemmisque locant; rapit ipsa cadentem
mater et arcanos iterat Cytherea liquores.
tunc puer e turba, manibus qui forte supinis
nobile gemmato speculum portaverat auro,

83 hunc (ϛ) bona *Courtney*: nunc nova M
91 cadentem *Schrader*: -tes M

other was entrusted with the power to soften the boy, but with silent skill Phoebus' son gently bade this body leave its sex, not shocked by any gash. Yet Cytherea is gnawed by worry, fearing the boy might suffer. Not yet had the leader's noble clemency begun to keep male children intact from birth.[6] Now 'tis forbidden to mollify sex and change manhood; rejoicing Nature sees only those she created. No more under an evil law do slave mothers fear to bear the burden of sons.

You too, had you been born later, would now be a young man, with shaded cheeks and limbs full-grown, stronger. More gifts than one[7] you would have sent rejoicing to Phoebus' shrine; as it is, let only the tress sail to your native shores. The Paphian used to steep it in plenteous perfume, a kindly Grace used to comb it. The severed lock of purple Nisus will yield to it, and that which proud Achilles was keeping for Sperchius.[8] When first it was decreed to crop your snow-white brow and unveil your gleaming shoulders, the tender winged ones with their Paphian mother run up and make ready your tresses and place a silken robe over your breast. Then they cut the lock with linked arrows and place it on gold and gems. Mother Cytherea herself catches it as it falls and anoints it once again with her secret essences. Then spoke a boy from the throng who had chanced to carry in upturned hands the mirror resplendent with jewelled gold: 'Let us give this too. No gift will be

---

[6] Domitian had forbidden child emasculation (Earinus had not been castrated); cf. Suetonius, *Domitian* 7.1, Martial 6.2; 9.5, 7.   [7] Beard as well as hair.

[8] *Iliad* 23.146.

95 'hoc quoque demus' ait 'patriis nec gratius ullum
munus erit templis, ipsoque potentius auro,
tu modo fige aciem et vultus hic usque relinque.'
sic ait et speculum seclusit imagine rapta.
   At puer egregius tendens ad sidera palmas,
100 'his mihi pro donis, hominum mitissime custos,
si merui, longa dominum renovare iuventa
atque orbi servare velis. hoc sidera mecum
hoc undae terraeque rogant. eat, oro, per annos
Iliacos Pyliosque simul, propriosque penates
105 gaudeat et secum Tarpeia senescere templa.'
   Sic ait, et motas miratur Pergamos aras.

III.5

‹AD UXOREM CLAUDIAM›

Quid mihi maesta die, sociis quid noctibus, uxor,
anxia pervigili ducis suspiria cura?
non metuo ne laesa fides aut pectore in isto
alter amor; nullis in te datur ire sagittis
5 (audiat infesto licet hoc Rhamnusia vultu),
non datur. etsi egomet patrio de litore raptus
quattuor emeritis per bella, per aequora lustris
errarem, tu mille procos intacta fugares,
non imperfectas commenta retexere telas

   97 hic *Laetus*: huc M
   98 seclusit *Gronovius*: rec- M
   104 situs *Markland*
   pro titulo VIA DOMITIANA (*cf. IV.3.tit.*) M
   9 imperfectas *Barth*: inter- M

224

more welcome to his native temple; it will be more potent than the gold itself. Only do you fix a look therein and leave your face there forever.'[9] So he spoke and shut in the mirror, catching the likeness.

But the peerless boy, stretching his hands to the stars: 'In return for these gifts, gentlest guardian of mankind, may you long wish, if I have so deserved, to renew our lord's youth and preserve him for the world. The stars ask this with me, and the waters and the lands. Let him, I pray, pass through Ilian and Pylian years both, rejoicing that his own home and the Tarpeian temple grow old along with himself.'

So he spoke, and Pergamus wondered that the altars shook.

III.5

TO HIS WIFE CLAUDIA

Why, my wife, do you sorrow by day and fetch painful sighs in the nights we share, in sleepless worry? I have no fear lest faith be broken or another love be in your heart. No arrows have license to assail you (though she of Rhamnus hear and frown), no indeed. If I had been reft from my native shore and were wandering after four lustres spent in war and on the seas, untouched you would put a thousand suitors to flight—not devising to unravel an unfinished web,[1] but frankly and forthrightly, refusing marriage

[9] The Cupid's powers anticipated photography.

[1] As Penelope told her suitors to wait until she finished a shroud she was weaving for her father-in-law and then unravelled at night the work done in the day.

10 sed sine fraude palam, thalamosque armata negasses.
    dic tamen, unde alia mihi fronte et nubila vultus?
    anne quod Euboicos fessus remeare penates
    auguror et patria senium componere terra?
    cur hoc triste tibi? certe lascivia corde
15 nulla nec aut rabidi mulcent te proelia Circi
    aut intrat sensus clamosi turba theatri,
    sed probitas et opaca quies et sordida numquam
    gaudia.
          Quas autem comitem te rapto per undas?
    quamquam, etsi gelidas irem mansurus ad Arctos
20 vel super Hesperiae vada caligantia Thules
    aut septemgemini caput impenetrabile Nili,
    hortarere vias. etenim tua, nempe benigna
    quam mihi sorte Venus iunctam florentibus annis
    servat et in senium, tua, quae me vulnere primo
25 intactum thalamis et adhuc iuvenile vagantem
    fixisti, tua frena libens docilisque recepi,
    et semel insertas non mutaturus habenas
    usque premo. tu me nitidis Albana ferentem
    dona comis sanctoque indutum Caesaris auro
30 visceribus complexa tuis, sertisque dedisti
    oscula anhela meis; tu, cum Capitolia nostrae
    infitiata lyrae, saevum ingratumque dolebas
    mecum victa Iovem; tu procurrentia primis
    carmina nostra sonis totasque in murmure noctes
35 aure rapis vigili; longi tu sola laboris

---

11 alia *Aldus*: alta M   13 arguor *Heinsius*
15 rabidi *Wakefield*: rapidi M   16 cura *Markland*
28 tu *Politianus*: ter M
32 dolebas *Calderini*: -eres M

226

sword in hand. But say, why do I see your brow changed, your face in cloud? Is it because in my weariness I propose to return to my Euboean home and settle my old age in my native land? Why does this make you sad? For of a certainty you have no frolicking at heart, no contests of the crazy Circus have charm for you, you are deaf to the crowd of the noisy theatre; virtue is for you and sheltered peace and joys never vulgar.

But what are the waves through which I would hail you in my company? And yet, if I were going to the Arctic, there to stay, or beyond the darkling waters of Hesperian Thule or the impenetrable fount of sevenfold Nile, you would be urging departure. For sure 'tis you whom Venus joined with me by a kind destiny in the springtime of my years and keeps with me till old age, 'twas you that pierced me with my first wound, untouched as I was by wedlock and still a young wanderer, and yours were the reins I received in willing obedience and to this day press the bit that once in my mouth I shall never change. As I bore Alba's gift on my shining hair, wearing Caesar's sacred gold,[2] 'twas you that clasped me to your bosom and gave panting kisses to my chaplet. When the Capitol said nay to my lyre, 'twas you that grieved for Jove's[3] cruelty and ingratitude, sharing my discomfiture. 'Tis you that catch with sleepless ear the first notes of my songs as they run forth and whole nights of murmuring. Only you know my long

[2] When Statius won the prize, a gold wreath in the form of olive leaves, at the Alban festival instituted by Domitian and held at his residence (IV.2.65). But he failed to repeat the success at the Capitoline contest (V.3.231ff.).

[3] Tarpeian (Capitoline) Jupiter, not the Emperor (cf. V.3.233).

conscia, cumque tuis crevit mea Thebais annis.
qualem te nuper Stygias prope raptus ad umbras
cum iam Lethaeos audirem comminus amnes,
aspexi, tenuique oculos iam morte cadentes!
40   scilicet exhausti Lachesis mihi tempora fati
te tantum miserata dedit, superique potentes
invidiam timuere tuam. post ista propinquum
nunc iter optandosque sinus comes ire moraris?
heu ubi nota fides totque explorata per usus,
45   qua veteres, Latias Graias, heroidas aequas?
isset ad Iliacas (quid enim deterret amantes?)
Penelope gavisa domos, si passus Ulixes;
questa est Aegiale, questa est Meliboea relinqui,
et quam tam saevi fecerunt maenada planctus.
50   nec minor his tu nosse fidem vitamque maritis
dedere. sic certe cineres umbramque priorem
quaeris adhuc, sic exsequias amplexa canori
coniugis ingentes iterasti pectore planctus
iam mea. nec pietas alia est tibi curaque natae;
55   sic et mater amas, sic numquam corde recedit
nata tuo, fixamque animi penetralibus imis
nocte dieque tenes. non sic Trachinia nidos
Alcyone, vernos non sic Philomela penates
circumit amplectens animamque in pignora transfert.
60   te nunc illa tenet, viduo quod sola cubili
otia tam pulchrae terit infecunda iuventae?
sed venient, plenis venient conubia taedis;

    49 quam tam saevi *Cruceus*: quamquam s- M: quam vesani
Owen: anne si quam s-?   50 *anne* marito*?
    56 illa tuo *Markland*   60 te *Phillimore*: et M
    61 tam *Politianus*: iam M

labour, my *Thebaid* grew along with your years. How looked you lately when I was almost swept into the Stygian shade, already hearing Lethe's waters close at hand, and stayed my eyes already falling in death! Surely 'twas in pity for you that Lachesis granted my exhausted span more time, your reproach that the potent High Ones feared. After all this are you now delaying a short journey, to go with me to the delightful bay? Alas! where is your familiar loyalty, proven in so many trials, that puts you alongside the ancient heroines of Latium and Greece? Penelope would gladly have gone to the dwellings of Ilium (for what do lovers fear?) if Ulysses had suffered it. Aegiale made moan to be left behind, and Meliboea, and she whom cruel lamentation made Maenad;[4] and you know as well as they how to be loyal and give your life for your man. So at least you still seek the ashes and shade of him that was, so you embraced the obsequies of your songful spouse,[5] raining violent blows on your breast yet again, when you were already mine. Nor other is your devotion and care for your daughter. Such is your mother love, so does your daughter never leave your heart; night and day you hold her fast in the inmost recesses of your being. Not thus does Trachinian Alcyone flutter round her nest, nor thus Philomela round her vernal home, embracing it, giving her life's breath over to her young. Now is it she that holds you, because alone in her widowed bed she passes a youth so fair in barren idleness? But marriage will come, yea, come with all its

[4] Laodamia; cf. II.7.124.

[5] Name unknown. Apparently he had a reputation as a singer.

sic certe formaeque bonis animaeque meretur.
sive chelyn complexa quatit seu voce paterna
65 discendum Musis sonat et mea carmina flectit,
candida seu molli diducit bracchia motu,
ingenium probitas artemque modestia vincit.
nonne leves pueros, non te, Cytherea, pudebit
hoc cessare decus? nec tantum Roma iugales
70 conciliare toros festasque accendere taedas
fertilis: et nostra generi tellure dabuntur.
non adeo Vesuvinus apex et flammea diri
montis hiems trepidas exhausit civibus urbes:
stant populisque vigent. hinc auspice condita Phoebo
75 tecta Dicaearchi portusque et litora mundi
hospita, at hinc magnae tractus imitantia Romae
quae Capys advectis implevit moenia Teucris,
nostraque nec propriis tenuis nec rara colonis
Parthenope, cui mite solum trans aequora vectae
80 ipse Dionaea monstravit Apollo columba.
      Has ego te sedes (nam nec mihi barbara Thrace
nec Libye natale solum) transferre laboro,
quas et mollis hiems et frigida temperat aestas,
quas imbelle fretum torpentibus alluit undis.
85 pax secura locis et desidis otia vitae
et numquam turbata quies somnique peracti.
nulla foro rabies aut strictae in iurgia leges:
morum iura viris, solum et sine fascibus aequum.
      Quid nunc magnificas species cultusque locorum

64 quatit *Waller*: petit M: ferit *Markland*
75 Dicaearchi *Krohn*: dicarchei M   78 nostraque nec
Otto: nostra quoque et M: n- q- haud *Markland*
80 Dionea . . . columba *Politianus*: -eae . . . -bae M

flambeaux—so surely her gifts of beauty and mind deserve, whether she clasps and shakes the lute, or with voice to match her father's makes music for Muses to learn and modulates my verses, or spreads white arms wide in supple motion. Her goodness is greater than her talent, her modesty than her skill. Shall not your lightsome Loves, Cytherea, shall not yourself take shame that such charm is wasted? Nor is Rome alone fertile in making matches and kindling the festal torch. In my country too sons-in-law shall be given. Not so entirely has Vesuvius' summit and the flowing tempest of the dire mountain drained the terrified cities of their population; they stand and flourish with folk. On one side are the dwellings of Dicaearchus[6] founded under Phoebus' auspices and the harbour and world-welcoming strand, on the other the walls that Capys filled with Teucrian migrants, mimicking the expanses of great Rome. There also is our Parthenope, neither meagre in her own folk nor lacking in settlers; to her, a traveller from overseas, Apollo himself showed a gentle soil with Dione's dove.

This is the dwelling place (for I was not born in barbarous Thrace or Libya) to which I am trying to bring you, tempered by mild winter and cool summer, washed by the lazy waves of an unwarlike sea. Peace secure is there, the leisure of a quiet life, tranquillity undisturbed, sleep that runs its course. No madness in the Forum, no laws unsheathed for brawling. Our men are ruled only by manners and right that needs no rods.

Why should I now praise the splendid sights and adorn-

---

[6] Puteoli. Capua and Naples follow.

90 templaque ‹et› innumeris spatia interstincta columnis
    et geminam molem nudi tectique theatri
    et Capitolinis quinquennia proxima lustris,
    quid laudem lusus libertatemque iocandi,
    quam Romanus honos et Graia licentia miscent?
95 nec desunt variae circa oblectamina vitae,
    sive vaporiferas, blandissima litora, Baias,
    enthea fatidicae seu visere tecta Sibyllae
    dulce sit Iliacoque iugum memorabile remo,
    seu tibi Bacchei vineta madentia Gauri
100 Teleboumque domos, trepidis ubi dulcia nautis
    lumina noctivagae tollit Pharus aemula lunae
    caraque non molli iuga Surrentina Lyaeo,
    quae meus ante alios habitator Pollius auget,
    Venarumque lacus medicos Stabiasque renatas.
105 mille tibi nostrae referam telluris amores?
    sed satis hoc, coniunx, satis est dixisse: creavit
    me tibi, me socium longos astrinxit in annos.
    nonne haec amborum genetrix altrixque videri
    digna?
        Sed ingratus qui plura annecto tuisque
110 moribus indubito. venies, carissima coniunx,
    praeveniesque etiam. sine me tibi ductor aquarum
    Thybris et armiferi sordebunt tecta Quirini.

93 lusus *Baehrens*: litus M   iocandi *Markland*: menandri M
104 Venarum* *scripsi* (ve- *van Buren*): de- M
109 quid *van Kooten*

232

ments of the place, the temples, the spaces marked out
with countless columns, the theatres, open and covered, a
double mass, the quinquennial contests ranking next to the
lustres of the Capitol? Why the shows, the freedom of jest,[7]
a mingling of Roman dignity and Greek licence? Nor lack
surrounding entertainments to give life variety. You may
please to visit the seductive beach of steaming Baiae or the
prophetic Sibyl's numinous abode[8] or the hills made memorable by the Ilian oar;[9] or shall it be the flowing vineyards
of Bacchic Gaurus and the dwellings of the Teleboi, where
the Pharos raises a light like the night-wandering moon,
sweet to frightened sailors, where are the Surrentine hills
dear to Lyaeus in no gentle mood,[10] hills that my Pollius
above all others enhances with his residence, and the healing pools of the Veins,[11] and renascent Stabiae? Shall I rehearse for you my country's thousand darlings? But it is
enough, my dear, enough to say this: she created me for
you, bound me to be your partner for many a long year. Is
she not worthy to be deemed mother and nurse of us both?

But ingrate that I am, adding this, that, and the other,
doubting your character. You *will* come, dear wife, you will
even go ahead. Without me you will reck little of Tiber,
prince of waters, or the dwellings of arm-bearing Quirinus.

[7] See critical note. Like Courtney, I baulk at 'the freedom of
Menander' (cf. II.1.114).

[8] Cumae.

[9] Misenum.

[10] Surrentine wine was tart; emperor Tiberius called it 'noble
vinegar.'

[11] See Critical Appendix.

BOOK FOUR

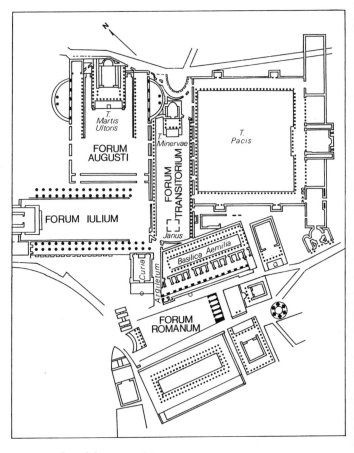

Plan of the imperial fora.
Drawing by S. L. Abraham; reproduced by permission

PREFATORY NOTES

1

Domitian became Consul for the seventeenth time on 1 January 95.

2

The description of Domitian's new palace (vv. 18–37) is likely to have been written not long after its completion in 92, but after the publication of Books I–III. Coleman (pp. 83f.) thinks it possible that the poem was composed in advance of the banquet which is its theme and recited during its course.

3

The Via Domitiana between Sinuessa and Puteoli was completed in the first half of 95 (Dio 67.14). This poem was written in the early summer (Coleman, p. xx).

4

Date: summer of 95. M. Vitorius Marcellus, to whom Statius dedicates Book IV, was Praetor that year and designated curator of the Via Latina for 96 (Coleman, pp. 135ff.). He became Consul suffect in 105. Probably a pupil of Quintilian, from whom he received the dedication of the treatise on the training of an orator, and a distinguished advocate (vv. 41–45), with the prospect of a military career (56–77). 'The general cast of this epistle is Horatian' (Coleman), without the Horatian informality.

5

In Alcaic metre, much favoured in Horace's Odes, written in the spring of 95 or perhaps of 94 (Coleman, p. xxi). Septimius Severus was a native of Lepcis Magna in Libya, also the home of L. Septimius Severus, grandfather of the future emperor (193–211). They may have been cousins.

6

Novius Vindex, a connoisseur of art, is mentioned by Martial (7.72.7) as an expert player of the board game called *latrunculi* ('Soldiers' not 'Robbers'; see my Loeb edition, III, p. 235, note c), also in connection with this same statuette of Hercules, which bore an ascription to Lysippus on its base. Statius' poem 'can be dated to winter 94/5' (Coleman). The metre is Sapphic, also a Horatian favorite.

7

'Probably written in 94 between spring and early autumn when regular sea-crossings were made, because St. implies that Vibius could return from Dalmatia at once if he so wished' (Coleman). In view of other prosopographical linkages Vibius Maximus is probably to be identified with the busy man of Martial 11.106. On the variant *Vivium* in the prefatory letter and the title (the latter deriving from the former) see Coleman. Vv. 13–20 show him to have

been a native of Dalmatia, where Vibii abounded, and this
one may best be identified with a Knight mentioned in an
inscription of 71; but there are other possibilities, dis-
cussed by Coleman.

8

Congratulating Pollius Felix' son-in-law on the birth of a
third child, a boy, written somewhere between the termi-
nals of 93 and 95.

9

The Saturnalia of December 94 were the occasion. Grypus
was a Senator and Statius his client (vv. 48–52). The lively
hendecasyllables 'recall Catullus and are evidently considered appropriate to Saturnalian jocularity' (Coleman,
comparing I.6).

LIBER QUARTUS

Inveni librum, Marcelle carissime, quem pietati tuae dedicarem. reor equidem aliter quam invocato numine maximi
imperatoris nullum opusculum meum coepisse; sed hic liber tres habet * * * se quam quod quarta ad honorem tuum
5 pertinet. primo autem septimum decimum Germanici
nostri consulatum adoravi; secundo gratias egi sacratissi-
mis eius epulis honoratus; tertio viam Domitianam miratus
sum qua gravissimam harenarum moram exemit, cuius
beneficio tu quo‹que› maturius epistulam meam accipies,
10 quam tibi in hoc libro a Neapoli scribo. proximum est lyri-
cum carmen ad Septimium Severum, iuvenem, uti scis, inter ornatissimos secundi ordinis, tuum quidem et condisci-
pulum, sed mihi citra hoc quoque ius artissime carum.
nam Vindicis nostri Herculem Epitrapezion secundum
15 honorem quem de me et de ipsis studiis meretur imputare
etiam tibi possum. Maximum Vibium et dignitatis et eloquentiae nomine a nobis diligi satis eram testatus epistula
quam ad illum de editione Thebaidos meae publicavi; sed

4 *lac. agnovit Hahn*
9 *add.* ⌐
13 citra *Nohl*: contra M

BOOK FOUR

STATIUS TO HIS FRIEND MARCELLUS GREETINGS

I have found a book, dearest Marcellus, that I can dedicate to your loyal affection. I think indeed that I have never begun any little work of mine without invoking the divinity of our great Emperor; but *this* book has three * * * than that the fourth is by way of honouring you. First, I have acclaimed the seventeenth Consulship of our Germanicus. Second, I have given thanks for the honour of his most sacred banquet. Third, I have admired the Domitian Way, by which he has eliminated a very irksome delay due to the sands. Thanks to him you will receive my letter more expeditiously, which I am writing to you from Naples in this volume. Next comes an ode to young Septimius Severus, one of the most distinguished members of the second Order, as you know, and a classmate of yours too, but a very close friend of mine apart from this relationship. As for the Hercules statuette of our friend Vindex, in addition to the honour that he deserves from me and from literature itself, I can also put it to your account. I had borne sufficient testimony to my regard for Maximus Vibius, based on his high standing and literary gifts, in the letter to him which I published concerning the appearance of my

nunc quoque eum reverti maturius ex Dalmatia rogo.
20 iuncta est ecloga ad municipem meum Iulium Mene-
craten, splendidum iuvenem et Polli mei generum, cui
gratulor quod Neapolim nostram numero liberorum
honestaverit. Plotio Grypo, maioris gradus iuveni, dignius
opusculum reddam, sed interim hendecasyllabos quos
25 Saturnalibus una risimus huic volumini inserui.

Quare ergo plura in quarto Silvarum quam in priori-
bus? ne se putent aliquid egisse qui reprehenderunt, ut
audio, quod hoc stili genus edidissem. primum superva-
cuum est dissuadere rem factam; deinde multa ex illis iam
30 domino Caesari dederam—et quanto hoc plus est quam
edere! exerceri autem ioco non licet? 'secreto' inquit. sed
et sphaeromachia spectantes et palaris lusio admittit. no-
vissime, quisquis ex meis invitus aliquid legit, statim se
profiteatur adversum. ita quare consilio eius accedam? in
35 summam, nempe ego sum qui traducor; taceat et gaudeat.
hunc tamen librum tu, Marcelle, defendes, si videtur; et
hactenus. sin minus, reprehendemur. vale.

30 exerceri (ς ?): -cere M
32 sphaeromachia spectantis *Phillimore*: -ias spectamus M
34 profitetur* *Aldus*
36 et *hic posui, ante* si M: *om. Goodyear*

Thebaid; but now I appeal to him to hasten his return from Dalmatia. Conjoined therewith is a poem addressed to my fellow townsman Julius Menecrates, a distinguished young man and my friend Pollius' son-in-law; I congratulate him for having brought honour to the city of Naples by the number of his children. To Plotius Grypus, a young man of senatorial rank, I shall be paying a worthier tribute, but in the meantime I have included in this volume some hendecasyllables over which we laughed at the Saturnalia.

So why are there more items in the fourth Book of my *Extempore Poems* than in its forerunners? Because I don't want those who, as I am told, criticized my publishing this kind of composition to think that their strictures have had any effect. First,[1] it is a waste of time to argue against a *fait accompli*. Second, I had already presented many of these items to our lord Caesar—and how much more is that than publication! Is there a law against practising in fun? 'Privately, no,' they say. But we watch ball games and are admitted to fencing matches. Finally, whoever reads something of mine with reluctance, let him declare himself my adversary; so why should I take his advice? In sum, I am the one under fire; let him hold his tongue and be thankful. As for this Book, however, you will defend it, Marcellus, if you think fit; and so much for that. If not, I shall live with the censure. Farewell.

[1] The following explains why he simply dismisses the critics. Possibly something connective has fallen out after *edidissem*.

SILVAE

IV.1

SEPTIMUS DECIMUS CONSULATUS IMP.
AUG. GERMANICI

Laeta bis octonis accedit purpura fastis
Caesaris, insignemque aperit Germanicus annum
atque oritur cum sole novo, cum grandibus astris,
clarius ipse nitens et primo maior Eoo.
5 exsultent leges Latiae, gaudete, curules,
et septemgemino iactantior aethera pulset
Roma iugo, plusque ante alias Evandrius arces
collis ovet. subiere novi Palatia fasces
et redit en! bis senus honos, precibusque receptis
10 curia Caesareum gaudet vicisse pudorem.
ipse etiam immensi reparator maximus aevi
attollit vultus et utroque a limine grates
Ianus agit. quem tu vicina Pace ligatum
omnia iussisti componere bella novique
15 in leges iurare fori. levat ecce supinas
hinc atque inde manus geminaque haec voce profatur:
     'Salve, magne parens mundi, qui saecula mecum

---

9 redit en *scripsi*: requiem M: rediit *Markland*: rediens *Courtney*   senus *Stange*: sextus M

---

[1] The Palatine.
[2] The Consulship, carrying twelve lictors; cf. I.2.174f. Against
this is set Dio's statement (67.4.3)that Domitian had twenty-four
lictors, whence Saenger's *bis saeptus* adopted by Coleman
(Courtney obelizes). But this could have been an innovation of
which Statius had not been informed. Had it been regular practice, Suetonius might have been expected to mention it (cf.
Domitian 13.3). As for *saeptus,* would Statius have risked the im-

244

IV.1

THE SEVENTEENTH CONSULSHIP OF EMPEROR
AUGUSTUS GERMANICUS

Joyfully does Caesar's purple join the twice eight en-
tries in the Calendar and Germanicus inaugurate a banner
year. He rises with the stars in their grandeur, himself
shining more brilliantly than they, greater than Eous. Let
Latium's laws exult, rejoice, ye curule chairs, and more
proudly let Rome knock at the sky with her Seven Hills;
above all the rest let Evander's summit[1] triumph. New
rods have entered the Palace, and the twelvefold honour[2]
returning. Its prayers heard, the Senate House rejoices to
have vanquished Caesar's modesty. Janus himself, greatest
renewer of measureless time, raises his hand and gives
thanks from either threshold;[3] you have tied his hands with
his neighbour Peace[4] and bidden him lay aside all warfare
and swear fealty to the laws of the new Forum.[5] See, he
raises upturned hands on this side and on that, and thus
with his two voices speaks:

'Hail, great Father of the world, who make ready with

plication that the number had been doubled for the Emperor's
protection—from his adoring subjects?

[3] In Forum Transitorium; plan of fora on page 236. See Coleman's discussion.

[4] A temple of Peace had been built by Vespasian. Statius gives
the credit to Domitian, who seems to have altered and perhaps re-
dedicated it; see Coleman on IV.3.17.

[5] The Forum Transitorium begun by Domitian, later known as
Forum Nervae. Janus, associated with warfare (cf. II.3.12), has
Domitian's orders to take an oath binding him to 'abide by the rule
of law administered by the civic authorities' (Coleman).

instaurare paras! talem te cernere semper
mense meo tua Roma cupit; sic tempora nasci,
20   sic annos intrare decet. da gaudia fastis
continua; hos umeros multo sinus ambiat ostro
et properata tuae manibus praetexta Minervae.
aspicis ut templis alius nitor, altior aris
ignis et ipsa meae tepeant tibi sidera brumae
25   moribus aequa tuis? gaudent turmaeque tribusque
purpureique patres, lucemque a consule ducit
omnis honos. quid tale, precor, prior annus habebat?
dic age, Roma potens, et mecum, longa Vetustas,
dinumera fastos nec parva exempla recense,
30   sed quae sola meus dignetur vincere Caesar.
ter Latio⟨s⟩ deciesque tulit labentibus annis
Augustus fasces, sed coepit sero mereri;
tu iuvenis praegressus avos. et quanta recusas,
quanta vetas! flectere tamen precibusque senatus

25 aequa *Bursian*: atque M: alme *Schwarz*
31 Latios *Gronovius*: -io M

---

6 *Instaurare* = resume or repeat an activity, particularly ritual,
here probably referring to the inauguration of the Consuls at the
beginning of the year rather than to Domitian's Secular games
seven years previously. See Coleman.

7 Minerva herself, mythically expert at the loom, makes her
favourite Domitian's consular robe, the purple-bordered *toga
praetexta*.

8 I.e. your gentleness and clemency.

9 The common people and Senators. The latter wore a broad
purple stripe on their tunics but not the purple-bordered gown
(*toga praetexta*), unless they were curule magistrates.

me to renew[6] the ages! Rome desires ever to see you thus in my month: thus, 'tis meet that times be born, thus that the years make entrance. Give joys continual to the Calendar. Let the fold surround these your shoulders with plenteous purple, and the bordered gown from your own Minerva's hastening hands.[7] See you how a new gleam is in the temples, how the flame mounts higher on the altars, and how the very stars of my midwinter grow warm for you, matching your manners?[8] Knights and tribes and purple-clad Fathers[9] rejoice, every office draws lustre from our Consul. Did any former year, I pray you, have the like?[10] Come, tell me, mighty Rome, and long Antiquity, count with me the annals, nor rehearse petty examples but only those that my Caesar would deign to surpass. Thrice and ten times as the years rolled by did Augustus bear the Latian rods,[11] but 'twas long before he began to deserve them: you were young when you outdid grandsires. And how much you refuse,[12] how much you forbid! Yet you

[10] I.e. 'did anyone in the past hold so many Consulships?' *Prior annus* is not 'the previous year' but 'a (i.e. any) previous year.' The answer is that only Augustus with thirteen Consulships can be compared, but the comparison is to his disadvantage, and not only numerically.

[11] Courtney keeps *Latio*, against which see Coleman. In case it be objected to *Latios* that Consuls did not carry the *fasces* themselves, cf. Silius 13.268f. *alter ut aequus / portaret fasces nostro de nomine consul.*

[12] Domitian had declined a triumph for his Sarmatian victory (III.3.171). *Quanta* is to be understood generally, not as 'how many Consulships' (Vollmer), which would be less than tactful seeing that Domitian had held the office every year of his reign but two.

35   permittes hunc saepe diem. manet insuper ordo
longior, et totidem felix tibi Roma curules
terque quaterque dabit. mecum altera saecula condes
et tibi longaevi renovabitur ara Tarenti.
mille tropaea feres; tantum permitte triumphos.
40   restat Bactra novis, restat Babylona tributis
frenari, nondum ⟨in⟩ gremio Iovis Indica laurus,
nondum Arabes Seresque rogant; nondum omnis hono-
       rem
annus habet, cupiuntque decem tua nomina menses.'
   Sic Ianus clausoque libens se poste recepit.
45   tunc omnes patuere dei laetoque dederunt
signa polo, longamque tibi, dux magne, iuventam
annuit atque suos promisit Iuppiter annos.

IV.2

EUCHARISTICON AD IMP.
AUG. GERM. DOMITIANUM

Regia Sidoniae convivia laudat Elissae
qui magnum Aenean Laurentibus intulit arvis,
Alcinoique dapes mansuro carmine monstrat

35 permittes *Calderini*: promittitis M (*et* promitte 39): pro-
mittes ς   38 Tarenti *Britannicus*: parentis M
   41 *add. Livineius*   46 dux* *Markland*: rex M

---

13 I.e. you shall celebrate the Secular games a second time.
14 See on I.4.18.   15 The laurels on the fasces of a messenger of victory were laid on the statue of Capitoline Jupiter.
That these prophecies of martial glory negate the promise of uni-

will be prevailed upon and will often promise this day to
the Senate's prayers. A longer series remains beyond, and
thrice and four times shall fortunate Rome bestow as many
curule chairs upon you. With me you shall found a second
century[13] and for you the altar of ancient Tarentus[14] shall
be renewed. You shall bear a thousand trophies, only permit the triumphs. Bactra and Babylon have still to be
curbed with new tributes, not yet are Indian laurels in
Jove's bosom,[15] not yet do Arabs and Seres make petition,
not yet does all the year have its honour, ten months still
crave your name.'[16]

So Janus, and gladly withdrew behind his closed portal.
Then all the gods opened wide[17] and gave signs in a joyful
heaven, and Jupiter accorded you, great leader, a long
youth and years as many as his own.

IV.2

THANKSGIVING TO EMPEROR
AUGUSTUS GERMANICUS DOMITIANUS

He that brought great Aeneas to the fields of Lauren-
tum extols the royal feast of Sidonian Elissa, and he that
wore out Ulysses with much seafaring portrays Alcinous'

versal peace in v. 14 does not worry Statius. Latin poets could tol-
erate or ignore inconsistency, as when they speak of navigation
prior to Argo.   [16] September and October had already been
renamed Germanicus and Domitianus.

[17] To receive the people's vows for their new Consul; cf. IV.8.1
pande fores superum. Whereas Janus' temple doors were closed,
those of the other gods opened wide. So Vollmer; *stupuere* (Watt,
read by Coleman) seems unnecessary.

aequore qui multo reducem consumpsit Ulixem:
5 ast ego, cui sacrae Caesar nova gaudia cenae
nunc primum dominamque dedit contingere mensam,
qua celebrem mea vota lyra, quas solvere grates
sufficiam? non, si pariter mihi vertice laeto
nectat adoratas et Smyrna et Mantua lauros,
10 digna loquar. medius videor discumbere in astris
cum Iove et Iliaca porrectum sumere dextra
immortale merum. steriles transmisimus annos;
haec aevi mihi prima dies, hic limina vitae.
tene ego, regnator terrarum orbisque subacti
15 magne parens, te, spes hominum, te, cura deorum,
cerno iacens? datur haec iuxta, datur ora tueri
vina inter mensasque, et non assurgere fas est?

    Tectum augustum, ingens, non centum insigne
        columnis,
sed quantae superos caelumque Atlante remisso
20 sustentare queant. stupet hoc vicina Tonantis
regia, teque pari laetantur sede locatum
numina (nec magnum properes escendere caelum).
tanta patet moles effusique impetus aulae
liberior campi multumque amplexus operti
25 aetheros et tantum domino minor; ille penates

---

6 dominamque dedit contingere mensam *Waller*: -naque d-
consurgere mensa M   7 qua solvere *Vollmer*
   9 adoratas: od- M   22 *anne* ne*?   escendere Ɫ
Gronovius: exced- M   23 effusique* *scripsi*: -saeque M

---

1 Virgil in the *Aeneid* and Homer in the *Odyssey*.

2 *Non surgere* (Markland for *cons-*), read by Courtney, pre-
empts the climax in v. 17 (Coleman).

repast in immortal verse.[1] But I, now that for the first time
Caesar has granted me novel joy of his sacred banquet,
granted me to attain to[2] his imperial board, with what lyre
am I to celebrate my answered prayers, what thanks shall I
avail to render? Not though Smyrna and Mantua both
were to bind holy laurel on my happy head should I find
fitting utterance. Meseems I recline with Jupiter among
the stars and take immortal liquor proffered by Ilian
hand.[3] Barren are the years behind me. This is the first day
of my span, here is the threshold of my life. Do I behold
you as I recline, sovereign of the lands, great parent of a
world subdued, you, hope of mankind, you, care of the
gods? Is it granted me indeed to gaze at this face from
nearby amid wine and tables, and lawful for me not to rise?

An august edifice,[4] vast, magnificent not with a hundred columns[5] but as many as might support heaven and
the High Ones were Atlas let go. The Thunderer' neighbouring palace[6] views it amazed, the deities rejoice to see
you established in a residence equal to their own (nor hasten you to ascend the great sky!);[7] so wide the pile, such the
thrust of the hall, freer than a spreading plain,[8] embracing
much of heaven within its shelter; he fills the household

[3] Ganymede.

[4] Domitian's new palace on the Palatine.

[5] Like Picus' palace in *Aeneid* 7.170 or the Hecatostylon in
Rome (Martial 2.14.9).   [6] The Capitoline temple.

[7] A rather confusing interjection. Perhaps read *ne* for *nec:* 'so
that you will not hasten,' the gods being concerned for the world's
welfare.

[8] Grammatically 'freer than that of'—*impetu* understood with
campi. See also Critical Appendix.

implet et ingenti genio gravat. aemulus illic
mons Libys Iliacusque nitet, ⟨tum⟩ multa Syene
et Chios et glaucae certantia Doridi saxa
Lunaque portandis tantum suffecta columnis.
30 longa supra species: fessis vix culmina prendas
visibus auratique putes laquearia caeli.
hic cum Romuleos proceres trabeataque Caesar
agmina mille simul iussit discumbere mensis,
ipsa sinus accincta Ceres Bacchusque laborat
35 sufficere. aetherii felix sic orbita fluxit
Triptolemi, sic uvifero sub palmite nudos
umbravit colles et sobria rura Lyaeus.
    Sed mihi non epulas Indisque innixa columnis
robora Maurorum famulasque ex ordine turmas,
40 ipsum, ipsum cupido tantum spectare vacavit,
tranquillum vultus et maiestate serena
mulcentem radios summittentemque modeste
fortunae vexilla suae; tamen ore nitebat
dissimulatus honos. talem quoque barbarus hostis
45 posset et ignotae conspectum agnoscere gentes.
non aliter gelida Rhodopes in valle recumbit
dimissis Gradivus equis; sic lubrica ponit
membra Therapnaea resolutus gymnade Pollux,
sic iacet ad Gangen Indis ululantibus Euhan,
50 sic gravis Alcides post horrida iussa reversus
gaudebat strato latus acclinare leoni.
parva loquor necdum aequo tuos, Germanice, visus:

---

26 gravat *Schwarz*: iuvat M   27 *add. Elter*: nitent et *Avan-*
tius   simul atra *Watt, alii alia*   28 Doridi *Politianus*: -de M
    36 uvifero *Krohn*: vitif- M   41 vultus et *Politianus*: -tu
sed M   52 visus *Markland*: vultus M

and weighs it down with his mighty being.[9] Here contend the mountains of Libya and the gleaming stone of Ilium, dark Syene too and Chios, and rocks to rival the grey-green sea,[10] and Luna, substituted only to support the columns.[11] Far aloft extends the view; your weary eyes could scarce attain the roof, you would think it the gilded ceiling of heaven. When Caesar bade Romulus' magnates and the columns of robed Knights recline here together at a thousand tables, Ceres herself with her dress girt up and Bacchus toil to supply their wants. So flowed the bounteous path of sky-borne Triptolemus; so Lyaeus shaded bare hills and sober fields under his clustered vines.

But not for the viands or the Moorish wood resting on Indian columns[12] or the ordered troops of servants had my eager gaze the time; for him, only him—calm of visage, softening its radiance with serene majesty, modestly lowering the banner of his fortune; yet the hidden splendour shone in his face. Even thus would a barbarian envoy and races unknown have recognized him had they seen him. Not otherwise does Gradivus recline in Rhodope's chill valley, horses dismissed; so Pollux lays down his slippery limbs, relaxing from Therapne's wrestling bout, so lies Euhan by Ganges, as Indians howl, so ponderous Alcides, returning from a grim behest, was fain to lean his flank against the outspread lion. I speak of little[13] things, nor yet, Germanicus, do I match your aspect. So looks the leader of

9 Genius.
10 From Carystos.
11 Marble from Luna was plain white.
12 Tables of citrus wood with ivory supports.
13 I.e. comparatively little.

talis, ubi Oceani finem mensasque revisit
Aethiopum sacros diffusus nectare vultus
55 dux superum secreta iubet dare carmina Musas
et Pallenaeos Phoebum laudare triumphos.
    Di tibi (namque animas saepe exaudire minores
dicuntur) patriae bis terque exire senectae
annuerint fines. rata numina miseris astris
60 templaque des habitesque domos. saepe annua pandas
limina, saepe novo Ianum lictore salutes,
saepe coronatis iteres quinquennia lustris.
qua mihi felices epulas mensaeque dedisti
sacra tuae, talis longo post tempore venit
65 lux mihi, Troianae qualis sub collibus Albae,
cum modo Germanas acies, modo Daca sonantem
proelia Palladio tua me manus induit auro.

IV.3

VIA DOMITIANA

Quis duri silicis gravisque ferri
immanis sonus aequori propinquum
saxosae latus Appiae replevit?
certe non Libycae sonant catervae
5 nec dux advena peierante bello
Campanos quatit inquietus agros
nec frangit vada montibusque caesis
inducit Nero sordidas paludes,

---

14 Victory over the Giants.
15 Or *domos* may be taken as earthly dwellings.
16 The crown of golden olive leaves, symbolic of Minerva.

the High Ones when he revisits Ocean's limits and the banquets of the Ethiopians, his sacred countenance diffused with nectar, and bids the Muses sing secret songs and Phoebus laud Pellene's triumphs.[14]

May the gods (for 'tis said they often give ear to lesser souls) grant that you pass twice and thrice the limits of your father's eld. May you send established deities skyward, give temples—and live in your home.[15] Often may you throw open the yearly threshold, often greet Janus with new lictors, often repeat the quinquennial festival with wreathed lustrations. The day you gave me the auspicious banquet and the rites of your table, such it came to me as that day long ago when under Trojan Alba's hill your hand invested me with Pallas' gold[16] as I sang now of German battles, now of Dacian.[17]

IV.3

THE DOMITIAN WAY

What monstrous sound of hard flint and heavy iron has filled paved Appia on the side that borders the sea? For sure 'tis not the sound of Libyan squadrons,[1] neither does a restless foreign captain shake Campania's fields in perfidious warfare. Nero is not breaching the waters and cleaving the mountains as he brings in murky swamps:[2] but he who

---

[17] Domitian's campaigns against the C(h)atti and the Dacians in 79, the year before Statius' victory.

[1] Hannibal's cavalry.

[2] Nero's abortive attempt to run a canal from Avernus to the mouth of the Tiber is chronicled by Tacitus, *Annals* 15.42.

sed qui limina bellicosa Iani
10 iustis legibus et foro coronat,
quis castae Cereri diu negata
reddit iugera sobriasque terras,
quis fortem vetat interire sexum
et censor prohibet mares adultos
15 pulchrae supplicium timere formae;
qui reddit Capitolio Tonantem
et Pacem propria domo reponit,
qui genti patriae futura semper
sancit limina Flaviumque caelum,
20 hic segnes populi vias gravatus
et campos iter omne detinentes
longos eximit ambitus novoque
iniectu solidat graves harenas,
gaudens Euboicae domum Sibyllae
25 Gauranosque sinus et aestuantes
septem montibus admovere Baias.

Hic quondam piger axe vectus uno
nutabat cruce pendula viator
sorbebatque rotas maligna tellus
30 et plebs in mediis Latina campis
horrebat mala navigationis;
nec cursus agiles, sed impeditum
tardabant iter orbitae tenaces,
dum pondus nimium querens sub alta
35 repit languida quadrupes statera.

---

13 qui ⊊
19 limina ⊊: lum- M   caelum *Turnebus*: calvum M
20 segnis (⊊) . . . gravatus *Heinsius*: senis . . . gravatas M
33 tenaces *Davies*: tacentes M

girdles Janus' warlike threshold with just laws and a Forum,[3] laws by which he restores to chaste Ceres acres long denied her, sober fields,[4] by which as Censor he forbids strong sex to perish and grown males to fear the punishment of fair form;[5] he who restores the Thunderer to the Capitol and puts Peace back in her own house,[6] who consecrates an everlasting dwelling and a Flavian sky to his father's race:[7] he it is who, impatient of routes that retard the people and plains that check their every journey, eliminates long distances and with new paving makes solid the clinging sands, glad to bring the home of Euboea's Sibyl and the fields of Gaurus and steaming Baiae closer to the Seven Hills.

Here once the tardy traveller borne on a single axle would sway on a pendulous pole[8] as the malignant earth sucked in his wheels, and the Latian folk feared the woes of navigation in the midst of the plain. No nimble runs; sticky ruts slowed the hampered journey, while the fainting beasts crawled beneath their high yoke, grumbling at too

[3] The Forum Transitorium containing the new temple of Four-faced Janus (cf. Martial 10.28.6).

[4] Domitian issued an edict against viticulture in Italy and the provinces but it was not enforced (Suetonius, *Domitian* 7.2).

[5] On the face of it *adultos* should refer to emasculation after puberty, but this could only have been exceptional. Statius must have been thinking of boys before puberty as opposed to infants, but his wording seems indefensible. The edict presumably banned such emasculation at any age.   [6] See on IV.1.13.

[7] Domitian had built a temple to the Flavian *gens* and deified his father Vespasian, his brother Titus, and his sister Domitilla.

[8] With one of the two wheels stuck in the mud, the traveller clings to the pole (*crux* = pole and yoke).

at nunc quae solidum diem terebat
horarum via facta vix duarum.
non tensae volucrum per astra pennae
nec velocius ibitis carinae.

40   Hic primus labor incohare sulcos
et rescindere limites et alto
egestu penitus cavare terras;
mox haustas aliter replere fossas
et summo gremium parare dorso,

45   ne nutent sola, ne maligna sedes
⟨d⟩et pressis dubium cubile saxis;
tunc umbonibus hinc et hinc coactis
et crebris iter alligare gomfis.
o quantae pariter manus laborant!

50   hi caedunt nemus exuuntque montes,
hi ferro scolopas trabesque levant,
illi saxa ligant opusque texunt
cocto pulvere sordidoque tofo,
hi siccant bibulas manu lacunas

55   et longe fluvios agunt minores.
hae possent et Athon cavare dextrae
et maestum pelagus gementis Helles
intercludere ponte non natanti;
his parens, nisi di viam vetarent,

60   Inous freta miscuisset Isthmos.
       Fervent litora mobilesque silvae.
it longus medias fragor per urbes
atque echo simul hinc et inde fractam

---

46 det *Heinsius*: et M   51 scolopas *Nisbet*: scopulos M
    59 parens *Postgate*: parvus M: ruptus *coni. Courtney*   di
viam *Barth*: deviae *vel* cle- M   62 it *Calderini*: et M

heavy a load. But now the route that used to wear out a
solid day barely takes two hours. The stretched wings of
birds flying through the stars will go no faster, nor ships
either.

The first task here was to start on furrows and cut out
borders[9] and hollow out the earth far down with a deep ex-
cavation. Next, to fill the trenches they dug with other material and prepare a basin for the raised spine, so that the
foundations do not wobble nor a niggardly bottom offer a
treacherous bed for the packed stones. After that, to knit
the road with blocks close set on either side and with frequent wedges. Oh, how many hands work in unison! Some
fell the forest and strip the mountains, some with iron
smooth stakes and beams; others bind stones together,
weaving the work with baked sand and grimy tufa; others
toil to dry up thirsty puddles and lead off lesser streams.
These hands could have hollowed out Athos and separated
lamenting Helle's mournful sea with a bridge that did not
float.[10] To these obedient, Ino's isthmus might have mingled seas did the gods not forbid passage.[11]

The shore and waving woods are astir. The lengthy din
travels through the towns between and grapy Massicus

---

[9] The meaning of *sulcos* and *limites* is doubtful. Coleman has
'cut back the existing track' in her note and 'cut back the edges' in
her translation. Rather perhaps, *limites* are ditches on either
side. *Fossae* in v. 43 are excavations along the track itself, the plural being explained 'as referring to the construction of the road in
sections to accommodate the gradual shifts in angle of direction.'

[10] As Xerxes' did, but *his* bridge was of boats.

[11] Several attempts to cut through the Isthmus of Corinth had
failed, most recently one by Nero.

259

Gauro Massicus uvifer remittit.
65   miratur sonitum quieta Cyme
et Literna palus pigerque Safon.
    At flavum caput umidumque late
crinem mollibus impeditus ulvis
Vulturnus levat ora, maximoque
70   pontis Caesarei reclinus arcu
raucis talia faucibus redundat:
    'Camporum bone conditor meorum,
qui me, vallibus aviis refusum
et ripas habitare nescientem,
75   recti legibus alvei ligasti,
en nunc ille ego turbidus minaxque,
vix passus dubias prius carinas,
iam pontem fero perviusque calcor!
qui terras rapere et rotare silvas
80   assueram, (pudet) amnis esse coepi.
sed grates ago servitusque tanti est
quod sub te duce, te iubente, cessi,
quod tu maximus arbiter meaeque
victor perpetuus legere ripae.
85   et nunc limite me colis beato
nec sordere sinis malumque late
deterges sterilis soli pudorem,
ne me pulvereum gravemque caeno
Tyrrheni sinus obluat profundi
90   (qualis Cinyphius tacente ripa
Poenos Bagrada serpit inter agros),
sed talis ferar ut nitente cursu
tranquillum mare proximumque possim
puro gurgite provocare Lirim.'
95   Haec amnis, pariterque se levarat

sends back to Gaurus the echo broken at either end. Quiet
Cyme wonders at the noise, and the Liternian marsh and
sluggish Savo.

But Vulturnus raises his face, his yellow head and mop
of watery hair tangled with soft sedge. Leaning against the
mighty arch of Caesar's bridge, he pours from his hoarse
throat such words as these:

'Kind orderer of my plains, who bound me in the law of
a straight channel when I spread over distant valleys nor
knew to keep my limits, see, now I, the turbulent bully,
that in time past barely tolerated imperilled barks, I bear a
bridge and am tramped by crossing feet. I that was wont to
carry off land and whirl woods, begin (ah, shame!) to be a
river. But I give you thanks and my servitude is worthwhile
because I have yielded under *your* guidance at *your* command, and because men shall read of you as supreme arbiter and conqueror of my bank. And now you tend me with a
copious channel nor let me lie in squalor, and broadly wipe
away the sorry shame of barren soil, so that the gulf of the
Tyrrhene sea does not wash against my sandy, mud-heavy
current, even as Cinyphian Bagrada glides by his silent
banks amid Punic fields, but I so flow that I can challenge
the smooth sea with my shining course and neighbouring
Liris with my limpid stream.'

Thus the river; and as he spoke a marbled stretch of

261

ingenti plaga marmorata dorso.
huius ianua prosperumque limen
arcus, belligeri ducis tropaeis
et totis Ligurum nitens metallis,
100   quantus nubila qui coronat imbri.
illic flectit iter citus viator,
illic Appia se dolet relinqui.
tunc velocior acriorque cursus,
tunc ipsos iuvat impetus iugales,
105   ceu fessis ubi remigum lacertis
primae carbasa ventilatis aurae.
ergo omnes, age, quae sub axe primo
Romani colitis fidem parentis
prono limite commeate gentes,
110   Eoae, citius venite, laurus:
nil obstat cupidis, nihil moratur.
qui primo Tiberim reliquit ortu
primo vespere naviget Lucrinum.
    Sed quam fine viae recentis imo,
115   qua monstrat veteres Apollo Cumas,
albam crinibus infulisque cerno?
visu fallimur, an sacris ab antris
profert Chalcidicas Sibylla laurus?
cedamus; chely, iam repone cantus:
120   vates sanctior incipit, tacendum est.
en et colla rotat novisque late
bacchatur spatiis viamque replet!
tunc sic virgineo profatur ore:
    'Dicebam: "veniet (manete campi

⁹⁸ belligeri *Calderini*: -is M
¹⁰⁰ iri ς

262

road had risen in a great spine. Its doorway and auspicious threshold was an arch, gleaming with the warrior leader's trophies and all Liguria's quarries, large as the bow that crowns the clouds with rain. There the swift traveller makes a turn, there Appia grieves to find herself abandoned. Then quicker and livelier grows the pace and the beasts themselves enjoy the rush, as when rowers' arms are weary and a first breeze fans the sails. Come therefore, all you peoples that under eastern sky maintain allegiance to the Roman Father, flock down the easy road; laurels of the Orient, come faster. Nothing stands in the way, nothing delays your eager advent. Let him that left Tibur at daybreak sail the Lucrine at earliest eve.[12]

But who is this that I see at the furthest end of the new road, where Apollo points to ancient Cumae?[13] Her hair and fillets are white. Do my eyes deceive me, or does the Sybil bring Chalcidian laurels forth from her sacred cave? Let us retire. Lyre, now put aside your song. A holier bard begins, we must be silent. See! She whirls her neck and wanders at large over the new spaces, filling the road. Then thus she speaks with virgin lips:

'I said it: "He will come. Fields and river, wait! He will

[12] Turning at v. 112 from messengers with news of eastern victories, who would land at Puteoli on their way to Rome, to travellers in general. But perhaps Coleman's rearrangement (see critical note) should be preferred.

[13] Apollo's ancient temple on its height (*Aeneid* 6.8ff.).

---

101 flectit iter citus *Cartault*: fectitur excitus M
112 reliquit ⊂: -inquit M
123 nunc *coni. Courtney*

125   atque amnis), veniet favente caelo,
         qui foedum nemus et putres harenas
         celsis pontibus et via levabit."
         en hic est deus, hunc iubet beatis
         pro se Iuppiter imperare terris,
130   quo non dignior has subit habenas
         ex quo me duce praescios Averni
         Aeneas avide futura quaerens
         lucos et penetravit et reliquit.
         hic paci bonus, hic timendus armis,
136   hic si flammigeros teneret axes
135   Natura melior potentiorque,
         largis, India, nubibus maderes,
         undaret Libye, teperet Haemus.
            Salve, dux hominum et parens deorum,
140   provisum mihi conditumque numen!
         nec iam putribus evoluta chartis
         sollemni prece Quindecimvirorum
         perlustra mea dicta, sed canentem
         ipsam comminus, ut mereris, audi.
145   vidi quam seriem virentis aevi
         pronectant tibi candidae Sorores.
         magnus te manet ordo saeculorum;
         natis longior abnepotibusque
         annos perpetua geres iuventa
150   quos fertur placidos adisse Nestor,
         quos Tithonia computat senectus,
         et quantos ego Delium poposci.
         iuravit tibi iam nivalis Arctus;
         nunc magnos Oriens dabit triumphos.
155   ibis qua vagus Hercules et Euhan
         ultra sidera flammeumque solem

come by heaven's favour, he that shall raise the foul forest and powdery sand with lofty bridge and causeway." See! He is a god, him Jupiter commands to rule the happy earth in his stead. None worthier has held these reins since Aeneas with me to guide both entered and left Avernus' prescient grove, eager to learn the future. He is friend to peace, formidable in arms. If he had the flaming sky in his keeping, better and mightier than Nature, India would be damp with generous clouds, Libya watered, Haemus warm.

Hail, leader of men and parent of gods, deity by me foreseen and placed on record! Do not now scan my words unrolled on crumbling sheets to the ritual prayers of the Fifteen;[14] but listen to me face to face as I sing, as you deserve. I have seen the procession of slow time that the white-clad Sisters[15] weave for you. A great chain of centuries awaits you. Longer lived than your sons and great-great-grandsons, in perpetual youth you shall spend such tranquil years as Nestor is said to have attained, such as Tithonus' age computes, and as many as I asked of the Delian.[16] Already the snowy north has sworn you fealty; now the east shall give you great triumphs. You shall go where Hercules and Euhan[17] went, beyond stars and flam-

---

[14] Cf. on I.2.176.

[15] The Fates, wearing white in token of benignity.

[16] See on I.4.126.

[17] To the land of the Hyperboreans and to India, far north and far east.

135–36 *inter se traiesit Russell*

145 virentis *Heinsius*: meren- M

et Nili caput et nives Atlantis,
et laudum cumulo beatus omni
scandes belliger abnuesque currus,
160   donec Troicus ignis et renatae
Tarpeius pater intonabit aulae,
haec donec via te regente terras
annosa magis Appia senescat.'

IV.4

EPISTULA AD VITORIUM MARCELLUM

Curre per Euboicos non segnis, epistula, campos,
hac ingressa vias qua nobilis Appia crescit
in latus et molles solidus premit agger harenas,
atque ubi Romuleas velox penetraveris arces,
5   continuo dextras flavi pete Thybridis oras,
Lydia qua penitus stagnum navale coercet
ripa suburbanisque vadum praetexitur hortis.
illic egregium formaque animisque videbis
Marcellum et celso praesignem vertice nosces.
10 cui primum solito vulgi de more salutem,
mox inclusa modis haec reddere verba memento:

---

18 I.e. far south. Statius follows *Aeneid* 6.795f. *extra sidera . . .
extra anni solisque vias,* meaning 'south of the zodiac and the
ecliptic.' So Housman, *Cl. Papers* 650ff., explaining the astronom-
ical background. 'Nile's fount' too refers to the south, as according
to Housman does 'Atlas' snows,' but there, I think, he mistakes.
Atlas is where he usually is in the far west, the remaining quarter.

19 I.e. triumphal.   20 The sacred flame in the temple
of Vesta.   21 Not necessarily an impossibility. 'Older than
Appia' could refer to Appia's present age.

266

ing sun[18] and Nile's fount and Atlas' snows. Warrior blest with every pile of glory, you shall ascend chariots[19] and refuse them, so long as Trojan fire[20] endures and the Tarpeian Father thunders in his renascent hall, until this road grows older than ancient Appia,[21] while you rule the earth.'

IV.4

A LETTER TO VITORIUS MARCELLUS

Run, letter, through the Euboean plains and loiter not, beginning your journey by the road wherewith famed Appia grows sideways[1] and a solid embankment presses down the soft sands. And when you have made your swift way into the heights of Romulus, forthwith seek the right bank of yellow Tiber where the Lydian shore from deep down confines the naval pool[2] and the water is fringed by suburban villas.[3] There you shall see Marcellus, eminent in form and spirit, and know him by his conspicuously lofty stature. First you shall greet him in ordinary everyday form, then be sure to give him this message in verse:

[1] The letter travels from Naples along the new Via Domitiana which had branched off from the Via Appia at Sinuessa.

[2] Probably the lake created by Augustus for naval spectacles rather than a similar lake created by Domitian (see Coleman). *Penitus* may be taken in the sense that the confinement began deep down, the depth of the river parallel with the depth of the pool.   [3] Not 'gardens.' *Horti* is a suburban residence (villa), a fact that will not be learned from P. Grimal's *Les Jardins romains;* see Martial 5.62. It would have grounds of course, more or less extensive.

'Iam terras volucremque polum fuga veris aquosi
lassat et Icariis caelum latratibus urit;
ardua iam densae rarescunt moenia Romae.
15   hos Praeneste sacrum, nemus hos glaciale Dianae
Algidus aut horrens aut Tuscula protegit umbra,
Tiburis hi lucos Anienaque frigora captant.
te quoque clamosae quae iam plaga mitior Urbi
subtrahit? aestivos quo decipis aëre soles?
20   quid tuus ante omnes, tua cura potissima, Gallus,
nec non noster amor, dubium morumne probandus
ingeniine bonis? Latiis aestivat in oris,
anne metalliferae repetit iam moenia Lunae
Tyrrhenasque domos? quod si tibi proximus haeret,
25   non ego nunc vestro procul a sermone recedo.
certum est: inde sonus geminas mihi circumit aures.
sed tu, dum nimio possessa Hyperione flagrat
torva Cleonaei iuba sideris, exue curis
pectus et assiduis temet furare labori.
30   et sontes operit pharetras arcumque retendit
Parthus et Eleis auriga laboribus actos
Alpheo permulcet equos et nostra fatiscit
laxaturque chelys. vires instigat alitque
tempestiva quies; maior post otia virtus.
35   talis cantata Briseide venit Achilles
acrior et positis erupit in Hectora plectris.
te quoque flammabit tacite repetita parumper
desidia et solitos novus exsultabis in actus.
certe iam Latiae non miscent iurgia leges,
40   et pacem piger annus habet messesque reversae

---

13 lassat *Behotius*: laxat M   18 quae iam *Otto*: quaenam M
31 actis *Markland*

'Already the flight of watery spring wearies earth and whirling sky and burns heaven with Icarian barking.[4] Already the lofty buildings of crowded Rome are less populous. Some sacred Praeneste shelters, some Diana's hilly wood,[5] or shivering Algidus,[6] or Tusculum's shade, yet others make for the groves of Tibur and Anio's cool. You too, what gentler clime now draws you from the clamourous city? With what air do you trick the suns of summer? What of your chief care, your favourite, Gallus, whom I too love (to be praised for gifts of character or mind, who shall say?)? Does he spend the season on Latium's coast or does he revisit the walls of quarried Luna and his Tyrrhene home? But if he stays close to you, I do not go far from your talk, that's certain, and that's why my ears are buzzing. But while the grim mane of Cleonae's star[7] blazes in the grip of too powerful Hyperion, strip your breast of its cares and steal yourself from ceaseless work. The Parthian covers his guilty quiver and unstrings his bow, the charioteer bathes his horses in Alpheus, hard-driven in the labours of Elis; my lyre too grows weary, its strings relax. Timely rest stimulates and fosters strength, energy is greater after ease. So came Achilles the fiercer after he had sung of Briseis; putting by his quill, out he burst against Hector. You also shall idleness silently inflame, sought again for a little while, and you shall leap up fresh to your wonted activities. Sure it is that Latium's laws now cease their wrangling, the lazy season enjoys peace and re-

---

[4] See Index. The bitch Maera became the dogstar Sirius by some accounts, genders notwithstanding.   [5] At Nemi.
[6] The name means 'cold.'   [7] The lion killed by Hercules at Cleonae became the constellation Leo.

dimisere Forum, nec iam tibi turba reorum
vestibulo querulique rogant exire clientes.
cessat centeni moderatrix iudicis hasta,
qua tibi sublimi iam nunc celeberrima fama
45 eminet et iuvenes facundia praeterit annos.
felix curarum, cui non Heliconia cordi
serta nec imbelles Parnasi e vertice laurus,
sed viget ingenium et magnos accinctus in usus
fert animus quascumque vices. nos otia vitae
50 solamur cantu ventosaque gaudia famae
quaerimus. en egomet somnum et geniale secutus
litus ubi Ausonio se condidit hospita portu
Parthenope tenues ignavo pollice chordas
pulso, Maroneique sedens in margine templi
55 sumo animum et magni tumulis accanto magistri.
    At tu, si longi cursum dabit Atropos aevi
(detque precor) Latiique ducis sic numina pergent
(quem tibi posthabito studium est coluisse Tonante
quique tuos alio subtexit munere fasces
60 et spatia obliquae mandat renovare Latinae).
forsitan Ausonias ibis frenare cohortes
aut Rheni populos aut nigrae litora Thules
aut Histrum servare latus metuendaque portae

42 negant *Burman*: *anne* vocant*?
57 pergent *Markland*: -gant M
63 latus *Calderini*: da- M: datur *Imhof*

8 Sales of enemy or confiscated property were conducted *sub hasta*. Why the symbolic spear also served as emblem for the civil Court of a hundred is uncertain, like many other things about this institution.

270

turning harvests have discharged the Forum. Defendants no longer throng your anteroom nor querulous clients ask you to come out. Idle stands the Spear[8] that rules the Hundred Judges, whereby your eloquence is already borne far and wide conspicuous on the wings of Fame, outstripping your youthful years. Happy in your avocations, you care not for Helicon's garlands or peaceable laurels from Parnassus' peak; vigorous your wit, girt up for great employments your mind shoulders whatever betides, while I solace a leisured life with song and seek the fickle joys of fame. Look! Pursuing sleep and the genial shore where stranger Parthenope[9] found refuge in Ausonian haven, I idly strike the slender strings; sitting on the verge of Maro's shrine,[10] I take heart and sing at the tomb of the great master.

But you, if Atropos grant long course of life—and I pray she grant it, so may the deity of Latium's leader proceed,[11] him whom you study to worship before the Thunderer, who has attached another function to your rods,[12] commissioning you to renovate the zigzag reaches of the Latin Way—perchance you shall go to bridle Ausonian cohorts: either it is appointed you to guard the peoples of the Rhine or the shores of dark Thule or the Histrian bank or the

---

[9] One of the three Sirens, who flung themselves into the sea after failing to entice Ulysses. One legend had it that she was washed ashore in the Bay of Naples and somehow founded the city. Statius has a different story; cf. III.5.79–9 and IV.8.47f. and see Coleman, pp. 209f.   [10] Virgil's tomb on the road from Naples to Puteoli became a cult object for admirers like Silius Italicus.   [11] I.e. continue to advance your career.

[12] *Fasces,* here signifying the Praetorship.

limina Caspiacae. nec enim tibi sola potentis
65 eloquii virtus: sunt membra accommoda bellis
quique gravem tarde subeant thoraca lacerti.
seu campo pedes ire pares, est agmina supra
nutaturus apex, seu frena sonantia flectes,
serviet asper equus. nos facta aliena canendo
70 vergimus in senium: propriis tu pulcher in armis
ipse canenda geres parvoque exempla parabis
magna Getae, dignos quem iam nunc belliger actus
poscit avus praestatque domi novisse triumphos.
surge agedum iuvenemque puer deprende parentem,
75 stemmate materno felix, virtute paterna.
iam te blanda sinu Tyrio sibi curia felix
educat et cunctas gaudet spondere curules.'
    Haec ego Chalcidicis ad te, Marcelle, sonabam
litoribus, fractas ubi Vesvius erigit iras
80 aemula Trinacriis volvens incendia flammis.
mira fides! credetne virum ventura propago,
cum segetes iterum, cum iam haec deserta virebunt,
infra urbes populosque premi proavitaque fato
rura abiisse pari? necdum letale minari
85 cessat apex. procul ista tuo sint fata Teate
nec Marrucinos agat haec insania montes.
    Nunc si forte meis quae sint exordia Musis
scire petis, iam Sidonios emensa labores

70 vergimus *Coleman*: -ur M   76 curia *Markland*: gloria M
79 erigit ⊊: -get M: egerit *Avantius*
83-4 fato . . . pari *Slater*: toto . . . mari M

---

13 Because of their size? But Coleman pronounces *tarde* intolerable and Courtney obelizes.

272

formidable threshold of the Caspian Gate. For potent eloquence is not your only strength. You have limbs well fitted
for war and arms slow (?)[13] to don a heavy corslet. If you
make to march on the level, your crest will wave above
the ranks; if you manage jingling reins, the mettlesome
charger will be your slave. I drift into old age singing other
men's deeds, whereas you, handsome in your own arms,
shall yourself perform acts deserving song and prepare
great examples for little Geta,[14] of whom his grandfather
already demands worthy feats, acquainting him of domes-
tic triumphs. Up then, boy, be doing, catch your young
parent, fortunate in your mother's lineage and your father's
valour! Already the happy Senate House fondly rears you
for herself in Tyrian[15] bosom and joys to promise you every
curule chair.'

This song I sing to you, Marcellus, on Chalcidian shores
where Vesuvius rears his broken wrath, rolling out fires to
rival Trinacrian flames. Wonderful but true! Shall future
progeny of men believe, when crops grow again and this
desert shall once more be green, that cities and peoples are
buried below and that an ancestral countryside vanished in
a common doom? Nor does the summit yet cease its deadly
thrust. Far be that fate from your Teate, nor let this madness drive Marrucinian mountains!

Now if perchance you would know what my Muse essays, the *Thebaid* has already accomplished her Sidonian

[14] C. Vitorius Hosidius Geta. His mother was granddaughter
(rather than daughter; see Coleman) to C. (possibly Cn.) Hosidius
Geta, who had received triumphal insignia for action in Claudius'
invasion of Britain (43 A.D.).

[15] Purple.

Thebais optato collegit carbasa portu
90 Parnasique iugis silvaque Heliconide festis
tura dedit flammis et virginis exta iuvencae
votiferaque meas suspendit ab arbore vittas.
nunc vacuos crines alio subit infula nexu:
Troia quidem magnusque mihi temptatur Achilles,
95 sed vocat arcitenens alio pater armaque monstrat
Ausonii maiora ducis. trahit impetus illo
iam pridem retrahitque timor. stabuntne sub illa
mole umeri an magno vincetur pondere cervix?
dic, Marcelle, feram? fluctus an sueta minores
100 nosse ratis nondum Ioniis credenda periclis?
       Iamque vale et penitus noti tibi vatis amorem
corde exire veta. nec enim Tirynthius almae
parcus amicitiae. cedet tibi gloria fidi
Theseos, et lacerum qui circa moenia Troiae
105 Priamiden caeso solacia traxit amico.

IV.5

ODE LYRICA AD SEPTIMIUM SEVERUM

Parvi beatus ruris honoribus,
qua prisca Teucros Alba colit lares,
    fortem atque facundum Severum
        non solitis fidibus saluto.

5 iam trux ad Arctos Parrhasias hiems
concessit altis obruta solibus,

101 noti ⌐: voti M   amorem *Calderini*: honorem M
103 parcus *Slater*: pectus M   *post* amic- *lac. suspicatus est*
Markland, post Tir- (102) *statuit Leo*

labours and furled her sails in longed-for haven. On Parnassus' ridges and the woods of Helicon she has given incense and the entrails of a virgin heifer to the festal flames and hung my chaplets from a votive tree. Now a different band comes to entwine my vacant locks: Troy I attempt and great Achilles, but the Father that bears the bow calls me elsewhere, pointing to the Ausonian leader's mightier arms. Impulse has long been drawing me that way, and fear draws me back. Will my shoulders hold fast under such a mass, or will my neck sink beneath the mighty load? Say, Marcellus, shall I bear it? Or is my ship, accustomed to sail lesser seas, not yet to be trusted to the perils of the Ionian?

And now farewell, and let not affection for the poet you know so well[16] pass from your heart. For neither was the Tirynthian sparing of fostering friendship. The glory of faithful Theseus shall yield to you, as shall he that dragged the torn son of Priam round the walls of Troy to solace his slain friend.

IV.5

LYRIC ODE TO SEPTIMIUS SEVERUS

Wealthy in the bounties of a small estate, where ancient Alba worships Teucrian hearth gods, I greet brave and eloquent Severus in no wonted strain. Now harsh winter has withdrawn to the Parrhasian north o'erwhelmed by high

---

[16] *Voti* = *devoti* may be right; cf. *Thebaid* 2.736 *virgineis votae Calydonides aris.*

iam pontus ac tellus renident
    in zephyros Aquilone fracto.

nunc cuncta veris frondibus annuis
10   crinitur arbos, nunc volucrum novi
    questus inexpertumque carmen
      quod tacita statuere bruma.

nos parca tellus pervigil et focus
culmenque multo lumine sordidum
15   solantur exemptusque testa
      qua modo fer‹b›uerat Lyaeus.

non mille balant lanigeri greges
nec vacca dulci mugit adultero,
    unique si quando canenti
20   mutus ager domino reclamat.

sed terra primis post patriam mihi
dilecta curis; hic mea carmina
    regina bellorum virago
      Caesareo redimivit auro,

25   cum tu sodalis dulce periculum
conisus omni pectore tolleres,
    ut Castor ad cunctos tremebat
      Bebryciae strepitus harenae.

tene in remotis Syrtibus avia
30   Lepcis creavit? iam feret Indicas
    messes odoratisque rara
      cinnama praeripiet Sabaeis.

suns, now sea and land are smiling as the North Wind soft-
ens into zephyrs. Now every tree is coiffed with spring's
yearly leaves, now come new plaints of birds and song untried, song that in silent winter they disused. To me a patch
of land, an unsleeping hearth, and a roof darkened by
abundant light[1] bring comfort, along with Lyaeus taken
from the jar in which lately he had fermented.[2] No bleat of
a thousand woolly flocks, no lowing of cow for her sweet
paramour; the fields are mute save when they echo to their
owner should he sing. But the land is dear to me, first in my
affections after my birthplace. Here the virgin queen of
battles[3] crowned my songs with Caesar's gold, when you
strove with all your might to buoy up your friend's sweet
peril, even as Castor trembled at every sound of the Be-
brycian arena.

Did Lepcis, remote in the distant Syrtes, give you
birth? Soon she will be bearing Indian harvests and fore-

---

[1] I.e. the hearth fire and lamps.

[2] Lyaeus (Bacchus) = wine. Statius' wine was of recent vintage,
therefore inexpensive.

[3] Minerva at the Alban festival.

---

[8] in (ad *Coleman*) . . . fracto *Buecheler, Krohn*: iam . . . fractos
M

[9] vernans *Markland*

[17] balant ⊊: lavant M

[22] hic *Laetus*: hinc M

[24] redimivit *Baehrens*: peramavit M: decora- *Markland*

[30] Lepcis *Coleman*: leptis M

quis non in omni vertice Romuli
reptasse dulcem Septimium putet?
35   quis fonte Iuturnae relictis
            uberibus neget esse pastum?

nec mira virtus: protinus Ausonum
portus vadosae nescius Africae
       intras adoptatusque Tuscis
40   gurgitibus puer innatasti.

hinc parvus inter pignora curiae
contentus ⟨artae⟩ lumine purpurae
       crescis, sed immensos labores
            indole patricia secutus.

45   non sermo Poenus, non habitus tibi,
externa non mens: Italus, Italus.
       sunt Urbe Romanisque turmis
            qui Libyam deceant alumni.

est et frementi vox hilaris Foro,
50   venale sed non eloquium tibi,
       ensisque vagina quiescit
            stringere ni iubeant amici.

sed rura cordi saepius et quies,
nunc in paternis sedibus et solo
55   Veiente, nunc frondosa supra
            Hernica, nunc Curibus vetustis.

42 *add. Burman duce Turnebo*
58 passu *Markland*: -um M

278

stall the perfumed Sabaeans with rare cinnamon. Who but would think that sweet Septimius had crawled on every hill of Romulus? Who deny that when he left the breast he drank from Juturna's fountain?

No wonder you excel. Straightway, knowing nothing of Africa's shallows, you entered an Ausonian harbour and, child of adoption, swam in Tuscan waters. Then in boyhood you grew up among sons of the Senate House, content with the brilliance of narrow purple,[4] but by nature a patrician seeking unmeasured toils. Your speech was not Punic, nor foreign your dress or your mind: Italian, Italian! In the City and Rome's squadrons there are some worthy to be fosterlings of Libya.[5]

Cheerful your voice ever when the Forum roars, but your eloquence is not for sale; your sword sleeps in its scabbard unless your friends tell you to draw it. But more often rest and the countryside is to your mind, now in your father's seat on Veientine soil, now on the leafy heights of

---

[4] The two narrow stripes on the tunic worn by Knights, though their sons were sometimes privileged to wear the senatorial broad stripe. The implication of *contentus* here is doubtful (see Coleman).   [5] A touch of unwonted acerbity; Vollmer compares III.*epist.* 12 *cum lugeret, quod iam rarissimum est, lacrimis senem patrem* (cf. III.3.21). Coleman's rendering, 'there are foster-children to do Libya credit,' destroys the antithesis: Romans who would fit better in Africa as opposed to the African who has become quite a Roman. And to tell the latter that he is not the only African to bring credit to his country of origin would be a poor sort of compliment. Add that *sunt* (without *alii*) would lack coherence.

hic plura pones vocibus et modis
passu solutis; sed memor interim
   nostri verecundo latentem
60   barbiton ingemina sub antro.

IV.6

HERCULES EPITRAPEZIOS NOVI VINDICIS

Forte remittentem curas Phoeboque levatum
pectora, cum patulis tererem vagus otia Saeptis
iam moriente die, rapuit me cena benigni
Vindicis. haec imos animi perlapsa recessus
5 inconsumpta manet: neque enim ludibria ventris
hausimus aut epulas diverso a sole petitas
vinaque perpetuis aevo certantia fastis.
a miseri, quos nosse iuvat quid Phasidis ales
distet ab hiberna Rhodopes grue, quis magis anser
10 exta ferat, cur Tuscus aper generosior Umbro,
lubrica qua recubent conchylia mollius alga!
nobis verus amor medioque Helicone petitus
sermo hilaresque ioci brumalem absumere noctem
suaserunt mollemque oculis expellere somnum,
15 donec ab Elysiis prospexit sedibus alter
Castor et hesternas risit Tithonia mensas.

      60 ingemina *Gronovius*: -as M
      10 ferax *Phillimore*

the Hernici, now in ancient Cures. Here most of your compositions shall be in free words and measures,[6] but remember me sometimes and once and again strike the lyre that
hides in your shy grotto.

IV.6

THE HERCULES STATUETTE OF NOVIUS VINDEX

It happened as I wandered idly at sunset in the spacious
Enclosure,[1] my tasks put by and my mind relieved of Phoebus, that kindly Vindex took me off to dine. That dinner
slid into the inmost recesses of my mind and stays un-
consumed. For we swallowed no stomach's mockery, fare
sought from a distant clime and wine rivalling our perpetual Calendar in age.[2] Ah, wretched are they that care to
know how the bird of Phasis differs from Rhodope's winter
crane, what goose gives offal rather than another, why the
Tuscan boar is nobler than the Umbrian, what seaweed
makes the most comfortable bed for slippery shellfish.
True affection and talk sought from the heart of Helicon
and many jests induced us to exhaust a winter's night and
banish soft sleep from our eyes until the other Castor[3]
looked out from Elysian abode and Tithonia laughed[4] at

[6] In prose.   [1] The Saepta Julia in the Campus Martius,
a great shopping centre. People might walk there in search of a
dinner invitation (Martial 2.14.5), but not so Statius here since
cena usually began before sunset (Coleman).   [2] The Annual
Register (*fasti*).   [3] I.e. when Castor or Pollux, whichever
was taking his twenty-four hour turn in the Underworld, comes to
replace his brother.   [4] Indulgently. The state of the table
suggested that the diners had made a night of it.

o bona nox iunctaque utinam Tirynthia luna!
nox et Erythraeis Thetidis signanda lapillis
et memoranda diu geniumque habitura perennem!
20   Mille ibi tunc species aerisque eborisque vetusti
atque locuturas mentito corpore ceras
edidici. quis namque oculis certaverit usquam
Vindicis artificum veteres agnoscere ductus
et non inscriptis auctorem reddere signis?
25 hic tibi quae docto multum vigilata Myroni
aera, laboriferi vivant quae marmora caelo
Praxitelis, quod ebur Pisaeo pollice rasum,
quid Polycliteis iussum spirare caminis,
linea quae veterem longe fateatur Apellen,
30 monstrabit: namque haec, quotiens chelyn exuit, illi
desidia est, hic Aoniis amor avocat antris.
   Haec inter castae genius tutelaque mensae
Amphitryoniades multo mea cepit amore
pectora nec longo satiavit lumina visu:
35 tantus honos operi finesque inclusa per artos
maiestas. deus ille, deus, seseque videndum
indulsit, Lysippe, tibi, parvusque videri
sentirique ingens; et cum mirabilis intra
stet mensura pedem, tamen exclamare libebit,
40 si visus per membra feres: 'hoc pectore pressus
vastator Nemees; haec exitiale ferebant
robur et Argoos frangebant bracchia remos.'
dant spatium tam magna brevi mendacia formae.

19 habitura *Laetus*: -umque M
25 hic *edit. pr.*: haec M   30 illi *Gevartius*: ille M
35 artos *Politianus*: artus M
43 dant *Ziehen*: ac M

282

yesterday's board. What a night that was! Would it had
been Tirynthian with double moon![5] A night to be marked
with Thetis' Erythraean gems,[6] long to be remembered,
whose spirit will live for ever.

There it was and then that I learned of a thousand
shapes of bronze and antique ivory and of false bodies
in wax, ready to speak. For who would ever rival Vindex'
eyes in recognizing the hands of old masters and restor-
ing its maker to an untitled statue? He shall show you
which bronzes cost skilled Myron many a wakeful night,
which marbles live from the chisel of laborious Praxite-
les, which ivory was smoothed by Pisaean thumb,[7] what
was bidden to breathe by Polyclitus' furnace, what line
proclaims ancient Apelles from afar. For this is his idleness
whenever he lays aside his lyre, this the passion that calls
him away from Aonian grottoes.

Amid all this the guardian spirit of the temperate
board, Amphitryon's son, took my heart captive in fond
love. Long as I looked, he left my eyes unsatisfied. Such
was the dignity of the work, the majesty confined in narrow
limits. A god he was, a god! And he granted you, Lysippus,
to behold him, small to the eye but huge to the sense. The
marvellous measure was no more than a foot, yet if you let
your vision travel over his limbs you will be fain to cry: 'this
was the breast that crushed the ravager of Nemea, these
the arms that bore the deadly club and broke Argo's oars.'[8]
So mighty the deception that makes the small figure large!

[5] Like the long night of Hercules' conception.
[6] Pearls.
[7] Phidias, creator of the ivory statue of Zeus at Olympia.
[8] As he does in Valerius Flaccus 3.476f.

quis modus in dextra, quanta experientia docti
45 artificis curis, pariter gestamina mensae
fingere et ingentes animo versare colossos!
tale nec Idaeis quicquam Telchines in antris
nec stolidus Brontes nec, qui polit arma deorum,
Lemnius exigua potuisset ludere massa.
50 nec torva effigies epulisque aliena remissis
sed qualem parci domus admirata Molorchi
aut Aleae lucis vidit Tegeaea sacerdos,
qualis et Oetaeis emissus in astra favillis
nectar adhuc torva laetus Iunone bibebat.
55 sic mitis vultus, veluti de pectore gaudens,
hortatur mensas. tenet haec marcentia fratris
pocula, at haec clavae meminit manus; aspera sedes
sustinet et cultum Nemeaeo tegmine saxum.
        Digna operi fortuna sacro. Pellaeus habebat
60 regnator laetis numen venerabile mensis
et comitem occasus secum portabat et ortus,
prensabatque libens modo qua diademata dextra
abstulerat dederatque et magnas verterat urbes.
semper ab hoc animos in crastina bella petebat,
65 huic acies semper victor narrabat opimas,
sive catenatos Bromio detraxerat Indos
seu clusam magna Babylona refregerat hasta
seu Pelopis terras libertatemque Pelasgam
obruerat bello; magnoque ex agmine laudum
70 fertur Thebanos tantum excusasse triumphos.

57 clavae *Markland*: levae M
62 prensabat *Calderini*: prestabat M

---

9 If they had crafted anything so small, it would have been a *jeu*

What precision in the hand, what daring in the cunning master's artistry, at once to fashion a table ornament and in his mind imagine forms gigantic! No such work from so tiny a lump could the Telchines in Ida's caverns or stolid Brontes or the Lemnian who furbishes the weapons of the gods have wrought for sport.[9] The figure is not grim or unsuited to a free and easy feast, but such as frugal Molorchus' home surveyed him or the admiring Tegean priestess[10] in Alea's groves; or such as sent to the stars from Oeta's embers he happily drank nectar, though Juno still scowled. So does the gentle countenance, as though rejoicing from the heart, encourage the board. One hand holds his brother's[11] mellow goblet, but the other remembers the club. A rough seat supports him, a stone adorned with Nemean hide.

The sacred work has a worthy history. Pella's ruler[12] had it on his cheerful board, a venerable deity, and used to carry it with him west and east. Gladly would he grasp it with the hand that had just taken crowns away and bestowed them and overturned great cities. From it he ever sought courage for the morrow's warfare, to it, victorious, he would always narrate glorious battles, whether he had taken chained Indians from Bromius or burst open barred Babylon with his great spear or overwhelmed with war the lands of Pelops and Pelasgian freedom; and from the great column of his glories he is said to have made excuse only for his triumph over Thebes.[13] He too, when the Fates

d'esprit; but such a masterpiece was beyond them.

[10] Auge.   [11] Bacchus and Hercules were both sons of Jupiter.   [12] Alexander the Great.

[13] Hercules' birthplace, destroyed by Alexander.

ille etiam, magnos Fatis rumpentibus actus,
cum traheret letale merum, iam mortis opaca
nube gravis vultus alios in numine caro
aeraque supremis timuit sudantia mensis.
75 Mox Nasamoniaco decus admirabile regi
possessum, fortique deo libavit honores
semper atrox dextra periuroque ense superbus
Hannibal. Italicae perfusum sanguine gentis
diraque Romuleis portantem incendia tectis
80 oderat et cum epulas, et cum Lenaea dicaret
dona deus castris maerens comes ire nefandis,
praecipue cum sacrilega face miscuit arces
ipsius ⟨im⟩meritaeque domos ac templa Sagunti
polluit et populis furias immisit honestas.
85 Nec post Sidonii letum ducis aere potita
egregio plebeia domus. convivia Sullae
ornabat semper claros intrare penates
assuetum et felix dominorum stemmate signum;
nunc quoque, si mores humanaque pectora curae
90 nosse deis. non aula quidem, Tirynthie, nec te
regius ambit honos, sed casta ignaraque culpae
mens domini, cui prisca fides coeptaeque perenne
foedus amicitiae. scit adhuc florente sub aevo
par magnis Vestinus avis, quem nocte dieque
95 spirat et in carae vivit complexibus umbrae.

---

14 Alexander was supposed to have been poisoned.

15 Hannibal was of course a citizen of Carthage; Statius makes him sound like a tribal monarch.

16 Hercules was the patron deity of Saguntum, the Spanish town whose people destroyed themselves rather than surrender to Hannibal.

were breaking off his mighty deeds and he drank the fatal liquor[14] and death's dark cloud oppressed him, was afraid at the changed look of his beloved deity and the bronze sweating on his final table.

Presently the wondrous treasure became the property of the Nasamonian king.[15] Hannibal, ever savage of hand and proud in treacherous sword, gave libation to the valiant god, who hated him, steeped as he was in the blood of the Italian race, carrying dire conflagration to Romulean dwellings, even as he offered him viands and Lenaean bounty; grieving he accompanied that wicked army, above all when Hannibal with sacrilegious torch mangled the god's own towers, defiling the houses and temples of innocent Saguntum and filling her people with a noble frenzy.[16]

After the death of the Sidonian captain 'twas no common house that gained possession of the peerless bronze. Ever accustomed to enter famous homes and fortunate in the line of his owners,[17] the statue adorned the banquets of Sulla. Fortunate now also,[18] if the gods care to know human manners and hearts. No palace, Tirynthian, or royal pomp surrounds you, but your master's soul is innocent, knowing no fault. Old-time loyalty is his and pact of friendship perennial once begun. Vestinus knows it, that still in life's flower equalled his great ancestors, Vestinus, whose spirit Vindex breathes night and day, living in the

---

[17] I.e. the series of owners as stated, not their individual pedigrees; cf. Martial 8.6.3 *argenti fumosa sui cum stemmata narret. Felix* may reflect Sulla's self-assumed agnomen.

[18] *Nunc quoque* (sc. *felix es*) is usually taken with *non aula* ff., starting a new paragraph and depriving *quoque* of significance.

hic igitur tibi laeta quies, fortissime divum
Alcide, nec bella vides pugnasque feroces
sed chelyn et vittas et amantes carmina laurus.
hic tibi sollemni memorabit carmine quantus
100 Iliacas Geticasque domos quantusque nivalem
Stymphalon quantusque iugis Erymanthon aquosis
terrueris, quem te pecoris possessor Hiberi,
quem tulerit saevae Mareoticus arbiter arae.
hic penetrata tibi spoliataque limina Mortis
105 concinet et flentes Libyae Scythiaeque puellas.
nec te regnator Macetum nec barbarus umquam
Hannibal aut saevi posset vox horrida Sullae
his celebrare modis. certe tu, muneris auctor,
non aliis malles oculis, Lysippe, probari.

IV.7

ODE LYRICA AD VIBIUM MAXIMUM

Iam diu lato spatiata campo
fortis heroos, Erato, labores
differ atque ingens opus in minores
    contrahe gyros,

5   tuque, regnator lyricae cohortis,
da novi paulum mihi iura plectri,
si tuas cantu Latio sacravi,
    Pindare, Thebas.

98–9 *aut* tempora (98) *aut* pectine (99) *Markland*
1 spatiata ⊊: sociata M: sati- *edit. pr.*

arms of the dear shade. Here then you have happy repose, Alcides, most valiant of the gods. You see no wars and fierce fighting, but lyre and garlands and song-loving laurels. In solemn verse he shall recount[19] in what might you terrified Ilian and Getic homes and snowy Stymphalos and Erymanthos' watery ridges; in what guise you came upon the owner of the Iberian herd and the Mareotic ruler of the savage altar. He shall sing of the gates of Death that you invaded and despoiled and of the weeping girls of Libya and Scythia. Neither the ruler of the Macetae nor barbarous Hannibal nor the harsh voice of savage Sulla could ever have hymned you in such strains. Assuredly you, Lysippus, author of the gift, would not have wished approval by other eyes than these.

IV.7

A LYRIC ODE TO VIBIUS MAXIMUS

Long, valiant Erato, have you ranged the spreading plain; now defer heroic labours and narrow your mighty work into lesser circuits;[1] and you, Pindar, ruler of the lyric band, grant me for a little while the right to change my quill, if I have hallowed your Thebes in Latian song: for

---

[19] Exploits of Hercules follow, including some of his twelve labours: capture of Troy, mares of Diomedes, birds of Stymphalos, Erymanthian boar, Geryon, Busiris, Cerberus, Hesperides, Amazons.

[1] 'The discipline of the training-ring' (Coleman).

Maximo carmen tenuare tempto.
10 nunc ab intonsa capienda myrto
serta, nunc maior sitis, at bibendus
        castior amnis.

quando te dulci Latio remittent
Dalmatae montes, ubi Dite viso
15 pallidus fossor redit erutoque
        concolor auro?

ecce me natum propiore terra
non tamen portu retinent amoeno
desides Baiae liticenque notus
20   Hectoris armis.

torpor est nostris sine te Camenis
tardius sueto venit ipse Thymbrae
rector et primis meus ecce metis
        haeret Achilles.

25 quippe te fido monitore nostra
Thebais multa cruciata lima
temptat audaci fide Mantuanae
        gaudia famae.

sed damus lento veniam, quod alma
30 prole fundasti vacuos penates.
o diem laetum! venit ecce nobis
        Maximus alter.

Maximus I essay to trim my verse.[2] Now my garlands must be taken from unpruned myrtle,[3] now my thirst is livelier but I have to drink of a purer river.[4]

When shall Dalmatia's mountains send you back to sweet Latium—Dalmatia, where the miner sees Dis and returns all pale, the colour of the gold he has dug out? As for me, born though I was in a less distant land, yet lazy Baiae does not hold me in her pleasant haven nor the trumpeter[5] known to Hector's arms. My Muse is in torpor without you. Thymbra's ruler himself comes more slowly than is his wont and, see, my Achilles is stuck at the first turning point. For 'tis with you as my trusty counsellor that my *Thebaid,* tortured by much filing, essays with daring string the joys of Mantuan fame.

But we forgive your dallying, since you have founded your empty hearth with fostering progeny. O happy day! Behold, we have a second Maximus! Childlessness must be

[2] See Critical Appendix.

[3] I.e. a new source: the shrub is to be myrtle instead of laurel and hitherto untouched. Myrtle, sacred to Venus, suits Erato, who is associated with love poetry, even though this is no love poem.

[4] Reminiscent of Callimachus' 'Assyrian river' contrasted with the stream 'pure and undefiled' (*Hymns* 2.108ff.).

[5] Misenus.

---

11 at* *scripsi*: et M

19-20 liticenve notus H- armis *Politianus*: laticemve motus H- amnis M

orbitas omni fugienda nisu,
quam premit votis inimicus heres,
35   optimo poscens (pudet heu!) propinquo
           funus amico.

orbitas nullo tumulata fletu:
stat domo capta cupidus superstes
imminens leti spoliis et ipsum
40   computat ignem.

duret in longum generosus infans
perque non multis iter expeditum
crescat in mores patrios avumque
           provocet actis.

45   tu tuos parvo memorabis enses,
quos ad Eoum tuleras Oronten
signa frenatae moderatus alae
           Castore dextro.

ille ut invicti rapidum secutus
50   Caesaris fulmen refugis amaram
Sarmatis legem dederit, sub uno
           vivere caelo.

sed tuas artes puer ante discat,
omne quis mundi senium remensus
55   orsa Sallusti brevis et Timavi
           reddis alumnum.

---

⁴⁶ tuleris ꜱ   Oronten *Housman*: -em M

292

avoided at all cost. An unfriendly heir presses hard upon
it with his prayers, asking (ah, shame!) that death come
soon for his excellent friend.[6] Childlessness is entombed
without a tear; the greedy survivor stands in the captured
house, hovering over death's booty, calculating the very
pyre. Long life to the noble infant! May he grow into his
father's manners, travelling a path that few may tread, and
challenge his grandfather with his achievements! You shall
tell the little one of the swords you bore to eastern Orontes
when you commanded the standard of a bridled troop,
favoured by Castor. He[7] shall relate how he followed
unconquered Caesar's swift bolt and imposed harsh terms
on the fleeing Sarmatians—they must live under one sky.
But first let the boy learn your skills, whereby you traced
back all the world's antiquity, giving us again the writings
of terse Sallust and Timavus' foster son.[8]

[6] *Optimo . . . amico* (or *optimi . . . amici*) after *inimicus* is
ironic. The heir pretends to be on the best of terms with the friend
whose death he prays for.

[7] The grandfather.

[8] Apparently Maximus had written a world history, probably
compendious. Sallust (whose terseness was proverbial) and Livy
were not world historians and probably owe their mention to their
preeminence in Latin historiography; the former's contribution to
Maximus' production, other than stylistic, cannot have amounted
to much. He might have owed more to Pompeius Trogus, whose
work survives only in Justin's epitome of uncertain date. The association of Livy's birthplace Patavium (Padua) with the river
Timavus derives from their juxtaposition in *Aeneid* 1.242–49.

IV.8

GRATULATIO AD IULIUM MENECRATEN

Pande fores superum vittataque templa Sabaeis
nubibus et pecudum fibris spirantibus imple,
Parthenope: clari genus ecce Menecratis auget
tertia iam suboles. procerum tibi nobile vulgus
5   crescit et insani solatur damna Vesevi.
nec solum festas secreta Neapolis aras
ambiat: et socii portus dilectaque miti
terra Dicaearcho nec non plaga cara madenti
Surrentina deo sertis altaria cingat,
10   materni qua litus avi, quem turba nepotum
circumit et similes contendit reddere vultus.
gaudeat et Libyca praesignis avunculus hasta,
quaeque sibi genitos putat attollitque benigno
Polla sinu. macte, o iuvenis, qui tanta merenti
15   lumina das patriae! dulci tremit ecce tumultu
tot dominis clamata domus. procul atra recedat
Invidia atque alio liventia pectora flectat:
his senium longaeque decus virtutis et alba
Atropos et patrius lauro\<s\> promisit Apollo.
20   Ergo quod Ausoniae pater augustissimus urbis
ius tibi tergeminae dederat laetabile prolis,

    8 Dicaearcho *Krohn*: dicachen M
    15 dulci . . . tumultu* *Calderini*: -cis . . . –tus M   strepit
Burman: fremit *Heinsius*   19 lauros ς: -o M

---

    [1] Two sons and a daughter (τρεῖς ἐμοὶ μυρίοι).
    [2] Maternal, probably a son of Pollius Felix who had won a
military decoration (*hasta pura*) in Africa.

IV.8

POEM OF CONGRATULATION TO
JULIUS MENECRATES

Fling wide, Parthenope, the doors of the High Ones and fill the garlanded temples with Sabaean clouds and the breathing entrails of beasts. A third scion now gives increase to Menecrates' line. Your noble crowd[1] of grandees grows, solacing the losses of mad Vesuvius. And let not Naples only in isolation surround the festal altars; let fellow havens, land beloved of gentle Dicaearchus and the Surrentine region, dear to the madid god, gird their altars with chaplets, the shore where lives his maternal grandfather, surrounded by a throng of children vying to resemble his features. And let their uncle[2] rejoice, distinguished by Libyan spear, and Polla who thinks them her own sons and raises them to her benignant bosom. Bravo, young man, who give so many shining lights to your deserving country. Lo, the house vibrates with sweet tumult, clamorous with so many masters.[3] Let black Envy get her gone afar, turning her malicious breast[4] elsewhere. White Atropos has promised them old age and glory of lengthy achievement, their country's Apollo[5] his laurels.

So it was an omen that the most august Father of the Ausonian city gave you the heartening privilege of triple

---

[3] See Critical Appendix.

[4] I.e. heart; but Markland's *lumina,* read by Coleman, is attractive.

[5] Cf. v. 47 and Coleman thereon.

omen erat. venit totiens Lucina piumque
intravit repetita larem. sic fertilis, oro,
stet domus et donis numquam mutata sacratis.
25 macte, quod et proles tibi saepius aucta virili
robore! sed iuveni laetanda et virgo parenti
(aptior his virtus, citius dabit illa nepotes),
qualis maternis Helene iam digna palaestris
inter Amyclaeos reptabat candida fratres,
30 vel qualis caeli facies, ubi nocte serena
admovere iubar mediae duo sidera lunae.
    Sed queror haud faciles, iuvenum rarissime, questus
irascorque etiam, quantum irascuntur amantes.
tantane me decuit vulgari gaudia fama
35 noscere? cumque tibi vagiret tertius infans,
protinus ingenti non venit nuntia cursu
littera, quae festos cumulare altaribus ignes
et redimire chelyn postesque ornare iuberet
Albanoque cadum sordentem promere fumo
40 et creta signare diem, sed tardus inersque
nunc demum mea vota cano? tua culpa tuusque
hic pudor. ulterius sed enim producere questus
non licet; en hilaris circumstat turba tuorum
defensatque patrem! quem non hoc agmine vincas?

26 laetanda et *Saenger, praeeunte Baehrens*: letum dat M
27 *damn. Markland*
29 certabat *Grasberger*
40 creta *Bentley*: cantu M

offspring;[6] so often came Lucina, again and again entering your pious home. So fruitful, I pray, may your house stand, its sacred gifts intact. Bravo too in that your stock has more often had increase in manly strength! But a maiden too brings happiness to a young parent (achievement belongs rather to them, but she will sooner give grandsons), the like of fair Helen as she crawled[7] between her Amyclaean brethren, already worthy of her mother's wrestling grounds; or like the sky's face on a clear night when two radiant stars from either side approach the moon.

But, rarest of fellows, I have a grievance, none of the lightest. I am angry even, so far as we can be angry with those we love. Was it fitting that I hear of such joy by common report? When your third child was wailing, did no letter come straightway posthaste to bring me word, telling me to heap my altar with festal fire and wreathe my lyre and decorate my doorway and bring out a jar begrimed with Alban smoke and mark the day with chalk? Only now, slow and sluggish, do I sing my vows?[8] Yours is the fault, yours this shame. But I may not further prolong my complaints. See, a merry throng surrounds you, your children, defending their father. With such a troop, whom would you not vanquish?

[6] The *ius trium liberorum,* carrying certain privileges. It was sometimes awarded to the childless.

[7] Spartan girls notoriously practised with men in the gymnasium, but not before they could walk. Here Helen and her brothers must all three be small children, not in the gymnasium but already showing signs of later prowess. *Certabat* is an easy change, but Menecrates' daughter was not of wrestling age.

[8] I.e. the fulfilment of my prayers.

45   Di patrii, quos auguriis super aequora magnis
litus ad Ausonium devexit Abantia classis,
tu, ductor populi longe migrantis, Apollo,
cuius adhuc volucrem laeva cervice sedentem
respiciens blande felix Eumelus adorat,
50   tuque, Actaea Ceres, cursu cui semper anhelo
votivam taciti quassamus lampada mystae,
et vos, Tyndaridae, quos non horrenda Lycurgi
Taygeta umbrosaeque magis coluere Therapnae:
hos cum plebe sua patriae servate penates.
55   sint qui fessam aevo crebrisque laboribus urbem
voce opibusque iuvent viridique in nomine servent.
his placidos genitor mores largumque nitorem
monstret avus, pulchrae studium virtutis uterque.
quippe et opes et origo sinunt hanc lampade prima
60   patricias intrare fores, hos pube sub ipsa,
si modo prona bonis invicti Caesaris adsint
numina, Romulei limen pulsare senatus.

49 Eumelus *Housman*: -liss M: -lis ⲅ
50 Actaea *Calderini*: acca M
54 patriae *Gronovius*: -rii M

298

Gods of our land, whom an Abantian fleet bore overseas
with great auguries to Ausonia's shore, and you, Apollo,
guide of the far-wandering folk, whose bird perched on
your left shoulder[9] fortunate Eumelus[10] still fondly eyes
and adores, and you, Actaean Ceres, for whom we silent
devotees ever wave the votive torch in our breathless
course,[11] and you, sons of Tyndarus, to whom Lycurgus'
grim Taygetus[12] and shady Therapnae gave no devouter
worship: protect this hearth and its folk for our country.
Let it be theirs to aid our city with voice and wealth, weary
as she is with time and many labours,[13] and keep her green
as her name. Let their father show them gentle ways and
their grandfather liberal splendour and both the pursuit
of fair virtue. For surely wealth and birth permit the girl
to enter patrician doors at first wedding torch, and the
brothers, if only the favouring deity of unconquered
Caesar befriend the good, to knock at the gate of Romulus'
Senate on manhood's first advent.

[9] Cf. III.5.79f. Statuary or painting is indicated here.

[10] 'A Eumelus is attested as an eponymous god of a Neapolitan
phratry' (Coleman), but his role here is problematical. The name
means 'rich in flocks.'

[11] There was a cult of Demeter (Ceres) in Naples analogous to
the Eleusinian mysteries.

[12] So II.2.90 *de monte Lycurgi,* suggestive of some special
connection between lawgiver and mountain otherwise unre-
corded (but cf. Plutarch, *Lycurgus* (16.1–2). The Spartan sons of
Tyndarus (Dioscuri, Castor and Pollux) had a temple in Naples
(see Coleman).

[13] Perhaps in allusion to the original foundation later called
Palaeopolis (Old City) that was replaced by a new one (Neapolis).
'Green' = 'youthful.'

IV.9

HENDECASYLLABI IOCOSI AD PLOTIUM GRYPUM

Est sane iocus iste, quod libellum
misisti mihi, Grype, pro libello.
urbanum tamen hoc potest videri
si post hoc aliquid mihi remittas.
5   nam si ludere, Grype, perseveras,
non ludis. licet ecce computemus.
noster purpureus novusque charta
et binis decoratus umbilicis
praeter me mihi constitit decussis:
10   tu rosum tineis situque putrem,
quales aut Libycis madent olivis
aut tus Niliacum piperve servant
aut Byzantiacos cocunt lacertos,
nec saltem tua dicta continentem
15   quae trino iuvenis Foro tonabas
aut centum prope iudices, priusquam
te Germanicus arbitrum sequenti
annonae dedit omniumque late
praefecit stationibus viarum,
20   sed Bruti senis oscitationes
de capsa miseri libellionis,
emptum plus minus asse Gaïano,
donas. usque adeone defuerunt
caesis pillea suta de lacernis
25   vel mantelia luridaeve mappae,

13 cocunt *Thomson*: colunt M

300

IV.9

JESTING HENDECASYLLABICS TO
PLOTIUS GRYPUS

A joke on your part, to be sure, Grypus, to send me a little book in return for a little book! But it can be thought amusing only if you were to send me a follow-up. For if you go on jesting, Grypus, it's no jest! Look, let's reckon up. Mine is purple, fresh paper, with a pair of handsome bosses.[1] Besides myself,[2] it cost me a ten-as piece. But yours! Motheaten and mouldering, like the sheets that soak up Libyan olives or keep incense or Nile pepper or cook Byantine tunny.[3] And it does not even contain your own speeches that as a young man you thundered in the triple Forum or before the Hundred Judges, ere Germanicus made you controller of the attendant corn supply[4] and general supervisor of relay stations on all the highways; but you give me the yawns of old Brutus,[5] a thing you bought for a Gaian as[6] more or less, from the case of a wretched bookseller. Were there really no caps for sale, stitched from cloak clippings, or towels, or yellowed nap-

---

[1] Knobs at each end of the roller (lit. 'navels').

[2] As author.   [3] Fish were cooked in wrapping material.

[4] *Sequenti annonae,* explained by Coleman as the supply train for Domitian's travels in Italy, so that the two functions mentioned are connected.

[5] No doubt Caesar's assassin, one of the leading orators of his day. *Senis,* here with a contemptuous flavour, does not refer to age but to remoteness in time. He died in 42 B.C. in his early forties.

[6] Coins, at any rate copper coins, of Caligula, whose memory had been condemned by the Senate, seem to have been as good as worthless.

chartae Thebaicaeve Caricaeve?
nusquam turbine conditus ruenti
prunorum globus atque cottanorum?
non enlychnia sicca, non replictae
30   bulborum tunicae? nec ova tandem
nec lenes halicae nec asperum far?
nusquam Cinyphiis vagata campis
curvarum domus uda cochlearum?
non lardum grave debilisve perna?
35   non Lucanica, non breves Falisci,
non sal oxyporumve caseusve
aut panes nitidantis aphronitri
aut passum psithiis suis recoctum
dulci defruta vel lutosa caeno?
40   quantum vel dare cereos olentes,
cultellum tenuesve codicillos?
ollares, rogo, non licebat uvas,
Cumano patinas vel orbe tortas
aut unam dare synthesin (quid horres?)
45   alborum calicum atque cacaborum?
sed certa velut aequus in statera,
nil mutas, sed idem mihi rependis.
quid si, cum bene mane semicrudus
illatam tibi dixero salutem,
50   et tu me vicibus domi salutes?

30 tandem* *Polster*: tantum M: saltem *Baehrens*
31 lenes *Heinsius*: leves M
34 breve *Markland*
35 breves *Coleman*: graves M
40 vel *Calderini*: nec M
43 vel *Heinsius*: in M

kins, writing paper, dates from Thebes[7] or figs from Caria?
Nowhere a handful of plums or bullaces stored in a cascading cone?[8] No dry lampwicks, no peeled-off onion jackets? No eggs even[9] or mild groats or rough spelt? Nowhere a slimy house of a sinuous snail[10] that had strayed over Cinyphian plains? No lump of bacon or mouldering ham? No Lucanian sausages or short Faliscans, no salt, no condiment, no cheese? Or rolls of furbishing soda or raisin wine boiled up with its own grapes or must muddy with its sweet lees? What does it save you not even to give me smelly candles or a knife or thin tablets? Could you not, I ask you, have sent some potted grapes or some dishes turned on a Cuman wheel[11] or a set[12] (don't be alarmed) of white cups and pots? But as though you were playing fair on an accurate scale, you change nothing, give me tit for tat. Come, if I bring you an early-morning greeting with an after-breakfast belch, are you to greet me at my home in return? Or

[7] In Upper Egypt. For full information on the items here listed see Coleman.

[8] Explained by Coleman as the bottom half of a jar (*cadus*) broken off from the top half.

[9] See Critical Appendix.

[10] Snail shells were used as oil containers.

[11] Cuman pottery was cheap.

[12] *Synthesis* ('combination') often = dinner suit.

aut cum me dape iuveris opima,
exspectes similes et ipse cenas?
irascor tibi, Grype. sed valebis;
tantum ne mihi, quo soles lepore,
55   et nunc hendecasyllabas remittas.

[54] quo . . . lepore *Calderini*: quod . . . -ri M

when you've treated me to a slapdash dinner, are you to expect a similar meal yourself? Grypus, I'm angry with you. But farewell. Only this time please don't send me back hendecasyllables in your usual witty style!

BOOK FIVE

PREFATORY NOTES

1

Flavius Abascantus, entitled *Aug(usti) lib(ertus) ab epistulis* in inscriptions of his freedmen, had charge of the imperial correspondence. His wife probably died in 95 (mention of the temple to the Flavian family in v. 240).

2

Crispinus, a boy of sixteen (v. 12) at the time of writing (probably summer of 95; cf. v. 163), is known only from this poem. He was the son of M. Vettius Bolanus, Consul Suffect in 66, with a distinguished career as Corbulo's right hand in Armenia, governor of Britain, and Proconsul of Asia.

3

Statius' father died some five to fifteen years before the publication of Book V. According to v. 29 the lament was written three months later, which is at odds with the mention of the festivals in vv. 219–33 (Vollmer, p. 9, n. 10, Coleman, pp. xviii f.). Whenever written, it was not published in the poet's lifetime.

4

No indication of date.

5

Mention of the completed *Thebaid* and the start of the *Achilleid* point to the summer of 95 (v. 36; cf. IV.4.94, V.2.163).

LIBER QUINTUS

Omnibus affectibus prosequenda sunt bona exempla, cum
publice prosint. pietas quam Priscillae tuae praestas et
morum tuorum pars et nulli non conciliare te, praecipue
marito, potest. uxorem enim vivam amare voluptas est, de-
5   functam religio. ego tamen huic operi non ut unus e turba
nec tantum quasi officiosus assilui. amavit enim uxorem
meam Priscilla et amando fecit mihi illam probatiorem.
post hoc ingratus sum si lacrimas tuas transeo. praeterea
latus omne divinae domus semper demereri pro mea
10   mediocritate conitor. nam qui bona fide deos colit amat et
sacerdotes. sed quamvis propiorem usum amicitiae tuae
iampridem cuperem, mallem tamen nondum invenisse
materiam.

V.1

EPICEDION IN PRISCILLAM ‹ABASCANTI›
UXOREM

Si manus aut similes docilis mihi fingere ceras
aut ebur impressis aurumve animare figuris,

310

BOOK FIVE

STATIUS TO HIS FRIEND ABASCANTUS
GREETINGS

Good examples should be unreservedly honoured since they are for the public benefit. The devotion you give your Priscilla is both part of your own character and must win you everyone's sympathy, every husband's especially. To love a living wife is pleasure, to love a dead wife is religion. However, I have not jumped to this work as one of a multitude nor as performing an obligation. Priscilla loved my wife and by loving her made her stand higher in my eyes; after that, I am an ingrate if I take no notice of your tears. Furthermore, I always do my humble best to oblige any appendage of the Divine House; for whoever worships the gods in good faith, loves their priests too. But although I desired for a long while past that my friendship with you become closer, I would rather not have found an occasion so soon.

V.1

A CONSOLATION ON THE DEATH OF PRISCILLA

If my hand were skilled to mould likenesses in wax or bring life to ivory or gold by impress of features, thence,

hinc, Priscilla, tuo solacia grata marito
conciperem. namque egregia pietate meretur
5 ut vel Apelleo vultus signata colore
Phidiaca vel nata manu reddare dolenti.
sic auferre rogis umbram conatur et ingens
certamen cum Morte gerit, curasque fatigat
artificum inque omni te quaerit amare metallo.
10 sed mortalis honos, agilis quem dextra laborat:
nos tibi, laudati iuvenis rarissima coniunx,
longa nec obscurum finem latura perenni
temptamus dare iusta lyra, modo dexter Apollo
quique venit iuncto mihi semper Apolline Caesar
15 annuat; haud alio melius condere sepulchro.
     Sera quidem tanto struitur medicina dolori,
altera cum volucris Phoebi rota torqueat annum.
sed cum plaga recens et adhuc in vulnere primo
nigra domus, miseram quis tunc accessus ad aurem
20 coniugis orbati? tunc flere et scindere vestes
et famulos lassare greges et vincere planctus
Fataque et iniustos rabidis pulsare querelis
caelicolas solamen erat. licet ipse levando
ad gemitus silvis comitatus et amnibus Orpheus
25 afforet atque omnis pariter matertera vatem,
omnis Apollineus tegeret Bacchique sacerdos,
nil cantus, nil fila deis pallentis Averni
Eumenidumque audita comis mulcere valerent:
tantus in attonito regnabat pectore luctus.
30 nunc etiam ad tactus refugit iam plana cicatrix

17 volucrem *Markland*
19 miseram quis tunc *Phillimore*: questu miseramque M: *post*
questu *lac. statuit Courtney*
30 ad tactus *Cartault*: ad planctus M: adtactus *Phillimore*

312

Priscilla, would I conceive a solace that your husband
should welcome. For by his extraordinary devotion he deserves to have you returned to his grief as Apelles would
have rendered your face in paint or Phidias' hand have
given you birth. So does he strive to rescue your shade
from the pyre and wages a mighty contest with Death,
wearying the efforts of artists and seeking to love you in
every material. But beauty created by toil of cunning hand
is mortal. Whereas I, rarest lady of applauded spouse,
essay with timeless lyre to give you obsequies that last long
nor end in oblivion, only let Apollo be propitious and
Caesar, who ever comes to me in Apollo's company,[1] nod
assent. In no other tomb will you be better laid to rest.

Late indeed is the medicine compounded for so great
an affliction, now that Phoebus' swift wheel brings round a
second year. But when the stroke was fresh and the house
still black in first shock, what access was there then to the
sad ear of the bereaved husband? Then all his consolation
was to weep and tear his clothes and weary his flocks of servitors, outdoing their laments, and assail the Fates and unjust sky-dwellers with frenzied plaints. Though Orpheus
himself with woods and rivers in attendance had been at
hand, though all his mother's sisters[2] alike, every priest
of Apollo and of Bacchus, surrounded the bard, naught
would his song have availed, naught the strings to which
the gods of dim Avernus and the locks[3] of the Eumenides
gave ear; such mourning reigned in his stunned breast.
Even today the scar now healed shrinks at touch, even as I

[1] As inspiration.

[2] The other eight Muses. The reader is left to take Calliope
herself for granted.   [3] Snakes.

dum canimus, gravibusque oculis uxorius instat
imber. habentne pios etiamnum haec lumina fletus?
mira fides! citius genetrix Sipylea feretur
exhausisse genas, citius Tithonida maesti
35   deficient rores aut exsatiata fatiscet
mater Achilleis hiemes affrangere bustis.
macte animi! notat ista deus qui flectit habenas
orbis et humanos propior Iove digerit actus,
maerentemque videt, lectique arcana ministri
40   hinc etiam documenta capit, quod diligis umbram
et colis exsequias. hic est castissimus ardor,
hic amor a domino meritus censore probari.
    Nec mirum si vos collato pectore mixtos
iunxit inabrupta concordia longa catena.
45   illa quidem nuptumque prior taedasque marito
passa alio, sed te ceu virginitate iugatum
visceribus totis animaque amplexa fovebat,
qualiter aequaevo sociatam palmite vitem
ulmus amat miscetque nemus ditemque precatur
50   autumnum et caris gaudet redimita racemis.
laudantur proavis et pulchrae munere formae
quae morum caruere bonis falsaeque potentes
laudis egent verae: tibi quamquam et origo niteret
et felix species multumque optanda maritis,
55   ex te maior honos, unum novisse cubile,
unum secretis agitare sub ossibus ignem.

33 Sipylea feretur *Heinsius*: si pelea fertur M
45 nuptumque ς: -uque M
51 proavis et *Politianus*: proavi seu M
52 falsaeque *Heinsius*: -soque M –saque *Meursius*

sing, and conjugal drops urge his heavy eyelids. Do these eyes have a husband's tears even yet? Wonderful, but true! Sooner shall the eyes of the mother of Sipylus be said to have run dry, sooner shall sad dews fail Tithonis or Achilles' parent be sated and weary of breaking storms against his tomb.[4] Honour to your soul! The god who governs the reins of all the world and nearer than Jupiter disposes of men's doings, he marks it and sees you grieving; and therefrom he takes private proof of his chosen servant, in that you love the shade and pay tribute to her obsequies. This is passion at its most chaste, a love that deserves the approval of a Censor master.

Neither is it any wonder that enduring Concord joined you by an unbroken chain, mingling heart with heart. She had indeed been through marriage before, known the torches with another spouse, but you she cherished, embracing you with all her heart and soul, as though a virgin bride; even as elm loves vine, sharing coeval branches, mingling foliage, praying for a bountiful autumn, rejoicing to be wreathed in the beloved clusters. Women who lack the moral virtues are praised for their ancestors or their gift of beauty; they have the false esteem, but lack the true. Your birth was splendid, your aspect pleasing as a husband could desire, but greater the dignity that came from yourself—to know one bed only, to cherish one flame

---

[4] The three weeping mothers are Niobe, Aurora (for her son Memnon), and Thetis.

illum nec Phrygius vitiasset raptor amorem
Dulichiive proci nec qui fraternus adulter
casta Mycenaeo conubia polluit auro.
60 si Babylonos opes, Lydae si pondera gazae
Indorumque dares Serumque Arabumque potentes
divitias, mallet cum paupertate pudica
intemerata mori vitamque rependere famae.
nec frons triste rigens nimiusque in moribus horror
65 sed simplex hilarisque fides et mixta pudori
gratia.
        Quod si anceps metus ad maiora vocasset,
illa vel armiferas pro coniuge laeta catervas
fulmineosque ignes mediique pericula ponti
exciperet. melius quod non adversa probarunt
70 quae tibi cura tori, quantus pro coniuge pallor.
sed meliore via dextros tua vota marito
promeruere deos, dum nocte dieque fatigas
numina, dum cunctis supplex advolveris aris
et mitem genium domini praesentis adoras.
75   Audita es, venitque gradu Fortuna benigno.
vidit quippe pii iuvenis navamque quietem
intactamque fidem succinctaque pectora curis
et vigiles sensus et digna evolvere tantas
sobria corda vices, vidit, qui cuncta suorum
80 novit et inspectis ambit latus omne ministris.
nec mirum: videt ille ortus obitusque, quid Auster
quid Boreas hibernus agat, ferrique togaeque
consilia atque ipsam mentem probat. ille gravatis

<hr />

[83] gravatis* *scripsi*: iubatis M: subactis *Avantius*

in your heart of hearts. That love no Phrygian ravisher would have sullied, no Dulichian suitors, nor that seducer of his brother's wife who polluted chaste wedlock with Mycenaean gold.[5] Had she been offered the wealth of Babylon, the weight of Lydian treasure, the potent riches of Indians and Seres and Arabians, she would rather have died inviolate in chaste poverty, paying life for reputation. Yet no stiff and frowning face was hers, no undue austerity in her manners, but gay and simple loyalty, charm blended with modesty.

But if some formidable danger had summoned her to a larger role, she would gladly have confronted armed bands or lightning fire or the hazards of mid ocean for her man. Happily no adversity proved your wifely care, your pallor for his peril. Instead, by a better path your vows on his behalf earned favouring gods, as day and night you wearied their deity, sinking in supplication at every altar and adoring the gentle genius of our lord here present.

You were heard, and Fortune came with benignant step. Surely he saw the devoted young man's quiet diligence, his untainted loyalty, his mind alert for business, his watchful intelligence, his sober judgement fitted to unfold great matters as they arose—*he* saw, who knows all about those near to him and surrounds every quarter with well-tried servants. No wonder: he sees east and west, what the South Wind is about and what the wintry North, probing counsels of sword and gown, ay, and the very heart. On

[5] Thyestes. Statius inverts the standard account, by which Aërope, wife of his brother Atreus, king of Mycenae, whom he had seduced, gave him a numinous golden lamb. Probably just a slip on the poet's part.

molem immensam umeris et vix tractabile pondus
85 imposuit (nec enim numerosior altera sacra
cura domo), magnum late dimittere in orbem
Romulei mandata ducis, viresque modosque
imperii tractare manu: quae laurus ab Arcto,
quid vagus Euphrates, quid ripa binominis Histri,
90 quid Rheni vexilla ferant, quantum ultimus orbis
cesserit et refugo circumsona gurgite Thule;
omnia nam laetas pila attollentia frondes
nullaque famosa signatur lancea penna.
praeterea, fidos dominus si dividat enses,
95 pandere quis centum valeat frenare, maniplos
inter missus eques, quis praecepisse cohorti,
quem deceat clari praestantior ordo tribuni,
quisnam frenigerae signum dare dignior alae;
mille etiam praenosse vices, an merserit agros
100 Nilus, an imbrifero Libye sudaverit Austro:
cunctaque si numerem, non plura interprete virga
nuntiat ex celsis ales Tegeaticus astris,
quaeque cadit liquidas Iunonia virgo per auras
et picturato pluvium ligat aëra gyro
105 quaeque tuas laurus volucri, Germanice, cursu
Fama vehit praegressa diem tardumque sub astris
Arcada et in medio linquit Thaumantida caelo.
    Qualem te superi, Priscilla, hominesque benigno
aspexere die, cum primum ingentibus actis
110 admotus coniunx! vicisti gaudia paene

84 pondus *Laetus*: tempus M
101 cuncta ego *coni. Courtney*
106 vehit *Calderini*: velut M
110 paene *Burman*: cene M: certe *Markland*

these burdened[6] shoulders he placed an enormous load, a weight almost beyond bearing. For no other charge in the sacred dwelling is so manifold: to send out the commands of the Romulean leader all over the great world and handle in writing the powers and modes of empire—what laurelled message comes from the north, what wandering Euphrates brings, or the bank of binamed Hister, or the standards of Rhine, how far the world's end has retreated and Thule surrounded by her roaring reflux; for every spear comes lifting joyous leaves[7] aloft and no lance is marked with infamous feather. Furthermore, if our lord should be distributing his faithful swords, to announce who is qualified to control a century (a Knight sent among infantry), who to command a cohort, who is right for the higher rank of illustrious Tribune, who more worthy to give the password to a troop of cavalry; also to forecast a thousand turns—has Nile drowned the fields, has Libya sweated with the rainy South Wind? If I were to enumerate all, no more messages does the winged Tegean announce from the stars with his go-between wand, nor Juno's maiden as she falls through the liquid air and binds the rainy atmosphere with her coloured arc, nor Fame that bears your laurels, Germanicus, outstripping the sun in her rapid flight, leaving the slow Arcadian beneath the stars and Thaumas' daughter in mid sky.

In what guise did gods and men see you, Priscilla, on that gracious day when your husband was first appointed to his great office! Your joy wellnigh surpassed his own, when

[6] Proleptic.

[7] Laurel in token of victory. A feather (indicating urgency?) meant the opposite.

ipsius, effuso dum pectore prona sacratos
ante pedes avide domini tam magna merentis
volveris. Aonio non sic in vertice gaudet
quam pater arcani praefecit hiatibus antri
115   Delius, aut primi cui ius venerabile thyrsi
Bacchus et attonitae tribuit vexilla catervae.
nec tamen hinc mutata quies probitasve secundis
intumuit; tenor idem animo moresque modesti
fortuna crescente manent. fovet anxia curas
120   coniugis hortaturque simul flectitque labores.
ipsa dapes modicas et sobria pocula tradit
exemplumque ad erile monet, velut Apula coniunx
agricolae parci vel sole infecta Sabino,
quae videt emeriti iam prospectantibus astris
125   tempus adesse viri, propere mensasque torosque
instruit exspectatque sonum redeuntis aratri.
parva loquor: tecum gelidas comes illa per Arctos
Sarmaticasque hiemes Histrumque et pallida Rheni
frigora, tecum omnes animo durata per aestus,
130   et, si castra darent, vellet gestare pharetras,
vellet Amazonia latus intercludere pelta,
dum te pulverea bellorum <in> nube videret
Caesarei prope fulmen equi divinaque tela
vibrantem et magnae sparsum sudoribus hastae.

113 Aonio ⲋ: ausonio M   117 hinc ⲋ: hic M
120 fulcitque *Watt*   123 Sabina *Heinsius*
127 ire *Nodell*   132 *add. Gevartius in textu*

---

8 Helicon, as in Virgil, *Georgics* 3.11. But why should a newly
appointed Pythia (Delphic prophetess) be there rather than on
Parnassus? More inadvertence?

9 *Primi thyrsi*, like *primi pili* in the military.

eagerly you threw yourself prostrate and grovelling at the sacred feet of the lord to whom you owe so much, pouring out your breast. Not so on Aonian summit[8] does she rejoice whom the Delian father has set over the mouth of his secret cave, or she to whom Bacchus has awarded the venerable right of First Wand[9] and the standard of his frenzied band. Yet her tranquillity was not changed thereby nor her goodness puffed up by prosperity. Her mind follows the same course and her modest manners remain as her fortune mounts. She cherishes anxiously her husband's cares, at once encouraging his labours and deflecting[10] them. She herself serves him his frugal meals and temperate cups, and admonishes him by his master's example;[11] even as some thrifty farmer's Apulian wife or sun-tanned Sabine, when she sees the stars are peeping out and it's nearly time for her man to come home from the day's work, smartly sets up the table and the couches and listens for the sound of the returning plough. I speak of little things. With you she would have travelled the frozen North and Sarmatia's winters and Hister and the pale frosts of Rhine, with you steeled her courage through every heat, and, if the army allowed, even been fain to bear a quiver and shield her flank with Amazonian targe, so long as she might see you in the dust-cloud of battles close to the thunderbolt that is Caesar's horse, brandishing divine[12] weapons and spattered with the sweat[13] of his great spear.

[10] I.e. making him take a break. Perhaps understand *in se* (cf. II.1.59). Not 'alleviating.'

[11] The Emperor was in fact a moderate eater and drinker (Suetonius, *Domitian* 21).

[12] Because provided by the Emperor.   [13] Blood.

SILVAE

135   Hactenus alma chelys. tempus nunc ponere frondes,
        Phoebe, tuas maestaque comam damnare cupresso.
            Quisnam impacta consanguinitate ligavit
        Fortunam Invidiamque deus? quis iussit iniquas
        aeternum bellare deus? nullamne notabit
140   illa domum torvo quam non haec lumine figat
        protinus et saeva proturbet gaudia dextra?
        florebant hilares inconcussique penates;
        nil maestum. quid enim, quamvis infida levisque,
        Caesare tam dextro posset Fortuna timeri?
145   invenere viam liventia Fata, piumque
        intravit vis saeva larem. sic plena maligno
        afflantur vineta Noto, sic alta senescit
        imbre seges nimio, rapidae sic obvia puppi
        invidet et velis obnubilat aura secundis.
150   carpitur eximium Fato Priscilla decorem,
        qualiter alta comam, silvarum gloria, pinus
        seu Iovis igne malo seu iam radice soluta
        deficit et nulli spoliata remurmurat aurae.
        quid probitas aut casta fides, quid numina prosunt
155   culta deum? furvae miseram circum undique leti
        vallavere plagae, tenduntur dura Sororum
        licia et exacti superest pars ultima fili.
        nil famuli coetus, nil ars operosa medentum
        auxiliata malis. comites tamen undique ficto
160   spem simulant vultu, flentem notat illa maritum.
        ille modo infernae nequiquam flumina Lethes
        incorrupta rogat, nunc anxius omnibus aris
        illacrimat signatque fores et pectore terget

139 notabit *Barth*: -avit M
149 obnubilat *Eden*: adn- M

322

So far the kindly lyre. Now 'tis time to lay aside your leaves, Phoebus, and doom my hair with sad cypress.

What god linked Fortune and Envy in truceless consanguinity? Who commanded these cruel goddesses to make everlasting war? Shall the one never mark a house but the other fix it with her grim gaze and drive out its joy with her savage hand? The home was prosperous, blithe and unshaken; nothing sad. For how could Fortune be feared, though faithless and fickle, when Caesar was so propitious? The jealous Fates found a way, and savage violence entered the blameless hearth. So full vineyards are blown upon by a malign sirocco, so a tall crop ages with too much rain, so an envious breeze meets a swift vessel, beclouding favouring sails.[14] Fate plucks away Priscilla's peerless beauty, as when a tall-crested pine, glory of the forest, wastes away, whether by Jove's fire or loosened root, and despoiled returns no whisper to the breeze. What avails probity or chaste loyalty or worship of gods' deity? On all sides the snares of dark Death encompassed the poor lady, the Sisters' pitiless skein is tightened, only the last scrap of the exhausted thread remains. The flocks of servitors, the painstaking skill of physicians brought no succour to her malady; yet her attendants all around feign hope, while she marks her husband weeping. As for him, he vainly implores Lethe's incorruptible stream, now sheds tears of anguish at every altar, leaving his marks on the doors and

[14] *Adnubilarunt* in the vulgate is a virtually unattested compound, for in Ammianus 27.6.15 *obnubilarunt* is accepted. So I read here, following P. T. Eden. The ill wind comes in opposition to the favourable wind under which the ship is sailing. The battle of the winds in Lucan 5.569ff. may be recalled.

limina, nunc magni vocat exorabile numen
165 Caesaris. heu durus Fati tenor! estne quod illi
non liceat? quantae poterant mortalibus annis
accessisse morae si tu, pater, omne teneres
arbitrium! caeco gemeret Mors clusa barathro,
longius et vacuae posuissent stamina Parcae.
170   Iamque cadunt vultus oculisque novissimus error
obtunsaeque aures, nisi cum vox sola mariti
noscitur. illum unum media de morte reversa
mens videt, illum aegris circumdat fortiter ulnis
immotas obversa genas, nec sole supremo
175 lumina sed dulci mavult satiare marito.
tum sic unanimum moriens solatur amantem:
    'Pars animae victura meae, cui linquere possim
o utinam quos dura mihi rapit Atropos annos,
parce, precor, lacrimis, saevo ne concute planctu
180 pectora, nec crucia fugientem coniugis umbram.
linquo equidem thalamos, salvo tamen ordine mortis
quod prior. exegi longa potiora senecta
tempora. vidi omni pridem te flore nitentem.
vidi altae propius propiusque accedere dextrae.
185 non in te Fatis, non iam caelestibus ullis
arbitrium: mecum ista fero. tu limite coepto
tende libens sacrumque latus geniumque potentem
irrequietus ama. nunc, quod cupis ipse iuberi,
da Capitolinis aeternum sedibus aurum,
190 quo niteat sacri centeno pondere vultus
Caesaris et propriae signet cultricis amorem.

    [172] reversae *Heinsius*

rubbing the threshold with his breast, now calls on Caesar's merciful deity. Alas, harsh course of fate! Is ought forbidden to Him? What stays might have accrued to mortal years if you, Father, were all-powerful! Death would have groaned far off in the sightless pit and the idle Fates have laid aside their spinning.

Now her face falls, her eyes wander one last time, her ears are dulled save when she recognizes her man's voice, his only. Him alone her mind sees, returning from the midst of death, him her failing arms tightly clasp as her stiffened eyes meet his; nor with final sunlight would she sate them, but rather with her sweet husband. Then dying, thus she comforts her true love:

'Part of my soul that shall live on, to whom I would that I might leave the years that harsh Atropos takes away from me,[15] spare your tears, I pray, beat not your breast with cruel lament, nor torture your wife's fleeing shade. I leave your marriage bed, 'tis true, but death's order is preserved, for I go first.[16] Better the time I have lived than a long old age. I have seen you this while shining in full flower, I have seen you draw closer and closer to the right hand on high. Not the Fates nor any sky-dwellers have power over you any longer; all that I take with me. Gladly pursue the path you have begun, love unremittingly the sacred presence and his potent guardian.[17] Now (and this my direction you yourself desire) give imperishable gold to the Capitoline temple in the weight of a hundred pounds in which Caesar's sacred countenance shall shine, betokening the love

---

[15] The years would have given her a normal lifetime.
[16] So she was older than her husband.
[17] Genius.

sic ego nec Furias nec deteriora videbo
Tartara et Elysias felix admittar in oras.'
    Haec dicit labens sociosque amplectitur artus
195 haerentemque animam non tristis in ora mariti
transtulit et cara pressit sua lumina dextra.
    At iuvenis magno flammatus pectora luctu
nunc implet saevo vacuos clamore penates,
nunc ferrum laxare cupit, nunc ardua tendit
200 in loca (vix retinent comites), nunc ore ligato
incubat amissae mersumque in corde dolorem
saevus agit, qualis conspecto coniugis igne
Odrysius vates positis ad Strymona plectris
obstupuit tristemque rogum sine carmine flevit.
205 ille etiam spretae rupisset tempora vitae,
ne tu Tartareum chaos incomitata subires,
sed prohibet mens fida duci firmandaque sacris
imperiis et maior amor.
                Quis carmine digno
exsequias et dona malae feralia pompae
210 perlegat? omne illic stipatum examine longo
ver Arabum Cilicumque fluit floresque Sabaei
Indorumque arsura seges praereptaque templis
tura Palaestinis simul Hebraeique liquores

---

202 alit *Heinsius*   conspecto coniugis igne* *Barth*: -ta -ge segnis M

205 spretae *Appelmann*: recte M: erecte M *prima manus*

207 duci *Calderini*: -is   firmandaque *Courtney*: mirandaque M

---

18 Priscilla herself. Domitian had ordained that statues of him-

of his own votaress.[18] Thus I shall see no Furies, no worser Tartarus,[19] and be admitted in happiness to Elysian regions.'

So she spoke as she sank, embracing the body she shares, and nothing loath transferred her lingering breath into her husband's mouth and closed her eyes with his beloved hand.

But the young man's heart was afire with mighty grief. Now he fills his widowed home with fierce clamour, now tries to unsheath his sword, now seeks high places (scarce do his companions hold him back), now, mouth glued to mouth, bends over his lost one and fiercely plies the sorrow hidden in his heart; even as the Odrysian bard at sight of his wife's fire[20] laid down his quill by Strymon's bank in a daze and songless wept the sad pyre. He would even have despised and broken his life's span, that you might not go down to Tartarus uncompanioned, but loyalty to the leader forbids, to be strengthened for the sacred commands, and a greater love.

Who could recount in worthy song the obsequies and funeral gifts of the sinister procession? There close-packed in lengthy abundance flows the springtime of Arabia and Cilicia, Sabaean flowers, Indian harvest for the flames, incense preempted from Palestinian temples,

self on the Capitol (cf. Martial 1.70.6, Pliny, *Panegyric* 52) must be of gold or silver not less than a certain weight (Suetonius, *Domitian* 13.2).

[19] Tartarus proper, as distinct from Tartarus = the Underworld as in v. 206 and often. Understood as 'worse than the Furies' the comparison is vapid.

[20] See Critical Appendix.

Coryciaeque comae Cinyreaque germina; at altis
215 ipsa toris Serum Tyrioque umbrata recumbit
tegmine. sed toto spectatur in agmine coniunx
solus, in hunc magnae flectuntur lumina Romae
ceu iuvenes natos suprema ad busta ferentem.
is dolor in vultu, tantum crinesque genaeque
220 noctis habent. illam tranquillo fine solutam
felicemque vocant: lacrimas fudere marito.
    Est locus ante Urbem qua primum nascitur ingens
Appia quaque Italo gemitus Almone Cybebe
ponit et Idaeos iam non reminiscitur amnes.
225 hic te Sidonio velatam molliter ostro
eximius coniunx (nec enim fumantia busta
clamoremque rogi potuit perferre) beato
composuit, Priscilla, tholo. nil longior aetas
carpere, nil aevi poterunt vitiare labores:
230 sic ca⟨u⟩tum membris, tantas venerabile marmor
spirat opes. mox in varias mutata novaris
effigies: hoc aere Ceres, hoc lucida Cnosis,
illo Maia luto, Venus hoc non improba saxo.
accipiunt vultus non indignata decoros
235 numina; circumstant famuli consuetaque turba
obsequiis, tunc rite tori mensaeque parantur
assiduae. domus ista, domus! quis triste sepulchrum
dixerit? hac merito visa pietate mariti

    214 at *Gronovius*: et M
    228 tholo *Polster*: toro M
    230 sic cautum *Phillimore*: sic catum M: siccatam ⌐
    233 luto *Baehrens*: tholo M

Hebrew essences too, Corycian strands and Cinyrean buds. She herself reclines on a lofty couch, shaded by cover of silk and Tyrian purple. But in the entire column the husband draws every eye. On him great Rome turns her gaze, as though he were bearing young sons to burial; such grief is in his face, such night upon his hair and cheeks.[21] Her they call free in a peaceful end and happy; they shed their tears for the husband.

There is a place before the City where great Appia begins and Cybele lays aside her grief in Italian Almo, no more remembering Ida's rivers.[22] Here your matchless consort softly laid you, Priscilla, covered by Sidonian purple in a wealthy dome; for he could not abide the smoke of burning and noise of the pyre. Length of time will have no power to wither nor labours of years to harm; such care is taken for your body, so much wealth the venerable marble breathes out. Soon you are made anew into various semblance: here shines Ceres in bronze, here the Cnosian maid,[23] in that clay is Maia, Venus (no wanton) in this stone. The deities accept your beauteous features without complaint. Servants stand around accustomed to obey. Then couches and tables are duly prepared, always at hand. It is a house, yes, a house! Who would call it a sombre sepulchre? Seeing the husband's devotion, one might

---

[21] Darkened by dust (not ashes; cf. vv. 226f.).

[22] The image of Cybele, who grieved for Attis, was ritually washed in the river Almo every 27 March.

[23] Ariadne; cf. I.2.133, *Thebaid* 12.676. Neither she nor Maia were usually regarded as divinities but both were celestial, Ariadne through the Crown, Maia as a Pleiad. The reason for their selection does not appear.

protinus exclames: 'est hic, agnosco, minister
240   illius, aeternae modo qui sacraria genti
condidit inque alio posuit sua sidera caelo.'
sic, ubi magna novum Phario de litore puppis
solvit iter iamque innumeros utrimque rudentes
lataque veliferi porrexit bracchia mali
245   invasitque vias, in eodem angusta phaselos
aequore et immensi partem sibi vindicat Austri.
    Quid nunc immodicos, iuvenum lectissime, fletus
corde foves longumque vetas exire dolorem?
nempe times ne Cerbereos Priscilla tremescat
250   latratus? tacet ille piis. ne tardior adsit
navita proturbetque vadis? vehit ille merentes
protinus et manes placidus locat hospite cumba.
praeterea si quando pio laudata marito
umbra venit, iubet ire faces Proserpina laetas
255   egressasque sacris veteres heroidas antris
lumine purpureo tristes laxare tenebras
sertaque et Elysios animae praesternere flores.
sic manes Priscilla subit; ibi supplice dextra
pro te Fata rogat, reges tibi tristis Averni
260   placat, ut expletis humani finibus aevi
pacantem terras dominum iuvenemque relinquas
ipse senex. certae iurant in vota Sorores.

261 pacantem *Avantius*: plac- M

330

exclaim forthwith: 'Yes, this is the minister of him that lately founded a shrine for his eternal race and set his stars in another firmament.'[24] So, when a great ship has started a new voyage from Pharian shore and already stretched countless ropes on either side and the broad arms of her sail-bearing mast, and launched out upon her way, a narrow pinnace on the same sea claims part of the measureless South Wind for herself.

Why now, most distinguished young sir, do you cherish immoderate tears in your heart and forbid long grief to leave it? You fear perhaps lest Priscilla tremble at Cerberus' bark? He is silent for the pious. Lest the ferryman come slowly or thrust her from the water? He conveys the deserving promptly, gently placing their ghosts in his hospitable boat. Moreover, if from time to time a shade comes with the praises of a devoted husband, Proserpine bids joyful torches go forth, bids the heroines of old leave their sacred grottoes and thin the gloomy darkness with gleaming light, strewing garlands and Elysian blooms before the soul. That was how Priscilla entered the world below. There she entreats the Fates on your behalf with suppliant hand, praying that when the term of human life is fulfilled you may leave your master giving peace to the world and still young, yourself a greybeard. The sure Sisters swear to honour her prayer.

[24] Domitian's temple of the Flavian race—a new heaven.

SILVAE

V.2

LAUDES CRISPINI VETTI BOLANI FILI

Rura meus Tyrrhena petit saltusque Tagetis
Crispinus; nec longa mora est aut avia tellus,
sed mea secreto velluntur pectora morsu
udaque turgentes impellunt lumina guttas,
5   ceu super Aegaeas hiemes abeuntis amici
vela sequar spectemque ratem iam fessus ab altis
rupibus atque oculos longo querar aëre vinci.
   Quid si militiae iam te, puer inclite, primae
clara rudimenta et castrorum dulce vocaret
10 auspicium? quanto manarent gaudia fletu
quosve darem amplexus! etiamne optanda propinqui‹s›
tristia? et octonos bis iam tibi circumit orbes
vita, sed angustis animus robustior annis,
succumbitque oneri et mentem sua non capit aetas.
15 nec mirum: non te series inhonora parentum
obscurum proavis et priscae lucis egentem
plebeia de stirpe tulit; non sanguine cretus
turmali trabeaque recens et paupere clavo
augustam sedem et Latii penetrale senatus
20 advena pulsasti, sed praecedente tuorum
agmine. Romulei qualis per iugera circi

3 sed *Gronovius*: et M
8–10 *distinxi*
11 propinquis ς: -qui M
12 et ς: ut M
18 trabeaque (ς) recens *Krohn*: trabeque ac remis M

V.2

PRAISES OF CRISPINUS, SON OF
VETTIUS BOLANUS

My friend Crispinus goes forth to Tyrrhenian fields and
Tagus' glades. Not for long his stay nor remote the land,
but a secret pang plucks at my heartstrings and my moist
eyes urge swelling drops, as though I were following the
sails of my departing friend over Aegean storms and
watching the ship wearily from some high cliff, complain-
ing of my eyes' defeat by stretch of air.

What if the bright beginnings of first soldiering, boy of
fame, and the fair auspices of the camp were summoning
you now?[1] With what tears my joy would flow, how close be
my embrace! Are friends to pray for sadness? And your life
has now rounded twice eight circuits, but your spirit is
sturdier than your few years. Your age sinks under the load,
unequal to the mind it bears. And no wonder. No unhon-
oured line of forbears brought you from plebeian stock,
obscure of ancestry and lacking ancient glory. Not born of
equestrian blood, fresh from trabea[2] and pauper stripe,[3]
did you knock as a newcomer at the august abode, the
sanctuary of Latium's Senate; a troop if kinsfolk came before you. As when in the spaces of Romulus' Circus a horse

---

[1] The scenario changes as the poem proceeds. The summons
to military duty abroad, here an apprehensive hypothesis, becomes a confident expectation, ending in a dramatic announce-
ment.   [2] Ceremonial dress of Knights.

[3] I.e. you came of a senatorial family and wore the broad stripe
on your tunic (cf. on III.2.124) before yourself becoming a Senator, not the two narrow ones like ordinary Knights.

cum pulcher visu, titulis generosus avitis
exspectatur equus, cuius de stemmate longo
felix demeritos habet admissura parentes,
25   illi omnes acuunt plausus, illum ipse volantem
pulvis et incurvae gaudent agnoscere metae:
sic te, clare puer, genitum sibi curia sensit
primaque patricia clausit vestigia luna.
mox Tyrios ex more sinus tunicamque potentem
30   agnovere umeri. sed enim tibi magna pararat
ad titulos exempla pater. quippe ille iuventam
protinus ingrediens pharetratum invasit Araxen
belliger indocilemque fero servire Neroni
Armeniam. rigidi summam Mavortis agebat
35   Corbulo, sed comitem belli sociumque laborum
ille quoque egregiis multum miratus in armis
Bolanum, atque uni curarum asperrima suetus
credere partirique metus: quod tempus amicum
fraudibus, exserto quaenam bona tempora bello,
40   quae suspecta fides aut quae fuga vera ferocis
Armenii. Bolanus iter praenosse timendum,
Bolanus tutis iuga quaerere commoda castris,
metiri Bolanus agros, aperire malignas
torrentum nemorumque moras tantamque verendi
45   mentem implere ducis iussisque ingentibus unus
sufficere. ipsa virum norat iam barbara tellus,
ille secundus apex bellorum et proxima cassis.
sic Phryges attoniti, quamquam Nemeaea viderent

25 illi* *Håkanson*: illum M
30 pararat *Courtney*: parabat M   37 uni *Heinsius*: illi M
39 exserto (*vide Courtney*): exorto M
43 metari *Calderini*   44 torrentum *Heinsius*: tot rerum M

is awaited, handsome of aspect and noble in glories of pedigree, from whose long family tree happy mating has produced meritable parents. For him all sharpen their applause; the very dust and rounded turning posts rejoice to recognize him as he flies: even so, illustrious boy, the Senate felt you as to its order born and set the patrician crescent[4] on your youthful steps. Soon your shoulder recognized the customary Tyrian folds[5] and the mantle of power. And indeed your father had prepared great examples for you to follow on your road to glory. For straightway as he crossed the threshold of manhood he carried war to quiver-bearing Araxes and Armenia that would not learn submission to savage Nero. Corbulo headed the stiff campaign, but he also much admired that splendid soldier Bolanus, comrade and partner of his toils. Only to him was he used to confide his sharpest cares, sharing his fears: what occasion favoured stratagem, what times were good for open fight, when to doubt the faith of the bold Armenian or when his flight was real. Bolanus would reconnoitre a dangerous route, Bolanus seek out a ridge suitable for safe encampment, Bolanus measure the terrain, open up malignant obstacles of torrent or forest, implement the great mind of his revered commander, and single-handed cope with his massive orders. Now even the barbarian land knew him; he was the second crest of the war, the proximate helmet. So the dismayed Phrygians saw the arms of Nemea and Cleonae's bow driving back their ranks and yet

[4] Worn by patricians on their shoes.

[5] Indicating, as Vollmer says, that the purple gown and tunic with purple stripe arrived when the boy was old enough to go out in public.

arma Cleonaeusque acies impelleret arcus,
50 pugnante Alcide tamen et Telamona timebant.
disce, puer, (nec enim externo monitore petendus
virtutis tibi pulcher amor: cognata ministret
laus animos, aliis Decii reducesque Camilli
monstrentur), tu disce patrem: quantusque nigrantem
55 fluctibus occiduis fessoque Hyperione Thulen
intrarit mandata gerens quantusque potentis
mille urbes Asiae sortito rexerit anno
imperium mulcente toga. bibe talia pronis
auribus, haec certent tibi conciliare propinqui,
60 haec iterent praecepta senes comitesque paterni.
        Iamque adeo moliris iter nec deside passu
ire paras. nondum validae tibi signa iuventae
irrepsere genis et adhuc tenor integer aevi,
nec genitor iuxta; Fatis namque haustus iniquis
65 occidit et geminam prolem sine praeside linquens
nec saltem teneris ostrum puerile lacertis
exuit albentique umeros induxit amictu.
quem non corrupit pubes effrena novaeque
libertas properata togae? ceu nescia falcis
70 silva comas tollit fructumque exspirat in umbras.
at tibi Pieriae tenero sub pectore curae
et pudor et docti legem sibi dicere mores;
hinc hilaris probitas et frons tranquilla nitorque

54 nigrantem *Avantius*: nega- M, *Courtney*

55 occiduis fessoque *Calderini*: -uis fessusque M: -uo fissis *Courtney*   56 potentis *Heinsius*: -es M   58 bibe *Heinsius*: tibi M   60 praecepta senes comitesque *Housman*: comites pr- senesque M   61 adeo *Markland*: alio M

73 hinc *Baehrens*: tunc M

they feared Telamon too with Alcides in the fray. Learn, my boy (for you do not have to seek fair love of valour from a stranger monitor; let kindred glory give you courage, let Decii and returning[6] Camilli be held up for others), learn of your father: in what greatness he entered Thule darkling in the waves of sunset, where Hyperion comes aweary, bearing his commission; how greatly too he governed the thousand cities of mighty Asia for his allotted year, given tempering command. Drink in such lore with attentive ears. All this let your family strive to commend to you, these precepts let old men and your father's companions ever set before you.

And now you prepare for a journey, making ready for departure at no sluggish pace. Not yet have the signs of strong manhood crept over your cheeks and your life's course is still to be determined. Your father is not by your side; for he died, swallowed by the cruel Fates and leaving two children without a guardian. He did not even strip boyhood's purple from your tender arms and clothe your shoulders in white. Who has not been corrupted by youth uncurbed and the hastened freedom of a new gown, as when a tree ignorant of the pruning hook rears up leaves and exhales its fruit in foliage? But in your heart were Pierian concerns, and modesty, and character taught to make its own law. Hence came blithe probity, a tranquil

---

[6] From exile to defeat the Gauls. Unlike *Decii*, *Camilli* is plural for singular.

luxuriae confine timens pietasque per omnes
75 dispensata modos: aequaevo cedere fratri
mirarique patrem miseraeque ignoscere matri
admonuit fortuna domus.
                                    Tibine illa nefanda
pocula letalesque manu componere sucos
evaluit, qui voce potes praevertere morsus
80 serpentum atque omnes vultu placare novercas?
infestare libet manes meritoque precatu
pacem auferre rogis. sed te, puer optime, cerno
flectentem visus et talia dicta parantem:
'parce, precor cineri. Fatum illud et ira nocentum
85 Parcarum crimenque dei, mortalia quisquis
pectora sero videt nec primo in limine sistit
conatus scelerum atque animos infanda parantes.
excidat illa dies aevo nec postera credant
saecula. nos certe taceamus et obruta multa
90 nocte tegi propriae patiamur crimina gentis.
exegit poenas hominum cui cura suorum,
quo Pietas auctore redit terrasque revisit,
quem timet omne nefas. satis haec lacrimandaque nobis
ultio. quin saevas utinam exorare liceret
95 Eumenidas timidaeque avertere Cerberon umbrae
immemoremque tuis citius dare manibus amnem.'
        Macte animo, iuvenis! sed crescunt crimina matris.
        Nec tantum pietas, sed protinus ardua virtus
affectata tibi. nuper cum forte sodalis
100 immeritae falso palleret crimine famae

[74] timens *Barth*: tenens **M**
[75] modos *Laetus*: domos **M**
[83] visus *Postgate*: iustis **M**: <a> iu- *Heinsius*

brow, elegance fearing luxury's borderline, family affection dispensed in all its forms. The fortune of your house admonished you to yield to your coeval brother,[7] admire your father, and forgive your unhappy mother.

Had she the heart to mix those wicked cups, those deadly juices, for you, who by your voice can forestall the bite of serpents and by your look placate any stepmother? Fain would I vex her shade, robbing her grove of peace with the curse she deserved. But best of boys, I see you turn your eyes away and prepare words such as these: 'Spare her ashes, I pray. It was Fate and the anger of the guilty Parcae, the fault of whatever god sees mortal hearts too late nor at first threshold arrests criminal attempts and minds planning the unspeakable. May that day fall out of time nor future generations credit it! Let us at least keep silence and suffer the family reproach to be covered up, buried in darkest night. *He*[8] exacted retribution who cares for his people, at whose instance Piety has returned and revisited the earth, whom every villainy fears. That is vengeance enough and I needs must weep for it. Nay, would it were permitted to implore the fierce Furies and keep Cerberus away from the timid shade and give the river of forgetfulness more speedily to your ghost!'

A blessing on your soul, young man! But your mother's guilt is all the blacker.

Nor piety only but high courage was your aspiration from the first. Not long ago it fell out that a friend of yours grew pale at false reproach of undeserved ill fame, and

[7] Mentioned again in v. 126, otherwise unknown. Nothing is known of their mother's scandalous fate outside this passage.

[8] The Emperor.

erigeretque Forum succinctaque iudice multo
surgeret et castum vibraret Iulia fulmen,
tu, quamquam non ante forum leges⟨que⟩ severas
passus sed tacita studiorum occultus in umbra,
105 defensare metus adversaque tela subisti
pellere, inermis adhuc et tiro, paventis amici.
haud umquam tales aspexit Romulus annos
Dardaniusque senex medii bellare togata
strage Fori. stupuere patres temptamina tanta
110 conatusque tuos; et te reus ipse timebat.
     Par vigor et membris promptaeque ad fortia vires
sufficiunt animo atque ingentia iussa sequuntur.
ipse ego te nuper Tiberino in litore vidi,
qua Tyrrhena vadis Laurentibus aestuat unda,
115 tendentem cursus vexantemque ilia nuda
calce ferocis equi, vultu dextraque minacem.
si qua fides dictis, stupui Martemque putavi.
Gaetulo sic pulcher equo Troianaque quassans
tela novercales ibat venator in agros
120 Ascanius miseramque patri flagrabat Elissam;
Troilus haut aliter gyro leviore minantes
eludebat equos, aut quem de turribus altis
Arcadas Ogygio versantem in pulvere turmas
spectabant Tyriae non torvo lumine matres.

103 *add.* ⊊
110 et te* *scripsi*: nec te M: nec tunc *Leo*
117 Martemque *Markland*: armatumque M
120 flammavit *Heinsius*
123 turmas *Markland*: metas M

BOOK V.2

Julia[9] roused up the Forum, as she rose girt with many a juryman, brandishing her chaste thunderbolt. You had never before experienced Forum and stern laws, hidden as you were in the silent shade of your studies. But you stepped up to avert your trembling friend's danger and repel the hostile weapons, you, a tiro, still unarmed. Never did Romulus and the old Dardanian[10] see so youthful a combatant in the gowned slaughter of the Forum. The Fathers were astonished at so daring a venture, at your enterprise; even the accused himself was in fear of you.[11]

No less vigour is in your limbs. Your strength, prompt to brave deeds, suffices for your spirit, following its massive commands. Lately I saw you myself on Tiber's bank, where the Tyrrhene wave foams on Laurentian waters, pressing your gallop and goading with naked heel the flanks of a mettlesome horse, menacing with face and hand. If you will believe what I say, I thought it was Mars. So fair Ascanius on his Gaetulian horse would ride hunting into his stepmother's[12] fields, setting poor Elissa aflame for his father;[13] not otherwise did Troilus[14] try to elude the threatening chariot in lighter circuit, or he[15] that Tyrian mothers watched from their towers (nor scowled) as he wheeled Arcadian squadrons in Ogygian dust.

[9] Augustus' Lex Julia de adulteriis. Domitian reenacted it, no doubt with additions (Martial 6.2 and 7).   [10] Aeneas. Their statues were in the Forum, where trials took place.

[11] See Critical Appendix.   [12] As though Dido And Aeneas were married; cf. I.2.53.   [13] In the *Aeneid* (1.657ff.) Cupid takes Ascanius' form and goes on Dido's lap, where he implants passion for Aeneas. Statius' reminiscence limps.

[14] See on II.6.33.   [15] Parthenopaeus.

125   Ergo age (nam magni ducis indulgentia pulsat
certaque dat votis hilaris vestigia frater)
surge animo et fortes castrorum concipe curas.
monstrabunt acies Mavors Actaeaque virgo,
flectere Castor equos, umeris quatere arma Quirinus,
130 qui tibi iam tenero permisit plaudere collo
nubigenas clipeos intactaque caedibus arma.
      Quasnam igitur terras, quem Caesaris ibis in orbem?
Arctoosne amnes et Rheni fracta natabis
flumina, an aestiferis Libyae sudabis in arvis?
135 an iuga Pannoniae mutatoresque domorum
Sauromatas quaties? an te septenus habebit
Hister et umbroso circumflua coniuge Peuce?
an Solymum cinerem palmetaque capta subibis
non sibi felices silvas ponentis Idumes?
140 quod si te magno tellus frenata parenti
accipiat, quantum ferus exsultabit Araxes
quanta Caledonios attollet gloria campos,
cum tibi longaevus referet trucis incola terrae:
'hic suetus dare iura parens, hoc caespite turmas
145 affari †vitae† speculas castellaque longe
(aspicis?) ille dedit cinxitque haec moenia fossa;
belligeris haec dona deis, haec tela dicavit
(cernis adhuc titulos); hunc ipse vocantibus armis

      125 magni *Calderini*: -no M
      130 iam *Polster*: tam M
      138 Solymum *Calderini*: solidum M
      145 late* *Waller*

---

    16 As one of the Salii, custodians of the shields of Mars that had dropped from the sky. *Collo clipeos* inverts *collum clipeis*.

Come then (for the leader's indulgence speeds you, and your blithe brother leaves sure footprints for your vows to follow), take heart of grace and think a soldier's gallant thoughts. Mavors and the Attic maiden shall show you battle arrays, Castor teach you to wheel chargers, Quirinus to shake shield with shoulder, the same that let you already beat cloud-born bucklers against your youthful neck and weapons untouched by slaughter.[16]

To what lands then shall you go, to which of Caesar's worlds? Shall you swim Arctic rivers or Rhine's shattered stream or sweat in the torrid fields of Libya? Or shall you shock Pannonia's ridges and nomad Sarmatians? Or shall sevenfold Hister have you, and Peuce, surrounded by her spouse's shady[17] stream? Or shall you tread Solyma's ashes and the captive palm-groves of Idume? Not for herself does she plant her fruitful woods. But if a land your great parent governed[18] shall receive you, how shall fierce Araxes rejoice, what glory exalt Caledonia's plains! Then shall an aged denizen of that cruel land tell you: 'Here was your father wont to dispense justice, from this mound to harangue his squadrons. The watchtowers and forts (see you?) he set far and wide (?)[19] and circled these walls with a ditch. These gifts he dedicated to the gods of war, these weapons—you shall see the legends. This cuirass he

[17] The epithet, which baffled Vollmer, will refer to the name of the island, Πεύκη = Pine, given according to Eratosthenes because of its pinewoods. After his fashion Statius transfers it to the river, in which the trees would be reflected.

[18] Bolanus governed Asia, not Armenia, but served in the latter under Corbulo.

[19] See Critical Appendix.

SILVAE

induit, hunc regi rapuit thoraca Britanno,'
150 qualiter in Teucros victricia bella paranti
ignotum Pyrrho Phoenix narrabat Achillem.
Felix qui viridi fidens, Optate, iuventa
durabis quascumque vias vallumque subibis,
forsan et ipse latus (sic numina principis adsint)
155 cinctus et unanimi comes indefessus amici,
quo Pylades ex more pius, quo Dardana gessit
bella Menoetiades. quippe haec <con>cordia vobis,
hic amor est, duretque, precor. nos fortior aetas
iam fugit; hinc votis tantum precibusque iuvabo.
160 ei mihi, sed coetus solitos si forte ciebo
et mea Romulei venient ad carmina patres,
tu deris, Crispine, mihi, cuneosque per omnes
te meus absentem circumspectabit Achilles.
sed venies melior (vatum non irrita currunt
165 omina), quique aquilas tibi nunc et castra recludit,
idem omnes properare gradus cingique superbis
fascibus et patrias dabit insedisse curules.
Sed quis ab excelsis Troianae collibus Albae,
unde suae iuxta prospectat moenia Romae
170 proximus ille deus, Fama velocior intrat
nuntius atque tuos implet, Crispine, penates?
dicebam certe: 'vatum non irrita currunt
auguria.' en ingens reserat tibi limen honorum
Caesar et Ausonii committit munia ferri!

150 ultricia *Baehrens*   paranti *Morel*: parentis M
154 si *Markland*   157 haec *Calderini*: et M
159 tantum *Markland*: animum M
160 ei *Calderini*: et M   coetus *Gronovius*: questus M
165 recludet* *Courtney*

donned himself at call to arms, this he took from a British king'—like Phoenix telling Pyrrhus about Achilles (to him unknown) as he planned victorious battles against the Teucrians.

Lucky are you, Optatus, who trusting in your green youth shall endure all roads and enter every rampart, perhaps yourself sword-girt (so help you our Prince's deity!) and tireless comrade of your friend, loyal after Pylades' fashion or as Menoetius' son[20] waged Dardan warfare. For such is the harmony between you, such the affection; and so, I pray, may it continue. As for me, robuster age already flies; from here I shall aid you only with vows and prayers. Alas! but if perchance I summon my wonted gatherings and the Romulean Fathers come to hear my songs,[21] you, Crispinus, will not be there for me and my Achilles will look around for you in vain on every bench. But you will return better than ever (not idle run poets' omens), and he who now opens up for you eagles and camps, the same shall grant you to hasten every step and be surrounded by the proud rods and sit on your father's curule chair.

But who is this messenger from Trojan Alba's lofty hills, where close at hand our god here present looks out upon the walls of his Rome? Swifter than Rumour he enters and fills your home, Crispinus. Did I not say so? Not idle run poets' auguries. Behold! Mighty Caesar unbars for you the doorway to office and entrusts you with the duties of

[20] Patroclus.
[21] Recitations of the *Achilleid*.

---

166 properare* *scripsi*: perferre M

175 vade, puer, tantisque enixus suffice donis.
felix qui magno iam nunc sub praeside iuras
cuique sacer primum tradit Germanicus ensem.
non minus hoc fortes quam si tibi panderet ipse
Bellipotens aquilas torvaque induceret ora
180 casside. vade alacer maioraque disce mereri.

V.3

EPICEDION IN PATREM SUUM

Ipse malas vires et lamentabile carmen
Elysio de fonte mihi pulsumque sinistrae
da, genitor praedocte, lyrae. neque enim antra moveri
Delia nec solitam fas est impellere Cirrham
5 te sine. Corycia quicquid modo Phoebus in umbra,
quicquid ab Ismariis monstrarat collibus Euhan,
dedidici. fugere meos Parnasia crines
vellera, funestamque hederis irrepere taxum
extimui tripodumque (nefas!) arescere laurum.
10 certe ego magnanimum qui facta attollere regum
ibam altum spirans Martemque aequare canendo.
quis sterili mea corda metu * * *
* * * * * * * * * quis Apolline merso
frigida damnatae praeduxit nubila menti?
stant circum attonitae vatem et nil dulce sonantes
15 nec digitis nec voce deae. dux ipsa silenti
fulta caput cithara, qualis post Orphea raptum

---

3 movere ⊊: -ri M
6 monstrarat *Phillimore*: -rabrat M: -rabat ⊊
9 sustinui *Markland*   tripodumque *Saenger*: trepidam- M

Ausonia's sword. Go, my boy, and do your utmost to be equal to so great a gift. Lucky you, that already take oath under our great chief and receive your first sword from Germanicus' hand. No less is this than if the Lord of Battle himself gave you access to the brave eagles and set the stern helmet on your head. Go boldly, and learn to expect greater things.

V.3

LAMENT FOR HIS FATHER

Yourself, most learned father, give me a sinister strength and a song of lamentation from Elysian fount and the touch of an ill-omened lyre. For without you the Delian grottoes may not be moved nor may I urge Cirrha as was my wont. Whatever Phoebus used lately to show me in Corycian shade, whatever Euhan from Ismarian hills, I have unlearned. The Parnassian fillets have fled my hair. To my terror, deadly yew has crept upon my ivy and the laurel of the tripods (horror!) has withered. He I am for sure whose lofty inspiration would exalt the deeds of great-souled kings and match their warfare in my lay. Who has <shadowed> my spirit with barren neglect * * *, drawn chill clouds over my sentenced mind, Apollo sunk? The goddesses stand around their poet in dismay, making no sweet sound with voice or finger. Their leader leans her head on her silent lyre, such as she stood by Hebrus af-

---

12 *lac. statuit Courtney*
14 sonantes *Calderini*: -tem **M**

astitit, Hebre, tibi, cernens iam surda ferarum
agmina et immotos sublato carmine lucos.
    At tu, seu membris emissus in ardua tendens
20   fulgentesque plagas rerumque elementa recenses,
quis deus, unde ignes, quae ducat semita solem,
quae minuat Phoeben quaeque integrare latentem
causa queat, notisque modos extendis Arati;
seu tu Lethaei secreto in gramine campi
25   concilia heroum iuxta manesque beatos
Maeonium Ascraeumque senem non segnior umbra
accolis alternumque sonas et carmina misces:
da vocem magno, pater, ingenium⟨que⟩ dolori.
nam me ter relegens caelo terque ora retexens
30   luna videt residem nullaque Heliconide tristes
solantem curas. tuus ut mihi vultibus ignis
irrubuit cineremque oculis umentibus hausi,
vilis honos studiis. vix haec in munera solvo
primum animum tacitisque situm depellere chordis
35   nunc etiam labente manu nec lumine sicco
ordior acclinis tumulo quo molle quiescis
iugera nostra tenens, ubi post Aeneia fata
stellatus Latiis ingessit montibus Albam
Ascanius, Phrygio dum pingues sanguine campos
40   odit et infaustae regnum dotale novercae.
hic ego te (nam Sicanii non mitius halat
aura croci, dites nec si tibi rara Sabaei

28 *add.* ⸋   29 caelum *Heinsius*
34 chordis *Schrader*: curis M   35 nec *Gronovius*: nunc M

[1] Homer or Hesiod.   [2] Not 'feebler' (Mozley). Parity in effort is claimed, not in achievement.

ter Orpheus' rape, viewing troops of beasts now deaf and
groves motionless now that his song was taken from them.

Discharged from your body and soaring to the heights,
do you review the shining regions and Nature's elements—
what is God, whence comes fire, what pathway leads the
sun, what cause dominates Phoebe and what can renew
her where she hides?—continuing the music of famed
Aratus? Or in the secluded herbage of Lethe's meadow,
among gatherings of heroes and blessed ghosts do you
keep company with the old Maeonian or him of Ascra,[1]
yourself no less busy[2] a shade, making music in turn, mingling song? Wherever you are, my father, give voice and
skill to my great grief. For thrice in the heavens has the
moon reassembled her visage and thrice taken it apart as
she sees me listless, not solacing my sadness with any of
Helicon's sisterhood. Since your fire reddened on my face
and I drank in your ashes with streaming eyes, little have I
cared for poetry. Hardly do I relax my mind for the first
time to do this office and start to brush away the dust from
my silent strings with hand still faltering and eyes not dry,
leaning upon the tomb in which you softly rest in your
own acres, where after Aeneas' death starred[3] Ascanius
piled Alba on the Latian hills, hating the fields soaked with
Phrygian blood and the dotal kingdom of an inauspicious
stepmother.[4] Here do I—for no more gently breathes[5]
the fragrance of Sicanian saffron or rare cinnamon, be it
plucked for you by wealthy Sabaeans, or odorous harvest

[3] See *Aeneid* 2.682ff.

[4] Lavinia, forced to wed Aeneas instead of Turnus (cf. I.2.245).

[5] An incongruous refinement on the basic idea: 'my poem
makes as worthy an offering as costly perfume.'

cinnama odoratas nec Arabs decerpsit aristas)
inferiis cum laude datis heu carmine plango
45 Pierio; sume ‹en› gemitus et vulnera nati
et lacrimas, rari quas umquam habuere parentes!
atque utinam Fortuna mihi dare manibus aras,
par templis opus, aëriamque educere molem
Cyclopum scopulos ultra atque audacia saxa
50 Pyramidum, et magno tumulum praetexere luco.
illic et Siculi superassem dona sepulchri
et Nemees lucum et Pelopis sollemnia trunci.
illic Oebalio non finderet aëra disco
Graiorum vis nuda virum, non arva rigaret
55 sudor equum aut putri sonitum daret ungula fossa,
sed Phoebi simplex chorus en frondentia vatum
praemia laudato, genitor, tibi rite ligarent!
ipse madens oculis, araeque animaeque sacerdos
praecinerem gemitum, cui te nec Cerberus omni
60 ore nec Orpheae quirent avertere leges.
atque tibi moresque tuos et facta canentem
fors et magniloquo non posthabuisset Homero,
tenderet aeterno ‹et› Pietas aequare Maroni.
    Cur magis incessat superos et aëna Sororum
65 stamina quae tepido genetrix super aggere nati
orba sedet, vel quae primaevi coniugis ignem

---

44 inferiis cum laude datis *Krohn*, heu *Courtney*: inferni cum
laude laci sed M   45 *add. Klotz*   52 ludum *Markland*
    56–7 en . . . ligarent* *scripsi*: et . . . –em M
    58 araeque *hic posui** (*pro* animaeque *Markland*): umbrarum
M
    63 aeterno ‹et›* *scripsi*: (temptet et aet- *Phillimore*): et torvo
M

culled by Arab—here do I alas! lament you in Pierian song,
making offering and praise. Take, oh take your son's groans
and wounds and tears, such tears as few parents ever had.
And would it were my fortune to build an altar to your
spirit, a work to match temples, and raise high an airy
mass, outdoing Cyclopean cliffs and the bold stones of the
Pyramids, and screen your tomb with a great grove! There
would I have surpassed the gifts bestowed on the Sicilian
sepulchre, and Nemea's forest, and the rituals of maimed
Pelops.[6] There no naked strength of Grecian athletes
would cleave the air with Oebalian disk, no sweat of horses
bedew the ground, nor hoof resound on crumbling trench;
only Phoebus' choir (behold!) would bind the leafy prize of
poets on your lauded brow, my father. I myself moist-eyed
would lead the dirge, priest of the altar and of your soul.[7]
Not Cerberus with all his mouths nor laws of Orpheus
could turn you away from it.[8] And as I there sang your ways
and deeds, Piety mayhap would have accounted me not inferior to mighty-mouthed Homer and striven to match me
with immortal[9] Maro.

Why should the bereaved mother sitting over her son's
warm mound in greater measure upbraid the High Ones
and the Sisters' brazen threads, or why the wife who sees

[6] Games held in honour of Anchises, Opheltes (Nemean), and
Pelops (Olympian). For *lucum* Courtney compares Virgil, *Georgics* 3.19. 'Maimed' refers to Pelops' ivory shoulder.

[7] On vv. 53–59 see Critical Appendix.

[8] The dead man's spirit would return to earth to attend the
proceedings, though the law of the Underworld forbade this, the
law that (ultimately) forbade Orpheus to retrieve Eurydice.

[9] See Critical Appendix.

aspicit obstantesque manus turbamque tenentem
vincit, in ardentem, liceat, moritura maritum?
maior ab his forsan superos et Tartara pulset
70 invidia, externis etiam miserabile visu
funus eat; sed nec mihi te Natura dolere
nec Pietas non iusta dedit. modo limine primo
Fatorum et viridi, genitor, ceu raptus ab aevo
Tartara dura subis. nec enim Marathonia virgo
75 parcius exstinctum saevorum crimine agrestum
fleverat Icarium Phrygia quam turre cadentem
Astyanacta parens; laqueo quin illa supremo⟨s⟩
inclusit gemitus, at te post funera magni
Hectoris Haemonio pudor est servisse marito.
80   Non ego quas fati certus sibi morte canora
inferias praemittit olor nec rupe quod atra
Tyrrhenae volucres nautis praedulce minantur
in patrios adhibebo rogos, non murmure trunco
quod gemit et durae queritur Philomela sorori,
85 nota nimis vati. quis non in funere †cuncto†
Heliadum ramos lacrimosaque germina dixit
et Phrygium silicem atque ausum contraria Phoebo
carmina nec fida gavisam Pallada buxo?

69 ab his *Schwarz*: aliis M   pulset ⊊ (?), *O. Mueller*: -em M
71 mihi *Calderini*: modo M   te . . . dolere* *scripsi*: se . . .
dolenti M   72 non iusta* *scripsi*: ini- M
76 fleverat *Watt*: -vit M
77 supremos ⊊: -mo M
85 cuncto M: fratris**temptavi*

10 Erigone.   11 Addressing Andromache.
12 Achilles' son Neoptolemus.

her young husband's pyre and overbears the opposing
hands of a restraining crowd to get to her burning spouse,
there to die if die she may? Greater reproach, it may be,
would assail the High Ones from these; even strangers
would pity as they watched the funeral train. But to me too
has Nature and Piety justly granted to grieve for you. To
me, father, you enter cruel Tartarus at the first threshold of
your destiny as though torn from life's springtime. For no
less bitterly had the maid of Marathon mourned for
Icarius, murdered by a crew of savage rustics, than his
mother for Astyanax as he fell from the Phrygian tower.
Nay, *she*[10] stifled her last groans with a noose, whereas
you[11] to your shame served a Haemonian husband[12] after
Hector's burial.

I shall not bring to my father's pyre the offering that the
swan, certain of his fate, sends before him at his tuneful
death, nor yet the sweet, sweet menace that the bird-maid-
ens of the Tyrrhenian[13] make to sailors from their black
rock, nor the mutilated murmur of Philomela's moans as
she complains to her pitiless sister.[14] All these the poet
knows too well. Who has not told of the branches of Helios'
daughters and their amber tears at their brother's burial
(?),[15] and of the Phrygian flint[16] and him who dared sing
against Phoebus, and of Pallas rejoicing at the faithless

[13] The Sirens, seemingly regarded as singing a lament
($\theta\rho\eta\nu\delta\lambda\alpha\lambda\omicron\iota$; cf. *RE* III A.297.51), which was really a threat.

[14] Cf. II.4.21n.   [15] Cf. Critical Appendix.

[16] Niobe's Mt Sipylus, as usually understood. Better perhaps,
the flint knife with which Marsyas, the Phrygian Satyr who lost his
contest with Apollo (flute versus lyre), was flayed. The tears of his
friends became a river bearing his name.

353

te Pietas oblita virum revocataque caelo
90 Iustitia et gemina plangat Facundia lingua
et Pallas doctique cohors Heliconia Phoebi,
quis labor Aonios seno pede ducere cantus,
et quibus Arcadia carmen testudine mensis
cura lyrae nomenque fuit, quosque orbe sub omni
95 ardua septena numerat Sapientia fama,
qui Furias regumque domos aversaque caelo
sidera terrifico super intonuere cothurno,
et quis lasciva vires tenuare Thalia
dulce vel heroos gressu truncare tenores.
100 omnia namque animo complexus es, omnibus auctor
qua fandi via lata patet, sive orsa libebat
Aoniis vincire modis seu voce soluta
spargere et effreno nimbos aequare profatu.
Exsere semirutos subito de pulvere vultus,
105 Parthenope, crinemque afflatu montis adustum
pone super tumulos et magni funus alumni,
quo non Munychiae quicquam praestantius arces
doctave Cyrene Sparteve animosa creavit.

---

92 ducere cantus *Gronovii amicus* (*cf. Ov. Trist.* 1.11.18): d-
campos M: currere c- *Heinsius*   94 cura lyrae *Gronovius*:
cydalibem M   98 quis . . . tenuare *Calderini*: qui . . . tenuere M
99 tenores *Calderini*: leones M   100 es *Saenger*: et M
auctor *Calderini*: utor M: usus *Wiman*   101 via *Markland*: vis
M   105 afflatu montis adustum *Heinsius*: -to –te sepultum M
108 doctave *Markland*: -aque M

---

17 Minerva hated the flute after seeing her reflection as she
played it, so would enjoy Marsyas' sufferings—an incidental detail.

boxwood?[17] Let Piety mourn you, forgetful of mankind, and Justice[18] recalled to heaven, and Eloquence in both tongues, and Pallas, and the Heliconian troop of poetic Phoebus: they whose toil it is to make song in six-foot measure, and they that regulate their poesy with Arcadian tortoiseshell—the lyre their care and name—and they whom under every sky lofty wisdom scores to her credit in sevenfold fame,[19] and they that on terrifying buskin have thundered Furies and kings' palaces and stars turned back in the sky, and they whose fancy it is to attenuate their powers with wanton Thalia or to maim heroic beats by a foot.[20] For your mind embraced all of these, in all you were a model, wherever the wide range of language extends, whether you were pleased to constrain your words in Aonian rhythms or to scatter them in free voice,[21] matching rainstorms in unbridled utterance.

Raise your half-buried countenance from the sudden shower of dust,[22] Parthenope, and place your locks, singed by the mountain's breath, on the tomb and body of your great foster son, than whom Munychia's towers created nothing finer, nor learned Cyrene or valiant Sparta. If you

[18] Cf. I.4.2, *Thebaid* 11.457f.

[19] Statius' father wrote poetry in various genres. After epic and lyric comes philosophical poetry (cf. II.7.76 *docti furor arduus Lucreti*), perhaps extending to didactic. The allusion to the Seven Wise Men seems to be cosmetic, though Solon at least wrote verse. For the meaning of *numerare*, to be added to dictionaries, see my note on Martial 4.29.7 (Loeb edition).

[20] Tragedy, comedy, and elegy are signified in vv. 96–9.

[21] Prose.

[22] Naples suffered comparatively little in the eruption; see Håkanson ad loc.

si tu stirpe vacans famaeque obscura iaceres
110 nil gentile tumens, illo te cive probabas
Graiam aque Euboico maiorum sanguine duci.
ille tuis totiens pressit sua tempora ser⟨t⟩is,
cum stata laudato caneret quinquennia versu
ora supergressus Pylii senis oraque regis
115 Dulichii, pretioque comam subnexus utroque.
   Non tibi deformes obscuri sanguinis ortus
nec sine luce genus, quamquam fortuna parentum
artior expensis. etenim te divite ritu
ponere purpureos Infantia fecit amictus
120 stirpis honore datos et nobile pectoris aurum.
protinus exorto dextrum risere Sorores
Aonides, pueroque chelyn commisit et ora
imbuit amne sacro iam tum tibi blandus Apollo.
nec simplex patriae decus, et natalis origo
125 pendet ab ambiguo geminae certamine terrae.
te de gente suum Latiis ascita colonis
Graia refert Hyele, Phrygius qua puppe magister
excidit et mediis miser evigilavit in undis.
maior at inde suum longo probat ordine vitae

---

109 vacans *Laetus* (?): vetas M   110 tumens *Markland* (*cf.*
Theb. 8.429): tenens M   111 aque *Markland*: atque M
112 pressit sua *Markland*: prestat sed M   114 senis ς: gregis
M: ducis *Slater*   115 pretioque *Saenger*: speciemque M
   118 expensis *Avantius*: exte- M   119 sumere *Markland*
fecit* *scripsi*: legit M: adegit *Calderini*   122 pueroque ς:
-rique M   commisit *Axelson ap. Håkanson*: summ- M
   123 tibi ς: mihi M   125 ab *Barth*: et M
   127 Hyele *Heinsius*: sele M   Phrygius *Avantius*: graius *vel*
gravis M

had lacked pedigree and lain unknown to fame, no heritage to boast, by that citizen you proved yourself Greek, sprung from blood of Euboean forbears. So often did he press his temples with your garlands when he sang at the regular quinquennial festival in lauded verse, after surpassing the eloquence of the Pylian ancient and of Dulichium's king,[23] binding his hair with either guerdon.

Your birth was not mean, your blood not obscure, nor your race without lustre, though your parents' fortune fell short of outgoings.[24] For rich was the ceremony wherein Infancy[25] made you lay aside your purple clothing, given in honour of your birth, and the noble gold upon your breast.[26] On your entry into life the Aonian Sisters smiled auspiciously, and in your boyhood Apollo put a lyre in your hands and dipped your face in his sacred stream, gracious to you even then. As for your country, the credit is complex; your birthplace depends on an undecided contest between two lands. Grecian Hyale,[27] adopted by Latian settlers, where the sleepy helmsman[28] fell from the poop and awoke in the midst of the waves, poor wight, claims you by race; but greater Parthenope proves you hers by

[23] Nestor and Ulysses, lauded as orators in the *Iliad*. Statius' father won prizes at the Augustalia in oratory and verse (cf. vv. 101–04).   [24] Or 'was narrowed by.' As Vollmer explains, the parenthesis tactfully alludes to a financial squeeze which had caused Papinius to make a living as a teacher and perhaps to forfeit equestrian status.

[25] Loosely for *Pueritia,* which will not scan in a hexameter.

[26] The purple-bordered gown (*toga praetexta*) and gold locket (*bulla*) worn by boys of free birth were laid aside at the coming of age ceremony.

[27] Velia, on the coast of Lucania.   [28] Palinurus.

SILVAE

⟨Parthenope⟩ * * * *

130 Maeoniden aliaeque aliis natalibus urbes
diripiunt cunctaeque probant; non omnibus ille
verus, alit fictas immanis gloria falsi.
atque ibi dum profers annos vitamque salutas,
protinus ad patrii raperis certamina lustri
135 vix implenda viris, laudum festinus et audax
ingenii. stupuit primaeva ad carmina plebes
Eubois et natis te monstravere parentes.
inde frequens pugnae nulloque ingloria sacro
vox tua. non totiens victorem Castora gyro
140 nec fratrem caestu virides plausere Therapnae.
sin pronum vicisse domi, quid Achaea mereri
praemia, nunc ramis Phoebi, nunc gramine Lernae,
nunc Athamantea protectum tempora pinu,
cum totiens lassata tamen nusquam avia frondes
145 abstulit aut alium tangit Victoria crinem?
    Hinc tibi vota patrum credi generosaque pubes
te monitore regi, mores et facta priorum
discere, quis casus Troiae, quam tardus Ulixes;
quantus equum pugnasque virum decurrere versu
150 Maeonides quantumque pios ditarit agrestes
Ascraeus Siculusque senex, qua lege recurrat

129 *lac. statuit Markland,* Parthenope *add. Vollmer*
132 fictas* *scripsi:* victos M: -tas *Bentley*
135 festinus et audax *Lipsius:* -na sed ut dux M
137 Eubois *Heinsius:* -oea M: Euboica *Laetus*
140 plausere* *Calderini:* clausero M
149 equum *Postgate:* equus M

29 See Critical Appendix.
30 I.e. festival, because of their religious context.

the long course of your life * * * Maeonides, and different
cities, different birthplaces tear him apart and all of them
make their case. He does not in truth belong to them all,
but the immense glory of the lie nourishes the pretend-
ers.[29] And while you there bear forward your years and
greet life's morning, you are straightway hurried to the
competitions of your native festival (scarcely can grown
men sustain them), hasty for glory and daring of wit. The
Euboean folk fell amazed at your youthful songs and parents pointed you out to their sons. From then on your voice
was heard at many a combat, nor was it inglorious at any
rite.[30] Less often did verdant Therapnae applaud[31] Castor
on the race course or his brother in the boxing ring. But if
victory at home was easy, what of winning Achaean prizes,
shielding your temples now with Phoebus' branches, now
with herbage of Lerna, now with Athamantean pine,[32]
when Victory, though so often weary, nowhere strayed or
took away her leaves or touched another head?

Hence parents' hopes were entrusted to you and noble
youth governed by your guidance, as they learned the
manners and deeds of men gone by: the tale of Troy, Ulysses' tardiness, Maeonides' power to pass in verse through
heroes' horses and combats, what riches the old man of
Ascra and the old man of Sicily gave honest farmers,[33] what

[31] See Critical Appendix.

[32] At Delphi with laurel, at Nemea with wild parsley, at the
Isthmus with pine (no mention of Olympia).

[33] Hesiod and Epicharmus. The latter lived till ninety. The ag-
ricultural work mentioned here is not certainly identified. Statius
may have confused him with a namesake mentioned by Columella
(1.1.8; cf. 7.3.6).

359

Pindaricae vox flexa lyrae volucrumque precator
Ibycus et tetricis Alcman cantatus Amyclis
Stesichorusque ferox saltusque ingressa viriles
155   non formidata temeraria Leucade Sappho,
quosque alios dignata chelys. tu pandere doctus
carmina Battiadae latebrasque Lycophronis atri
Sophronaque implicitum tenuisque arcana Corinnae.
sed quid parva loquor? tu par assuetus Homero
160   ferre iugum senosque pedes aequare solutis
versibus et numquam passu breviore relinqui.
quid mirum, patria si te petiere relicta
quos Lucanus ager, rigidi quos iugera Dauni,
quos Veneri plorata domus neglectaque tellus
165   Alcidae, vel quos e vertice Surrentino
mittit Tyrrheni speculatrix virgo profundi,
quos propiore sinu lituo remoque notatus
collis et Ausonii pridem laris hospita Cyme,
quosque Dicarchei portus Baianaque mittunt
170   litora, qua mediis alte permixtus anhelat
ignis aquis et operta domos incendia servant?
sic ad Avernales scopulos et opaca Sibyllae
antra rogaturae veniebant undique gentes
(illa minas divum Parcarumque acta canebat,

---

153 Ibycus *Politianus*: obsicus M
155 Leucade *anon. Italus*: chalcide M
156 docti *Markland*   170 permixtus ⊊: -issus M

---

34 I.e. the strophic structure of his verse.
35 Cranes, whom he asked to punish some robbers who had mistreated him.
36 See Critical Appendix.

law governs the recurring voice of Pindar's winding harp,[34]
and Ibycus, who prayed to birds,[35] and Alcman, sung in
austere Amyclae, and bold Stesichorus and rash Sappho,
who feared not Leucas but took the manly leap,[36] and
others by the lyre approved. You were skilled to expound
the songs of Battus' son,[37] the lurking places of dark
Lycophron, Sophron's mazes, and the secrets of subtle
Corinna. But why speak of trifles? You were wont to bear
equal yoke with Homer, matching his six feet with verse
turned to prose, never outpaced and left behind.[38] What
wonder if they left their homes to seek you? Lucania's
land sends them, and the acres of stern Daunus,[39] and
the dwelling mourned of Venus, and the land Alcides
neglected, or the maiden who gazes from Surrentum's
summit at the Tyrrhene deep and the hill on the nearer bay
marked by trumpet and oar, and Cyme[40] that long ago
welcomed Ausonia's household god, and the haven of
Dicarchus,[41] and Baiae's shore, where fire pants mingled
deep in the midst of water and hidden conflagrations preserve the houses.[42] Even so from all sides used to come the
peoples to Avernus' crags and the Sibyl's dark cave to ask
their questions; she would sing of the threats of gods and

[37] Callimachus.

[38] A prose paraphrase, probably in Latin.

[39] Apulia, followed allusively by Pompeii (with Venus for patron goddess), Herculaneum, Surrentum (with temple of Minerva
on the headland), Misenum.   [40] Later Cumae, ancient
Greek colony where Aeneas landed; *laris* seems to refer to his
worship after he disappeared from earth.   [41] Puteoli.

[42] I.e. do not harm them, by contrast with Pompeii and Herculaneum, destroyed by the highly visible fires of Vesuvius.

SILVAE

175 quamvis decepto vates non irrita Phoebo).
mox et Romuleam stirpem proceresque futuros
instruis inque patrum vestigia ducere perstas.
sub te Dardanius facis explorator opertae,
qui Diomedei celat penetralia furti,
180 crevit et inde sacrum didicit puer; arma probatis
monstrasti Saliis praesagumque aethera certis
auguribus, cui Chalcidicum fas volvere carmen,
cur Phrygii lateat coma flaminis; et tua multum
verbera succincti formidavere Luperci.
185 et nunc ex illo forsan grege gentibus alter
iura dat Eois, alter compescit Hiberos,
alter Achaemenium secludit Zeugmate Persen;
hi dites Asiae populos, hi Pontica frenant,
hi fora pacificis emendant fascibus, illi
190 castra pia statione tenent. tu laudis origo.
non tibi certassent iuvenilia fingere corda
Mentor et indomiti Phoenix moderator alumni,
quique tubas acres lituosque audire volentem
Aeaciden alio frangebat carmine Chiron.

180 probatis *Baehrens*: -atur M   186 Hiberos ς: -ras M
192 Mentor *Saenger*: nestor M

---

43 She refused him after he had granted her what she asked.
44 The Pontifex Maximus, under whose supervision the Vestals maintained the sacred flame brought by Aeneas from Troy. It is surely not incumbent to take this as a concrete reference to the existing Pontifex Maximus, Domitian.
45 The Palladium (statue of Pallas Athene = Minerva, stolen from her temple in Troy by Diomedes and Ulysses and supposedly kept in Vesta's temple).

the doings of the Fates, no vain prophetess though Phoebus was hoodwinked.[43] Presently too you instruct the stock of Romulus and notables to be, ceasing not to lead them in their fathers' footsteps. Under your direction grew up the Dardan inspector of the hidden fire,[44] who conceals the sanctuary of that which Diomedes stole,[45] and learned the ritual as a boy. You approved the Salii and showed them their arms, you showed the Augurs the sky that gives them foreknowledge, showed who is authorized to unroll the song of Chalcis[46] and why the hair of the Phrygian Flamen[47] is concealed; and greatly did the girt-up Luperci fear your stripes.[48] And now one of that company perhaps gives laws to eastern nations, another holds down Iberians, another with Zeugma keeps off the Achaemenian Persian.[49] These bridle the rich peoples of Asia, those the Pontic territories, these as magistrates of peace[50] correct our courts, these hold armies in loyal station. Their glory began with you. Mentor[51] would not have vied with you in moulding youthful hearts, nor Phoenix, guide of a tameless foster son, nor Chiron, who softened Aeacides with a different tune when he would fain have heard trumpets and clarions.

[46] The Sibylline Books kept by the Quindecimviri.

[47] The flamen (priest) of Cybele, like the other flamens, wore a special headgear (apex), but the implication of *lateat* is obscure.

[48] The future Luperci—the whipped becoming the whippers. 'Girt-up' applies to both.   [49] The ancient counterpart of the contemporary Arsacid king of Parthia.

[50] Lit. 'with peace-making rods,' i.e. civil magistrates.

[51] Substituted by conjecture for Nestor, who is not known as a pedagogue. But the poet may be at fault.

195   Talia dum celebras, subitam civilis Erinys
Tarpeio de monte facem Phlegraeaque movit
proelia. sacrilegis lucent Capitolia taedis
et Senonum furias Latiae sumpsere cohortes.
vix requies flammae necdum rogus ille deorum
200 siderat, excisis cum tu solacia templis
impiger et multum facibus velocior ipsis
concipis ore pio captivaque fulmina defles.
mirantur Latii proceres ultorque deorum
Caesar, et e medio divum pater annuit igni.
205 iamque et flere pio Vesuvina incendia cantu
mens erat et gemitum patriis impendere damnis,
cum Pater exemptum terris ad sidera montem
sustulit et late miseras deiecit in urbes.

    Me quoque vocales lucos Boeotaque tempe
210 pulsantem, cum stirpe tua descendere dixi,
admisere deae; nec enim mihi sidera tantum
aequoraque et terras, quae mos debere parenti,
sed decus hoc quodcumque lyrae primusque dedisti
non vulgare loqui et famam sperare sepulchro.
215 qualis eras Latios quotiens ego carmine patres
mulcerem felixque tui spectator adesses
muneris! heu quali confusus gaudia fletu
vota piosque metus inter laetumque pudorem!
quam tuus ille dies, quam non mihi gloria maior!
220 talis Olympiaca iuvenem cum spectat harena
qui genuit, plus ipse ferit, plus corde sub alto
caeditur; attendunt cunei, spectatur Achaeis

202 concipis *Markland*: concinis M   209 Boeotaque
Baehrens: biot- M (?)   212 quae mos *Krohn*: quam vos M
222 Achaeis *Imhof*: achates M

Such was your occupation when the Fury of civil war suddenly raised her torch from the Tarpeian mount and stirred battles as of Phlegra.[52] The Capitol was alight with sacrilegious brands, and Latian cohorts borrowed Senonian rage. Scarce was the flame at rest nor yet had that pyre of gods collapsed when, far swifter than the brands themselves, you hasten to conceive consolation for the razed shrines with pious voice and bewail the captive thunderbolts. Latium's magnates and Caesar, the gods' avenger, are wonderstruck, and from the midst of the conflagration the father of the gods nods approval. And now it was your purpose to weep Vesuvius' flames in pious melody and spend your tears on the losses of your native place, what time the Father took the mountain from earth and lifted it to the stars only to plunge it down upon the hapless cities far and wide.

Me too, as I knocked at the vocal groves and Boeotia's vales, claiming myself sprung from your stock, did the goddesses admit. For not only stars and sea and land, the common debt of son to parent, but this grace of the lyre, whatever it be, you were the first to give me: speech beyond the vulgar, hope of fame in the grave. What was your mien whenever I soothed the Latian Fathers with my song and you were present, happy spectator of your own gift! Ah, what confusion of joy and loving tears amid prayers and fears and joyous modesty! That day was yours, 'tis very sure; my glory was no greater. So, when his begetter watches a youth on Olympia's sand, 'tis *he* rather that strikes and deep in his heart is stricken, him the benches watch, on him rather the Achaeans gaze as he whelms his

[52] The fighting on the Capitol in 69.

ille magis, crebro dum lumina pulveris haustu
obruit et prensa vovet exspirare corona.
225 ei mihi quod tantum patrias ego vertice frondes
solaque Chalcidicae Cerealia dona coronae
te sub teste tuli! qualem te Dardanus Albae
vix cepisset ager, si per me serta tulisses
Caesarea donata manu! quod subdere robur
230 illa dies, quantum potuit dempsisse senectae!
nam quod me mixta quercus non pressit oliva
et fugit speratus honos, quam lustra parentis
invida Tarpei caperes! te nostra magistro
Thebais urguebat priscorum exordia vatum.
235 tu cantus stimulare meos, tu pandere facta
heroum bellique modos positusque locorum
monstrabas. labat incerto mihi limite cursus
te sine, et orbatae caligant vela carinae.
    Nec solum larga memet pietate fovebas:
240 talis et in thalamos; una tibi cognita taeda
conubia, unus amor. certe seiungere matrem
iam gelidis nequeo bustis; te sentit habetque,
te videt et tumulos ortuque obituque salutat,
ut Pharios aliae ficta pietate dolores
245 Mygdoniosque colunt et non sua funera plorant.

232 quam (ς) lustra *Markland*: qua dusce M

---

53 Not to be taken literally. The father identifies with the son
fighting in the arena. Cf. v. 228.
54 Winners in the Neapolitan Augustalia were crowned with
corn ears. 'Chalcidic' = Neapolitan; cf. II.2.94 n.
55 In the Alban contest (cf. III.5.28ff.) in which Statius won
a prize after his father's death; he subsequently failed in the

eyes with frequent draught of sand and prays to die once he has grasped the wreath.[53] Alas that with you to witness I only bore off native chaplets, only Ceres' gift of Chalcidic crown![54] How would it have been with you (scarce would Alba's Dardan field have contained you) had you through me borne off a garland bestowed by Caesar's hand?[55] What vigour that day might have given you, how much of old age taken away! For inasmuch as oak mingled with olive did not press my brow and the hoped-for honour eluded me, how calmly would you have taken[56] the grudging lustre of the Tarpeian Father.[57] With you as my mentor my *Thebaid* pressed close upon the works of ancient bards. You showed me how to spur my songs, how to set forth the deeds of heroes, the modes of warfare, the layout of places. Without you my course falters, uncertain my track, befogged the sails of the orphan craft.

Nor was it only I whom you cherished in abounding love: thus you were to your helpmate also. You knew marriage by a single torch, yours was a single love. 'Tis sure I cannot separate my mother from your tomb now cold. She feels and has you, sees you, greets your grave at rise and set of sun, as other women in feigned devotion observe Pharian and Mygdonian sorrows, mourning deaths not their own.[58]

Capitoline. *Ager* may mean the whole district or the grounds of Domitian's villa where the contest was held—not Papinius' property in the area.   [56] See Critical Appendix.

[57] Jupiter Capitolinus. The winners will probably have been chosen by a panel of judges, though the Emperor crowned them.

[58] Ritual mournings for Attis and Osiris in the cults of Cybele and Isis.

SILVAE

Quid referam expositos servato pondere mores,
quae pietas, quam vile lucrum, quae cura pudoris,
quantus amor recti? rursusque, ubi dulce remitti,
gratia quae dictis, animo quam nulla senectus?
250 his tibi pro meritis famam laudesque benignas
iudex cura deum nulloque e vulnere tristes
concessit. raperis, genitor, non indigus aevi,
non nimius, trinisque decem quinquennia lustris
iuncta ferens. sed me pietas numerare dolorque
255 non sinit, o Pylias aevi transcendere metas
et Teucros aequare senes, o digne videre
me similem! sed nec leti tibi ianua tristis;
quippe leves causae, nec segnis labe senili
exitus instanti praemisit membra sepulchro,
260 sed te torpor iners et mors imitata quietem
explicuit falsoque tulit sub Tartara somno.
  Quos ego tunc gemitus (comitum manus anxia vidit,
vidit et exemplum genetrix gavisaque novit),
quae lamenta tuli! veniam concedite, manes,
265 fas dixisse, pater: non tu mihi plura dedisses.
felix ille patrem vacuis circumdedit ulnis
vellet et Elysia quamvis in sede locatum
abripere et Danaas iterum portare per umbras.
  *   *   *   *   *
temptantem et vivos molitum in Tartara gressus

251 tristes *Markland*: -em M
258 tabe *Gronovius*   *lac. post 268 agnovit Housman, post*
272 *Heinsius*

BOOK V.3

Why should I tell of your manners—open but at no sacrifice of gravity, your loyalty, your contempt of lucre, your
sense of honour, your love of right? And again, when you
chose to relax, the charm of your conversation? Your mind
untouched by age? For these deserts the gods' protective
care allowed you fame and generous credit unsaddened by
any misfortune. You are taken, father, not starved of years
nor over-abounding, bearing ten quinquennia joined with
three lustres. But love and grief forbid me to count, O worthy to transcend the Pylian goals of life and equal Teucrian
ancients,[59] worthy to see me in your semblance![60] And yet
the door of Death held no sadness for you: for the causes
were light, no lingering departure sent your body in senile
decay ahead to the impending tomb; a lazy lethargy, a
death disguised as sleep stretched you out, bearing you to
Tartarus[61] in the guise of slumber.

What groans, what lamentations did I bring then! My
companions saw it, my mother saw and gladly noted the example.[62] Give me leave, spirit, be it no sin to say it, father:
you would have done no more for me. Happy he that
embraced his sire with ineffectual arms. Fain would he
have snatched him away, settled though he was in Elysian
abode, and carried him once more through Danaan shades
* * * he that the aged seer of Underworld Diana[63] took
down as he essayed to gain foreknowledge of the fates
awaiting his descendants and thought to bring living steps

59 Nestor and Priam and Tithonus.
60 As old as you were when you died.
61 The Underworld, as in v. 269.
62 It showed how Statius would one day mourn for her.
63 Hecate.

369

SILVAE

270 detulit infernae vates longaeva Dianae.
si chelyn Odrysiam pigro transmisit Averno
causa minor, si Thessalicis Admetus in oris
* * * * *
si lux una retro Phylaceida rettulit umbram,
cur nihil exoret, genitor, chelys aut tua manes
275 aut mea? fas mihi sit patrios contingere vultus,
fas iunxisse manus, et lex quaecumque sequatur.
    At vos, umbrarum reges Aetnaeaque Iuno,
si laudanda precor, taedas auferte comasque
Eumenidum; nullo sonet asper ianitor ore,
280 Centauros Hydraeque greges Scyllaeaque monstra
aversae celent valles, umbramque senilem
invitet ripis discussa plebe supremus
vector et in media componat molliter alga.
ite, pii manes Graiumque examina vatum,
285 illustremque animam Lethaeis spargite sertis
et monstrate nemus quo nulla irrupit Erinys,
in quo falsa dies caeloque simillimus aër.
    Inde tamen venias melior qua porta malignum
cornea vincit ebur, somnique in imagine monstra
290 quae solitus. sic sacra Numae ritusque colendos

271–72 si . . . si *Calderini*: sic . . . sic M
273 si lux *Heinsius*: silva M   275 sit ⊊: sic M
288 porta ⊊: parte M

---

64 In the sixth Book of the *Aeneid* the Sibyl of Cumae takes
Aeneas down to the Underworld, where he tries to embrace his father's phantom and hears him prophecy of Roman worthies in
time to come.
    65 Of Orpheus.

370

into Tartarus.[64] If a lesser occasion sent the Odrysian lyre[65] over to sluggish Avernus, if Admetus in the land of Thessaly ‹could rejoice when his wife was brought from below›, if one day retrieved the shade of him of Phylace,[66] why should your lyre, father, or mine win no boon from the ghosts? Only let me be permitted to touch my father's face and clasp his hand, no matter what law may follow.[67]

But you rulers of the shades and Juno of Enna,[68] if my prayers are praiseworthy, take away the torches and hair of the Furies. Let not the harsh warder bark with any mouth,[69] let remote valleys hide Centaurs and Hydra's swarm[70] and Scylla's monsters, and let the ferryman of the dead invite the aged shade to the bank, scattering the populace, and lay him softly among the weed. Go, righteous ghosts and multitude of Grecian bards, shower the illustrious soul with Lethaean garlands and point him to the grove which no Fury has invaded, where is false day and air most like to the sky.

Yet may you come thence, along that path wherein the kindlier gate of horn bests the unfriendly ivory,[71] and in sleep's semblance counsel me as you used. Even so in the

[66] Protesilaus, brought back to life for one day.

[67] Cf. v. 60. Three factors can be suggested: (a) The law of the Underworld forbidding return. (b) The law or ordinance forbidding Orpheus to look back on his way to the upper world. (c) The penalty for breach of b.

[68] Proserpine, carried off from Enna (or Aetna by some accounts) by Pluto to be his queen in the Underworld; a pleonasm after *reges,* which includes her.

[69] He had three.

[70] The Hydra had many heads.

[71] See *Aeneid* 6.894.

mitis Aricino dictabat Nympha sub antro,
Scipio sic plenos Latio Iove ducere somnos
creditur Ausoniis, sic non sine Apolline Sulla.

V.4

SOMNUS

Crimine quo merui, iuvenis, placidissime divum,
quove errore miser donis ut solus egerem,
Somne, tuis? tacet omne pecus volucresque feraeque
et simulant fessos curvata cacumina somnos,
5   nec trucibus fluviis idem sonus; occidit horror
aequoris et terris maria acclinata quiescunt.
septima iam rediens Phoebe mihi respicit aegras
stare genas; totidem Oetaeae Paphiaeque revisunt
lampades et totiens nostros Tithonia questus
10   praeterit et gelido spargit miserata flagello.
unde ego sufficiam? non si mihi lumina mille
quae sacer alterna tantum statione tenebat
Argus et haud umquam vigilabat corpore toto.
at nunc, heu, si aliquis longa sub nocte puellae
15   bracchia nexa tenens ultro te, Somne, repellit,
inde veni; nec te totas infundere pennas

[293] sic *Sudhaus*: nec M
[12] vafer *Heinsius*

---

[72] The elder Africanus, supposed to have contact with Jupiter in the Capitoline temple.

[73] He wore an image of Apollo, whom he chose to consider his protector.

Arician grot did the gentle Nymph instruct Numa in sacred lore and rites to be observed, so Scipio,[72] as Ausonians believe, passed slumbers full of Latian Jove, so Sulla was not without Apollo.[73]

V.4

SLEEP

For what cause, youthful Sleep, kindest of the gods, or what error have I deserved, alas, to lack your boon? All cattle are mute and birds and beasts, and the nodding treetops feign weary slumbers, and the raging rivers abate their roar; the ruffling of the waves subsides, the sea is still, leaning against the shore.[1] Now returning for the seventh time Phoebe sees my sick eyes stare; so many lights of Oeta and Paphos[2] revisit me, so often does Tithonia pass me by and in pity sprinkle me with her chill whip.[3] How am I to bear it? Not if I had the thousand eyes of sacred[4] Argos, who kept them alert only by turns, never wakeful over all his body. But now, alas, if one there be that clasping a girl's twining arms through the long night even thrusts you from him, O Sleep, come thence. Nor do I demand that you

---

[1] From *Aeneid* 4.522–27: the poetry of night, not the reality.

[2] The morning and evening star, imagined by Latin poets as appearing in the same twenty-four hour period. *Oetaeus* recalls Virgil, *Eclogue* 8.30, but the association with Mt Oeta is problematic. If Statius knew that both morning and evening stars are Paphian (i.e. the planet Venus), he seems to have forgotten it; cf *Thebaid* 6.238–41.

[3] With which she chases away the stars; cf. *Thebaid* 8.274.

[4] Protected by Juno.

luminibus compello meis (hoc turba precetur
laetior); extremo me tange cacumine virgae
(sufficit), aut leviter suspenso poplite transi.

V.5

EPICEDION IN PUERUM SUUM

Me miserum! neque enim verbis sollemnibus ulla
incipiam nunc Castaliae vocalibus undis
invisus Phoeboque gravis. quae vestra, Sorores,
orgia, Pieriae, quas incestavimus aras?
5   dicite; post poenam liceat commissa fateri.
numquid inaccesso posui vestigia luco?
num vetito de fonte bibi? quae culpa, quis error,
quem luimus tanti? morientibus ecce lacertis
viscera nostra tenens animamque avellitur infans,
10 non de stirpe quidem nec qui mea nomina ferret
oraque; non fueram genitor. sed cernite fletus
liventesque genas et credite planctibus orbi.
orbus ego. huc patres et aperto pectore matres
conveniant; cineremque oculis et crimina ferto,
15 si qua sub uberibus plenis ad funera natos
ipsa gradu labente tulit madidumque cecidit
pectus et ardentes restinxit lacte favillas.
quisquis adhuc tenerae signatum flore iuventae
immersit cineri iuvenem primaque iacentis

---

¹⁷ precetur ⌐: -catur M

² nunc *Scriverius*: nec M   ⁸ tanti* *scripsi*: -tis M: -tus
Politianus   ⁹ animamque ⌐: -aque M   ¹⁴ ferto *Politianus*:
-te M   ¹⁷ favillas *Calderini*: papillas M

pour all your wings upon my eyes (that be the prayer of those more fortunate): touch me with the final tip of your wand (it suffices) or pass by me lightly, knees in air.

V.5

LAMENT FOR HIS BOY

Alas, alas! For with no wonted words shall I make my opening, hateful as I now am to Castalia's vocal stress, misliked by Phoebus. What mysteries of yours, Pierian Sisters, have I profaned, what altars? Say. After punishment let me be permitted to confess the crime. Have I set foot in an untrodden grot, drunk from a forbidden spring? What is the fault, what the error for which I pay so dearly? See, a child is torn away as he grasps my heart and soul[1] with dying arms—not indeed of my stock, bearing my name and features; I was not his father. But see my tears and bruised cheeks, trust my lament, you that are bereaved: bereaved am I. Let fathers and mothers come hither with open bosom. And let her endure with her eyes the ashes and the crime whosoever under full breasts herself carried children to the pyre with faltering steps and pounded her moist bosom and quenched the glowing embers with her milk. Whoever has plunged into ash[2] a lad still adorned with the bloom of youth and seen the cruel flames creep

[1] *Animaque* in Courtney's text seems to be a mistake.
[2] If sound, *cineri* seems to be carelessly used for the flames of the pyre.

20   serpere crudeles vidit lanugine flammas
adsit et alterno mecum clamore fatiscat:
vincetur lacrimis et te, Natura, pudebit.
tanta mihi feritas, tanta est insania luctus.
hoc quoque cum ni⟨tor⟩ ter dena luce peracta
25   acclinis tumul⟨o et pla⟩nctus in carmina verto
discordesque m⟨odos et⟩ singultantia verba
molior. ista ly⟨rae vis est⟩ atque ira tacendi
impatiens; sed nec solitae mihi vertice laurus
nec fronti vittatus honos. en taxea marcet
30   silva comis hilaresque hederas plorata cupressus
excludit ramis; nec eburno pollice chordas
pulso sed incertam digitis errantibus amens
scindo chelyn. iuvat, heu, iuvat illaudabile carmen
fundere et incompte miserum laxare dolorem.
35   sic merui? sic me cantuque habituque nefastum
aspiciunt superi? pudeat Thebasque novumque
Aeaciden; nil iam placitum manabit ab ore.
ille ego qui quotiens blande matrumque patrumque
vulnera, qui vivos potui mulcere dolores,
40   ille ego lugentum mitis solator, acerbis
auditus tumulis et descendentibus umbris,
deficio medicasque manus fomentaque quaero
vulneribus subitura meis. nunc tempus, amici,
quorum ego manantes oculos et saucia tersi
45   pectora: reddite opem, saevas exsolvite grates.
nimirum cum vestra domus ego funera maestus

20 flammas *Calderini*: malas M
24 nitor ter dena *Gronorius*: in (*spat.*) terdana M
25 tumulo et (ς) planctus *Baehrens*: tumul (*spat.*) notus M
26 modos et ς: m (*spat.*) M

over his first down as he lies, let him come and grow weary
with me in alternate wail; he shall lose the contest of tears,
and you, Nature, shall be ashamed, so savage, so wild is my
mourning. Even as I make this effort after thirty days have
passed, leaning on the tomb, and turn blows into poetry, I
labour discordant measures and sobbing words. It is compulsion to sing and anger impatient of silence;[3] but the
wonted laurels are not on my head nor the grace of fillets
on my brow. See, yew leaves wither on my hair and
branches of lamented cypress shut out the merry ivy. I do
not strike the strings with ivory thumb but with wandering
fingers tear madly at the uncertain lyre. I am fain, fain alas,
to pour out song that none can praise and ease the cruel
pain in clumsy sort. Have I deserved so? So do the High
Ones see me, ill-omened in song and habit? Should
Thebes and my new Aeacides be shamed? Shall nothing
that pleases flow any more from my lips? I that (how often!) could gently soothe the wounds of mothers and fathers, the pain of widowhood, I, mild comforter of mourn-
ers, heard at untimely graves as ghosts descend, I fail, and
seek healing hands and compresses to aid my wounds.
Now is the time, friends, whose streaming eyes and
wounded breasts I stanched: return my help, pay the cruel
debt of gratitude. Like as not when I ‹bewailed› your be-

[3] See Critical Appendix.

27 ista* *scripsi*: orsa M   ly *(spat.)* M, *suppl. Krohn*: ly‹ra
dolor› *Sudhaus*   34 laxare *Unger*: laudare M: nud- *Markland*
    36 aspiciunt *scripsi*: -ciant M   37 placitum *Markland*:
-idum M   manabit ⊊: -bat M   43 subitura* *scripsi*: sed
summa M: sed nulla *Rothstein*   *post 46 lac. agnovit Baehrens*

*   *   *   *   *

increpitans: 'qui damna doles aliena, repone,
infelix, lacrimas et tristia carmina serva.'
verum erat. absumptae vires et copia fandi
50   nulla mihi dignumque nihil mens fulmine tanto
repperit. inferior vox omnis et omnia sordent
verba. ignosce, puer; tu me caligine mersum
obruis. a durus, viso si vulnere carae
coniugis invenit caneret quod Thracius Orpheus
55   dulce sibi, si busta Lini complexus Apollo
non tacuit. nimius fortasse avidusque doloris
dicor et in lacrimis iustum excessisse pudorem.
quisnam autem gemitus lamentaque nostra rep⟨r⟩endis?
o nimium felix, nimium crudelis et expers
60   imperii, Fortuna, tui qui dicere legem
fletibus aut fines audet censere dolendi!
incitat, heu, planctus. potius fugientia ripas
flumina detineas rapidis aut ignibus obstes
quam miseros lugere vetes. tamen ille severus,
65   quisquis is est, nostrae cognoscat vulnera causae.
      Non ego mercatus Pharia de puppe loquaces
delicias doctumque sui convicia Nili
infantem lingua nimium salibusque protervum
dilexi: meus ille, meus. tellure cadentem
70   excepi atque unctum geniali gramine fovi,
poscentemque novas tremulis ululatibus auras
inserui vitae. quid plus tribuere parentes?

52 mersum *Heinsius*: maestu M
53 durus *Politianus*: duro M
58 reprendis *Politianus*: repen- M
63 detineas *Boxhorn*: demneus M

reavements in sad strains * * * rebuking: 'You that grieve
for others' losses, put back your tears, unhappy man, and
keep your sad songs.' It was true. My strength is exhausted,
I have no store of speech, my mind finds nothing worthy of
such a thunderbolt. All utterance falls short, all words are
mean. Forgive me, boy; you smother me in a mist of sorrow. Ah, hard was Orpheus if he saw his dear wife's wound
and found a song that pleased him; hard Apollo if he kept
not silence as he embraced Linus' tomb. Perhaps I am
called extravagant and avid of grief, weeping beyond the
bounds of decency. But who are you that blame my groans
and lamentations? Ah, too fortunate is he, too cruel and ignorant, Fortune, of your dominion, who dares to lay down
rules for tears and decree limits to grieving. Alas, he but
adds fuel to lamentation. More easily might you hold back
rivers as they flee their banks or block devouring fire than
forbid the stricken to mourn. Yet let this austere critic,
whoever he be, take cognizance of my case and its pain.

I did not love a chatterbox favourite bought from some
Pharian boat, taught in infancy the chaff of his native Nile,
too glib of tongue, a pert jester: no, he was mine, mine. I
picked him up as he fell upon the ground, anointed him
with festal oil, took him in my arms, and as he demanded
the novel air with tremulous wails, I made him part of life.

---

67 delicias *Avantius*: aedituas M

68 nimium *Britannicus*: sumum M

70 excepi *Avantius*: aspexi M   geniali *Axelson ap. Håkanson*: -itali M   gramine (*an* germine ?) *Håkanson*: ca- M

71 noscentemque *Baehrens*

quin alios ortus libertatemque sub ipsis
uberibus tibi, parve, dedi, cum munera nostra
75   rideres ignarus adhuc. properaverit ille,
sed merito properabat amor, ne perderet ⟨ullum⟩
libertas tam parva diem. nonne horridus ⟨omnes⟩
invidia superos iniustaque Tartara pulsem?
nonne gemam te, care puer? quo sospite natos
80   non cupii, primo gremium qui protinus ortu
implicuit fixitque mihi, cui verba sonosque
monstravi questusque et vulnera caeca resolvi,
reptantemque solo demissus ad oscula dextra
erexi blandoque sinu iam iamque ⟨cadentes⟩
85   feci operire genas dulcesque accersere somnos.
cui nomen vox prima meum, ludusque tenello
risus et a nostro veniebant gaudia vultu.

74 cum *Politianus*: heu M
76 *add.* ⊊
77 *addidi**: ipsos ⊊
80 non cupii *Calderini*: concu- M   gremium *Heinsius*:
gemitum M
82 resolvi ⊊: ne solvam M: resolvens *Markland*
83 dextra ⊊: vestra M
84 *suppl. Baehrens*
85 feci operire *Phillimore*: excepere M

What more did his parents give? Nay, I gave you another birth, little one, your freedom, when you were still at the breast, though you laughed at my present nor yet knew gratitude. Hasty my love may have been, but hasty with good cause, lest so small a freedom should lose a single day. Shall I not grimly assail all[4] the High Ones and unjust Tartarus with my reproach? Shall I not bemoan you, dear lad? As long as you lived, I wanted no sons. At the first moment of your birth you enfolded my bosom, fastening firm. I showed you words and sounds, saw to your complaints and hidden hurts, stooped and lifted you to kisses as you crawled on the ground, and on my loving lap made you hide your drooping eyes (?) and summon sweet slumber. My name was your first utterance, my play your baby laughter, from my face came your joys.

[4] See Critical Appendix.

CRITICAL APPENDIX

Asterisked notes are repeated *mutatis mutandis* from my article in *Harvard Studies in Classical Philology* 91 (1987).273–82. Lemmata are from Courtney's text, with 'v' for consonantal 'u.'

BOOK I

I.epist. v. 29

> nam Claudi Etrusci testimonium †domonnum† est,
> qui balneolum suum intra moram cenae recepit.

The prefatory letter has cited recipients of the poems in this Book as witnesses for the claim that they were composed in a couple of days, or less. But the fifth poem, on Claudius Etruscus' baths, came into being in the course of a dinner party, and that is more than the public can be expected to swallow. So Etruscus' testimony has to be waived: *donandum est.*

I.2.22

> tu modo fronte rosas, violis modo lilia mixta
> excipis et dominae *niveis* a vultibus obstas.

Tu is the bridegroom. *Niveis* follows *niveos* in v. 20. Such repetitions need to be considered on their individual demerits. A colourless word like *locum* in II.2.15 can be followed by *loci* in 17 with little or no harm done, but *niveis a vultibus* after *niveos . . . artus,* referring to the same person, is a serious embarrassment. Moreover, *niveis* is inappropriate as well as inelegant. This is the face of a blushing bride (v. 12). For *nitidis* Ov. *Ars* 3.74 *perit in nitido qui fuit ore color* is especially relevant. *Nivei vultus* has its proper place in v. 244, where Lavinia's face *was* snow-white before she started to blush (*cum Turno spectante rubet*).

*I.3.29

> hic aeterna quies, nullis hic iura procellis,
> numquam fervor aquis. datur hic transmittere visus
> et voces et paene manus. *sic* Chalcida fluctus
> expellunt reflui, *sic* dissociata profundo
> Bruttia Sicanium circumspicit ora Pelorum.

The river Anio flows between the two parts of Vopiscus' villa but does not sunder them: v. 24 *litus utrumque domi, nec te mitissimus amnis / dividit.* Håkanson accepts the comparisons with the Euripus and the Straits of Messina, though finding them 'somewhat strange.' More recently Courtney in *Trans. Am. Phil. Ass.* 114 (1984).330f. observes that Statius 'has been incautious in the actual selection of his expressions.' As though anyone in his right mind would pick the two most notoriously turbulent narrows in the Mediterranean to liken to this profoundly peaceful stretch of river. (Methodologically, temporary insanity is a defence of last resort at best, but as concerns the author of II.3.57–60 not absolutely to be excluded; here there is no such compulsion.) And what of *dissociata* after *non dividit*? This is no likeness, but as violent a contrast as Statius could think of. Read *nec . . . nec*. No Euripus or Straits of Messina *here* (*hic,* v. 30).

CRITICAL APPENDIX

*I.3.70

    illic ipse antris Anien et fonte relicto
    nocte sub arcana glaucos exutus amictus
    huc illuc fragili *prosternit* pectora musco,
    aut ingens in stagna cadit vitreasque natatu
    plaudit aquas.

The river god moves this way and that in the stream, pushing the moss on its surface in front of him: *fragilis prosternit pectore muscos*—which could be what Statius wrote. However, I rather think he wrote *praesternit*, a rare verb found twice elsewhere in the *Silvae*, III.2.114 and V.1.257; in the first place it means 'spread beforehand,' in the second, 'spread in front.' Here it will correspond to the use of *sternere* in e.g. Cic. *Pro Mur.* 75 *stravit pelliculis haedinis lectulos Punicanos.* With regard to *huc illuc,* as remarked by Markland, 'Latini voculas *huc . . . illuc* cum verbis alienis coniungunt, quasi cogitatione addi debeat verbum accedendi aut veniendi'; cf. Ov. *Met.* 10.124 *nunc eques in tergo residens huc laetus et illuc / mollia purpureis frenabas ora capistris.*

Some take 72 as referring to movement on land; but the moss would then be under foot, not breast high. The god wades in the water, then dives and swims.

I.4.48

               Sic itur in alta
  pectora, sic mixto reverentia *fidit* amori.

Subjects stand in awe of an efficient ruler (like Gallicus) whether they love him or not. But Gallicus has known how to make himself loved as well as revered, in fact even more loved than revered: *mixto reverentia cedit*

amori. Fidit is nonsense, worse than in Hor. *Carm.*
3.24.20, where it has ousted *laedit* (*SCP*, p. 291).

I.4.58

> tunc deus, Alpini qui iuxta culmina dorsi
> signat Apollineos sancto cognomine lucos,
> respicit heu tanti pridem securus alumni
> progressus * * * * *
> * * que moras: 'hinc mecum, Epidauria proles, *sqq.*

Most editors read *praegressusque moras,* 'forestalling
delay,' i.e. acting at once and so precluding any postpone-
ment. Markland's comment was fair: 'non male ad sensum,
sed phraseos desunt exempla et derunt, si recte auguror.'
But is the phrase really too imaginative for Statius? As for
alternatives, Housman's *praecidensque* (not mentioned in
Courtney's apparatus) is perfect *per se,* but as he recognized *praecidens* could hardly be corrupted to *progres-
sus* and his ingenious explanation is rather hard to swallow. Courtney's proposed supplement (*exempli causa* of
course), *tandem est ex silva maestus opaca / abrumpensque
moras* seems to assume that Apollo is somewhere in the
'Apollonian groves' (v. 59; see my note), but this has not
been stated or implied; and what would Aesculapius be doing there?

I.4.82

> sed revocant fasti maiorque curulis
> nec *permissa* semel.

As governor of Asia Gallicus is recalled to Rome to hold
the Consulship and then the City Prefecture with prom-

ise of a second Consulship, which was duly fulfilled. M's *promissa* should be retained. Does not *permissa* sound a little grudging?

I.6.15

    et quod percoquit †aebosia† Caunos

Ebusos, modern Iviza in the Balearic Islands, was famous for its figs, Caunos in Caria more so (*Cauneae*). 'The Caunus of Ebusos' is a portmanteau expression on all fours with *Haemonium Pyladen* (II.6.54 q.v.), 'the Pylades of Thessaly,' i.e. Patroclus. Prosody varied, though the first syllable is short elsewhere. That the manuscript reading should be thus relevant to figs by sheer coincidence should be incredible.

1.6.35

    orbem, qua melior severiorque est,
    et gentes alis insemel togatas

V. 35 refers to the fourteen rows in the theatre reserved for Knights under the lex Roscia of 67 B.C. The institution was revised and reformed by Domitian, with exclusion of unqualified persons, thereby supplying Martial with the point of no less than eight of the epigrams in his fifth Book (dated 89). *Orbem* ('the Circle') covers the whole body of spectators except senators, who sat in the orchestra, and *qua melior severiorque* distinguished the fourteen rows from the part occupied by the general public (*gentes togatas*). It also, I suppose, prompts the reader to think of the recent reform. I have removed the misleading commas in 35.

I.6.85

> vixdum caerula nox subibat orbem,
> *descendit* media nitens harena
> densas flammeus orbis inter umbras.

To what lower area does the fiery ball descend as it shines in the middle of the arena? Statius goes on to say that it illuminated the whole sky, which it would hardly do from down below. I accept *escendit* (Stange).

I.6.94

> quis dapes *inemptas,*
> largi flumina quis canat Lyaei?

'*Inemptas* corruptum videtur' Courtney. Not when explained: the fare provided for the Emperor's guests was not bought in any market; it was produced on his own land.

BOOK II

II.epist. v. 5

> primum enim habet Glauciam nostrum, cuius *gratissima infantia* et qualem plerumque infelices sortiuntur †apud te complexus amabam iam non tibi†.

Calderini's *gratissimam infantiam* would have solved the problem if he and his successors had not been baffled by the conclusion of the sentence: Statius had loved the dead boy for Melior's sake. But after he had embraced him at Melior's home, it was no longer (*iam non*) for Melior's sake but for the boy's own. With *complexus* ending the colon and *amabam* integrated with *iam non tibi* the heroic clausula pilloried by Courtney has evaporated.

*II.2.14

placido lunata recessu
hinc atque hinc *curvas* perrumpunt aequora rupes

The reader envisages a bay backed by a shore in the
shape of a horseshoe with two cliffs at the extremities both
pointing inwards, between which the sea enters. In revision of my earlier opinion, I now think the text might stand
provided *hinc atque hinc* be taken with *curvas,* not *perrumpunt.* But *curvae* is so much easier that I have maintained it. In v. 80 an island strikes curving waves.

II.3.53

sic ait. illa dei veteres imitata calores
uberibus stagnis obliquo pendula trunco
incubat atque umbris scrutatur amantibus undas.
sperat et amplexus, sed aquarum spiritus arcet
nec patitur tactus. tandem eluctata sub *auras*
libratur fundo rursusque enode cacumen
ingeniosa levat, veluti *descendat in imos*
stirpe lacus alia.

On *imitata* see note. In vv. 53–59 (*levat*) the tree (*illa*),
representing Pan, starts from its root in the bank and
bends obliquely over the pool, then tries *unsuccessfully* to
enter it. At length it struggles to the surface (*sub auras*),
balances on the bottom, then shoots up on high as though
from a new root. Thus far its behaviour conforms to the
reasonably clear account in 2–5, where ⟨*in*⟩*curvata*
(*vadis*) will replace Havet's phonetically unwelcome ⟨*cur*⟩
curvata (for the dative see *TLL* VII.1.1095,32), with the
major exception that *sub auras* is a clangorous mistake
for *sub undas*—the tree cannot struggle up into the air

without first struggling down. This could be scribal error, despite *undas* in 55. But what follows, 'as though it descended into the depth of the pool,' is sheer nonsense in the context, and no conjectural solvent is about to convert *descendit in imos lacus* into *escendit in altum aëra*. The conclusion that the muddle was in the author's mind seems unavoidable.

II.6.40

> > torva atque virilis
> gratia nec petulans acies blandique severo
> igne oculi, qualis *liber* iam casside visu
> Parthenopaeus erat

Liber for *bellis* (i.e. *bellus*) might pass for Baehrens at his worst, but better judgments than his went astray. Amazingly both Håkanson and van Dam have lengthy notes supporting *liber.*

Philetos and Parthenopaeus were beautiful youths, but it is the *kind* of beauty that matters here. Philetos was not the standard *puer delicatus* that the non-Statian title dubs him. On the contrary, he was like Parthenopaeus *with* a helmet, i.e. after he had joined the army against Thebes (*iam;* its relevance is a minor casualty of the *Schlimmbesserung*); pretty, to be sure, but a soldier. *Dubiae crimina formae* ('reproach of ambiguous beauty') implies that there is something discreditable about an effeminate appearance. *Qualis* and *visu* in 42 go together. See *Classical Journal* 97.2 (2001–02). 177–78.

*II.6.103

> pone, precor, questus; alium tibi Fata Phileton,
> forsan et ipse *dabit,* moresque habitusque decoros
> *monstrabit* gaudens similemque *docebit amari.*

My objection to the third persons stands. The notion that the dead boy might provide Ursus with a successor and train him seems to be absolutely unexampled and even for Statius, one would hope, impossibly bizarre. The new favourite might be provided by Fate (home-born) or by Ursus himself (bought). *Amare* would be better than *amari* for M's *amori,* but *amorem* is clearly right (see van Dam).

II.7.52

> tu *carus* Latio memorque gentis
> carmen fortior exseres togatum.

Lucan was a Roman and, mindful of his race, wrote a Roman poem, leaving for others the stock themes of Greek mythology. Patriotism, not his countrymen's affection, made him do that. *Partus* (Saenger) gets the sense, but that participle is not so used. I read *cretus* with at least one classical parallel, Sil. 3.249 *undosa cretus Berenicide miles.*

II.7.79

> quid? maius loquar: ipsa te Latinus
> Aeneas venerabitur canentem.

This punctuation violates the rule (lex Shackletonii?) that *quid?* thus used is followed by a question or (what was probably the same thing to a Roman) an exclamation introduced by an interrogative particle, not a statement. Therefore: *quid maius loquar?* or *quin (Ϛ) maius loquar.*

BOOK III

III.1.91

'tune' inquit 'largitor opum, qui mente profusa
tecta Dicarchei pariter *iuvenemque* replesti
Parthenopen?

Iuvenemque, supposedly a vacuous play on Parthenope's name, should be peremptorily dismissed in favour
of *iuvenisque* (Klotz). The reference to Pollius' younger
days fits in perfectly with II.2.137 *iuvenile calens.*

*III.3.76

praecipuos sed enim merito surrexit in actus
nondum stelligerum senior dimissus in axem
Claudius et †longo† transmittit *habere* nepoti.

Etruscus' father had begun his service under Tiberius.
Gaius retained him, Claudius promoted him and handed
him on to Nero. Vollmer unwisely follows Barth in explaining *nepoti* as a collective singular, 'the long series of descendants, i.e. of successors on the imperial throne.'
Neroni (Markland) may well be right, but *nepoti* may pass
as a venial laxity, 'grandson' for 'grandnephew,' perhaps
made easier by the fact that Nero was Claudius' adopted
son. On the other hand *longo* as an epithet of *nepoti* (or
Neroni) is inexplicable and there is no plausible substitute.
The other thing to notice is that *habere,* though inoffensive
(cf. *Theb.* 1.616), has no needful function. Graphically it is
practically the equivalent of *ab aere,* which makes perfect
sense with *longo* when understood as 'after long service,' a
sense supported by *aera = stipendia* and the Ciceronian *in
meo aere est* in *Fam.* 13.62 and 15.14.

*III.3.179

>   haud aliter gemuit per Sunia Theseus
> litora, *qui* falsis deceperat Aegea velis.

Per Sunia for *periuria* deserves its place; but *qui . . . velis* is no way for a poet like Statius to convey a piece of well-known information. I read *quem,* which Mozley had already translated: 'Aegeus, whom his false sails had deceived.' The comma is not wanted.

III.5.60

> *et* nunc illa tenet viduo quod sola cubili
> otia iam pulchrae terit infecunda iuventae.

Te (Phillimore) for *et* deserves admission. Statius suggests that his wife does not want to leave Rome for Naples because her daughter (*illa*) needs another husband, going on to predict that a marriage will come anyway. Suggests, surely, rather than baldly states. This is a question. What is the subject of *tenet*? *Illa,* I think, with the usual comma after *tenet.*

III.5.104

> *venarumque* lacus medicos Stabiasque renatas

See critical note. 'The solution lies in reading *venarumque;* a proper name is not required. With the first word thus restored, the opening part of line 104 refers to the remarkable group of mineral springs which are still today a feature of that portion of the Stabian plain which lies along the edge of the gulf at the foot of the great limestone mass of the Surrentine promontory' (A. W. van Buren, *Amer. Journ. Phil.* 51 (1930) 378f.). But a proper name *is* required, not only for concinnity after a string of them, but

CRITICAL APPENDIX

because *venarum lacus* is gibberish. The name, I suggest, is *Venae,* covering the area. Van Buren does not mention any pools, but presumably some existed in Statius' time if not today.

BOOK IV

IV.epist.24 v. 32

> quisquis ex meis invitus aliquid legit, statim se *profitetur* adversum.

So Aldus for *profiteatur.* But why impose such a false-hood? Disapproval of a poem is not an automatic declara-tion of enmity to the poet; it need not even be declared.

IV.1.46

> longamque tibi, *rex* magne, iuventam

adnuit

Domitian is addressed. For *rex* 'there exists not one sin-gle good parallel' (Håkanson), a claim not invalidated by Coleman's note. The obvious alternative is *dux* (Mark-land); to parallels add Hor. *Carm.* 4.5.5 *dux bone.* I have replaced *rege* (assimilated from preceding *regum*) with *duce* in Val. Max. 1.8.ext.18 (Loeb edition) and pointed out the converse error in Housman's note on Lucan 7.268.

*IV.2.23

> tanta patet moles *effusaeque* impetus aulae
> liberior campi

Campi needs an epithet, whereas *aulae,* 'the hall' (of Domitian's palace) can easily do without one. One does not say 'more extensive than that of a plain.' Read *effusique;* cf. Luc. 6.270 *effuso laxat tentoria campo.*

394

IV.7.9

> Maximo carmen tenuare tempto;
> nunc ab intonsa capienda myrto
> serta, nunc †maior† sitis *et* bibendus
> castior amnis.

Having completed the *Thebaid,* Statius is turning for Maximus' sake to the narrower field of lyric; myrtle replaces laurel. For *maior* Courtney would like to substitute *sedit* or *sidit,* which might however seem less than complimentary to Maximus. On the contrary the poet is even *more* eager to work in the new style, *but* the theme is rarified. He must leave Callimachus' Assyrian river (surely in mind) for the fountain pure and undefiled (*Hymns* 2.108–12). So *at* for *et.*

*IV.8.15

> dulci *strepit* ecce tumulti
> tot dominis clamata domus. Procul atra recedat
> invidia atque alio liventia pectora flectat:
> his senium longaeque decus virtutis et alba
> Atropos et patrius *lauro* promisit Apollo.

I still can find nothing against *tremit* in v. 15, 'coming under the *OLD* heading "to be affected by vibratory motion" (*tremo* 3).' But I think Coleman and Courtney were wrong to discard the humanist correction *lauros.* The construction *et Atropos promisit senium decusque longae virtutis et Apollo lauros* does not seem impossible to me, whereas I cannot envisage Apollo promising the children a long and illustrious career (promised by Atropos anyway) *with his bay. His* gift was poetry. As for *patrius,* their father Menecrates may not have written verse since Statius does

not say he did, but their (maternal) grandfather, Statius'
friend and patron Pollius (cf. v. 10), made it his main occupation and Statius was not likely to leave it out.

IV.9.29

non replictae

bulborum tunicae? nec ova *tantum*
nec lenes halicae

Rightly rejecting *tantum,* Coleman ignores *tandem*
(Polster), which is clearly the right answer, virtually equivalent to *saltem*; see *SCP* 50.

BOOK V

V.1.83

ille †*iubatis*†

molem immensam umeris et vix tractabile pondus
imposuit

The archetype seems to have been damaged at the ends
of the lines in 81–84. In 83 *subactis* (Avantius) and *volen-
tis* (Watt) are not to be despised, but I have preferred
gravatis, proleptic like *subactis* (see Kühner-Stegmann,
Lateinische Grammatik I, p. 239).

V.1.202

qualis conspecta coniuge segnis

Odrysius vates positis ad Strymona plectris
obstupuit tristemque rogum sine carmine flevit.

Segnis (inactive), before *positis plectris* and *obstupuit,*
is a deadweight, while *coniuge* is inadequate (sc. *mortua*).
Conspecto coniugis igne (Barth) provides a double remedy
at slight palaeographical cost.

V.2.25

> *illum* omnes acuunt plausus, illum ipse volantem
> pulvis et incurvae gaudent agnoscere metae.

Illum is the star racehorse whom all spectators favour. That *illum acuunt* could mean 'make him keener' needs no demonstration (Courtney compares Mart. Cap. 9.925), but as Håkanson (78, also cited by Courtney) appreciated, the sense here is not 'all the applause makes him keener' but 'for him (as he enters?) everybody applauds more loudly' (he compares Langen on Val. Fl. 2.172). Håkanson's *illi* is the answer.

*V.2.107

> haud umquam tales aspexit Romulus annos
> Dardaniusque senex medii bellare togata
> strage Fori. stupuere patres temptamina tanta
> conatusque tuos, *nec tunc* reus ipse timebat.

Leo's *tunc* for *te* is off key; Crispinus' display was not a tranquillizer. Moreover it stultifies *ipse*, as implying without any warrant that the rest of the audience too was afraid of a conviction, though to a lesser degree. *Pro te* (Markland) might pass as a joke (the Nuremberg audience worrying lest the speaker strain a muscle), but that is not Statius' style. *Et te*, proposed in *Harvard Studies*, provides the needful and logical climax. The statues have never heard anything like this from one so young, the Senators are dumbfounded, and the defendant himself is frightened by his advocate's demonic eloquence. The court has become a bloody battleground (*bellare* and *strage*).

V.2.144

> hic suetus dare iura potens, hoc caespite turmas
> adfari; †vitae† speculas castellaque longe
> aspicis ille dedit, cinxitque haec moenia fossa.

For Vollmer *late*, with *aspicis?* in parenthesis, removed all difficulties and easily explained the corruption *vitae*. The latter cannot be said for Courtney's proposal *quas hinc*. But we need a parallel for *late speculas castellaque longe* = *longe lateque speculas castellaque*. I leave the obelus.

V.2.165–67

> quique aquilas tibi nunc et castra *recludet*
> idem omnes *perferre* gradus . . . dabit

Courtney changes *recludit* on the ground that Crispinus' military appointment is announced only in vv. 168ff. But that is a literary device: see my note on v. 8. By the time we reach 125 and 132 the posting is assumed to be settled in principle, the only question being to what part of the world Crispinus will go.

*Perferre, in its usual sense of 'endure,' is semi-ridiculous and in the sense of 'carry out thoroughly, perform' inappropriate with *dabit*. I can make nothing of *proferre* (Polster), though *gradum proferre*, 'step forward' is standard. Since the abbreviations of *per* and *pro* differ only slightly, my reading *properare* involves hardly more than the addition of one letter, confusion of f and p being routine.

V.3.53

> illic Oebalio non finderet aera disco
> Graiorum vis nuda virum, non arva rigaret

sudor equum aut putri sonitum daret ungula fossa,
sed Phoebi simplex chorus, *et* frondentia vatum
praemia laudato, genitor, tibi rite *ligarem.*
ipse madens oculis, *umbrarum* animaeque sacerdos
praecinerem gemitum

The ellipse of *esset* after *chorus,* followed by *et . . .
ligarem,* has a makeshift aura. The prize would be awarded
by the Muses rather than the poet, whose role begins at 58
ipse madens oculis. So *en . . . ligarent.*

In 58 *umbrarum* is the stumbling block, or should be.
In his fantasy Statius becomes the priest of his father's
spirit (which is summoned to attend the ceremony), but
surely not of spirits in general. Markland found the right
substitute, *araeque* (cf. v. 47), but the wrong place to put it.
It should replace *umbrarum,* not *animae,* which is exactly
and indispensably in point. The loss of *araeque* before
animaeque explains itself and produced *umbrarum* to
mend the metre.

V.3.61

atque *tibi* moresque tuos et facta canentem
fors et magniloquo non posthabuisset Homero
tenderet *et torvo pietas* aequare Maroni.

Read *ibi me* (Heinsus). *Torvo,* 'grim,' as a generalized
epithet of Virgil corresponding to *magniloquo* of Homer,
will hardly do. Phillimore had the answer, comparing Martial 11.52.18 *rura vel aeterno proxima Vergilio,* but his
temptet et aeterno leaves room for improvement. Read
tenderet aeterno <et>. I give *Pietas* her capital rather than
understanding 'your affection.'

V.3.85
> quis non in funere *ductos*
> Heliadum ramos lacrimosaque germina dixit
> et Phrygium silicem . . . ?

Ductos (Ellis) for *cunctos* does not appeal and *in funere* seems to need a more useful function than this text allows it. I obelize, but hazard *in funere fratris*. In Ov. *Met.* 2.325ff. Phaëthon is buried by Nymphs, but his mother and sisters find his tomb and weep at it. The sisters are changed into poplars and their tears become amber. Papinius père deserves a different sort of mourner.

V.3.118
> etenim te divite ritu
> *sumere* purpureos Infantia *legit* amictus
> stirpis honore datos et nobile pectoris aurum.

Misled by *Infantia* (see my note), Markland put *sumere* in place of *ponere;* but the ceremony is the coming of age, when the purple gown and gold locket were laid aside. No ceremony is known to have celebrated the assumption of these emblems of free birth, which does not seem to have been simultaneous. I can find no sense in *legit* (choice is not involved) and substitute *fecit*.

*V.3.130
> Maeoniden aliaeque aliis natalibus urbes
> diripiunt cunctaeque probant; non omnibus ille
> verus, alit *victos* immanis gloria falsi.

We do not hear elsewhere of a contest that decided the perennial question of Homer's birthplace. Had there been one, the defeated claimants would not continue to make a

CRITICAL APPENDIX

plausible case (*probant*) or thrive on the monstrous glory of a falsehood. For *victos* read *fictos*, 'the liars' (*OLD fictus* c), or better *fictas*, 'falsely pretended' (*victas* Bentley).

V.3.139

          non totiens victorem Castora gyro
nec fratrem caestu virides *auxere* Therapnae.

I see little to commend *auxere* (Watt) or *coluere* (Håkanson) *for clausero* in M. The latter is disfavoured rather than commended by IV.8.53f. *et vos, Tyndaridae, quos non horrenda Lycurgi / Taygeta umbrosaeque magis coluere Therapnae.* Håkanson pronounced *plausere* (ς) 'of course impossible, since this verb never occurs with an accusative.' In point of fact it does, but not, it is true, with accusative of the person applauded. But 'What is unique is not therefore wrong, and the next step is to look for examples of analogous constructions' (Housman, *Cl. Papers* 423). And here there are indeed analogies: *sibilare* (in Hor. *Sat.* 1.1.66, also unique), *latrare, plangere*. In Cicero *Ad Q. Fr.* 2.7.1 *foris valde plauditur* we seem to have a passive with subject (*hoc factum*) or the like understood, though I suppose *plauditur* could be impersonal. *Gaudere alicui* is normal, but *gaudere aliquem* or *aliquid* well established. With due hesitation I have accepted *plausere*, after several previous editors.

V.3.154

    Stesichorusque ferox saltusque ingressa viriles
non formidata temeraria *Chalcide* Sappho

I find it impossible to refer this to Sappho's metres (Vollmer) or to anything other than her famous leap, which legend located at Leucas, not Chalcis. *Viriles* and *temeraria* point to the reckless, unfeminine hardihood of the act. The substitution of *Leucade* for *Chalcide* is justified, unless the latter be regarded as a mistake. That unfortunately is a possibility not to be excluded, especially in a poem published posthumously.

*V.3.231

> nam quod me mixta quercus non pressit oliva
> et fugit speratus honos, quam *lustra* parentis
> invida Tarrpei *caneres*

Whatever may be thought of Courtney's *caneres* in itself (as a subject for paternal celebration Statius' disappointment at the Capitoline festival may seem unpromising), the faultless paradosis *caperes* should not be ousted. Had the father lived to see his son's failure, he would have taken it philosophically; cf. Sen. *Oed.* 82 *regium hoc ipsum reor, / adversa capere. Lustra* (Markland) comes rather closer to M's *dulce* than the alternative *iura* ('judgement, decision'). *Quam . . . caperes* deserves a mark of exclamation.

V.5.7

> quae culpa, quis error
>
> quem luimus *tantus*?

Tantus (Politian (?) for *tantis*) should have been discountenanced by the ugly homoeoteleuton, an important consideration in Statius' case; see my *Homoeoteleuton in Dactylic Latin Verse* (Teubner, 1994), p. 93. Read *tanti,* making better sense and carrying the emphasis required by the order, whereas *tantus* is merely accessory; cf. Sen., *Tro.* 193f. *non parvo luit / iras Achillis Graecia et magno luet.*

V.5.24

> hoc quoque cum ‹ni›tor, ter dena luce peracta,
> adclinis tumul‹o pla›nctus in carmina verto
> discordesque ‹modos et› singultantia verba.
> molior orsa ly‹ra (dolor) est atque ira tacendi
> impatiens), sed nec solitae mihi vertice laurus
> nec fronti vittatus honos.

The close parenthesis after *dolor* in 27 should have been an angle bracket. But my text runs as follows (see critical note):

> > singultantia verba
> molior. *ista* ly‹rae vis est› atque ira tacendi
> impatiens.

In this poem, Statius says, he is not inspired by Apollo and the Muses but driven by grief and anger. I take *lyrae vis* (Krohn) as equivalent to *canendi vis,* 'compulsion to sing'; cf. Suet. *Tib.* 61.5 *vis adhibita vivendi.*

V.5.33

> iuvat, heu, iuvat illaudabile carmen
> fundere et incompte miserum laxare dolorem.
> sic merui, sic me cantuque habituque nefastum
> *aspiciant* superi. pudeat Thebasque novumque
> Aeaciden. nil iam *placidum manabat* ab ore.

In *Harvard Studies* I remarked that *aspiciunt* and *manabit* (ς) should replace *aspiciant* and *manabat;* also that *placitum* (Markland) is as evidently right as *placitissima* for *placidi-* in *Theb.* 12.302 (add. *placitissime* in I.2.201); as for the latter, perhaps not wholly in vain, since *placitum* has found its way into Courtney's apparatus.

V.5.42

    deficio medicasque manus fomentaque quaero
vulneribus, *sed summa,* meis

Substituting for the comically forcible-feeble *sed
summa,* Rothstein's *sed nulla* could be right, but I far prefer *subitura = succursura;* cf. Sil. 1.566 *defessis subeant re-
bus.*

V.5.77

                      nonne horridus ⟨*ipsos*⟩
invidia superos iniustaque Tartara pulsem?

The standard supplement *ipsos* is inept. Who else but
the gods (or Fate) was he to reproach? *Omnes* or *ergo* offer
themselves.

INDEX OF NAMES

INDEX

killed his son Learchus in a
fit of madness: II.1.143
Athamantēus, adj.: V.3.143

Athēnae: I.3.93. II.7.28. See
also Actaeus, Atticus,
Cecropius, Munychius

Athos, mountain in northeast
Greece, through which
Xerxes hollowed a passage for
his fleet: IV.3.56

Atlās, Titan supposed to carry
the sky on his shoulders:
I.1.60. IV.2.19. V.3.157
(Atreus): cf. V.3.96

Atrīdēs: I.4.113 (Menelaus).
III.2.98 (Agamemnon)

Atropos, a Fate: III.3.127.
IV.4.56. IV.8.19. V.1.178

Atticus = Athenian, adj.:
I.1.102. II.1.114

Attis, shepherd beloved and
mourned by Cybele, cas-
trated himself: I.5.38. Cf.
II.2.87. III.4.41. V.3.245. *See
also* Sangarius

Augē, mother of Telephus by
Hercules: III.1.40. Cf. IV.6.52

(Augustālia): musical and gym-
nastic contest held every four
years in Naples: cf. II.2.6.
III.1.152. III.5.92. V.3.113,
134, 226

Augustus: IV.1.32. Cf. I.1.23.
See also Iulia, lex. As imperial
title IV.1.tit. IV.2.tit.

Aurōra, goddess of dawn:
I.2.218. I.6.9. *See also*
Tithonia, Tithonis

Ausones, early inhabitants of
Campania: IV.5.37
Ausonia = Italy: III.2.20.
–nii V.3.293. –nius, adj.
I.2.76, 175. I.4.24. II.1.195.
III.2.120. III.3.105, 116.
III.4.18, 32. IV.4.52, 61, 96.
IV.8.20, 46. V.2.174. V.3.168

Auster, South Wind: I.6.78.
II.4.28. III.1.72. III.3.96.
V.1.81, 100, 246. austri
II.1.106. II.2.27. III.3.129

Autumnus: II.1.217

Aventīnus: adj. from Aventinus
(mons): II.3.22

Avernus, lake near Cumae, sup-
posed to give entrance to the
Underworld: IV.3.131. V.1.27,
259. V.3.271
Avernālis, adj.: II.6.101.
V.3.172

Babylōn, city on the Euphrates:
II.7.95. III.2.137. IV.1.40.
IV.6.67. V.1.60

Bacchēis, fem. adj. perhaps
from Bacchis, legendary king
of Corinth and ancestor of its
ruling family, the Bacchiadae:
II.2.34

Bacchus (sometimes = wine):
I.6.96. II.1.98. III.3.62.
III.4.59. IV.2.34. V.1.26, 116.
Cf. I.4.21. III.1.41. IV.6.56.
IV.8.9. *See also* Bromius,
Euhan, Lenaeus, Lyaeus
Bacchēus, adj.: II.2.99.
III.5.99

409

INDEX

Bactra, mod. Balkh in Afghanistan: III.2.136. IV.1.40

Baetica, region of southern Spain: II.7.29

Baetis, river in Spain, mod. Guadalquivir: II.7.34, 35

Bagrada: river near Carthage, mod. Medjerda: IV.3.91

Baiae, resort on the Bay of Naples: III.5.96. IV.3.26. IV.7.19. *See* Lucrinus
    Baiānus, adj.: I.5.60. III.2.17. V.3.169

Bassarides, Bacchantes, from Bassareus, a name of Bacchus: II.7.7

Batracho(myo)machia, 'Battle of the Frogs (and Mice),' an early Greek poem: I.epist.8

Battiadēs, son of Battus, i.e. Callimachus: V.3.157

Bebrycius, adj. from Bebrycia, territory of Lampsacus in Mysia, scene of boxing match between its king Amycus and Pollux: IV.5.28

Bellipotens: I.4.34. V.2.179. *See also* Mars

Bistonius, adj. from Bistones, a people of Thrace: I.1.19. II.4.21

Blaesus, friend of Atedius Melior: II.1.191, 201. II.3.77

Boeōtus, adj. from Boeotia, region north of Attica: V.3.209

Bōlānus, (M.) Vettius, cos. suff. 66: V.2.tit., 2, 37, 41–43. Cf. V.2.31–60, 64–7, 76, 140–49,

167. His wife: V.2.76–96. *See also* Crispinus

(Bōlānus, M. Vettius), cos. ord. 111, son of the foregoing: cf. V.2.75, 126

Boreās, the North Wind: III.2.45. III.3.96. V.1.82. *See also* Aquilo

Brīsēis, daughter of Brisus, Achilles' slave and mistress: IV.4.35

(Britannia): *see* Caledonius, Thule
    Britannus, adj.: V.2.149

Bromius = Bacchus: II.2.4. II.3.38. IV.6.66

Brontēs, a Cyclops: I.1.4. III.1.131. IV.6.48

Brūma, winter: II.1.215

Bruttius, adj. from Bruttii, people living in mod. Calabria: I.3.33

Brūtus (L. Jūnius), first Consul: I.4.42

Brūtus (M. Jūnius), assassin of Julius Caesar: IV.9.20

(Būsīris), king of Egypt, who sacrificed strangers: cf. III.1.31. IV.6.103

Byzantiacus, adj. from Byzantium, mod. Istanbul: IV.9.13

Cācus, robber infesting the Aventine: II.3.12

Caelicus, adj. from Caelius (mons): II.3.14

Caesar, (C.) Iūlius (Dictator): I.1.28, 86. Cf. I.1.23. II.7.67
    Iūlius, adj.: I.1.29

410

INDEX

gle-handedly drawing off a grounded ship that was carrying Cybele's sacred objects to Rome: I.2.245

Claudia, Statius' wife: III.epist.22. Cf. III.5 *passim*. V.epist.6

Claudius, emperor: III.3.78

Claudius Etruscus: *see* Etruscus

Cleōnaeus, adj. from Cleonae near Nemea: IV.4.28. V.2.49

Cleopatra: III.2.120

Clīō, a Muse: I.5.14

Clītumnus, adj. from Clitumnus, river in Umbria: I.4.129

Clōthō, one of the three Fates: I.4.1

Clymenaeus, adj. from Clymene, mother of the Heliades: I.2.123

Cnōsis, fem. adj. subst. = Ariadne from Cnosus (Cnossos) in Crete: I.2.133. V.1.232

    Cnōsiacus, adj.: I.6.88

Colchis, fem. adj. subst. from Colchis, region on the southeast coast of the Black Sea = Medea: II.1.141

Concordia: I.1.31. I.2.240. II.2.155. V.1.44

Coös, Aegean island: I.2.252

Corbulō (Cn. Domitius), Roman general: V.2.35

Corinna, sixth-century Boeotian poetess: V.3.158

(Corinthus), Corinth: *see* Ephyre, Isthmos

Cōrycius, adj. from Corycus, (a) grotto on Mt Parnasus: V.3.5; (b) town in Cilicia, noted for saffron: V.1.214

Crēta, Crētē: I.4.101. II.6.67
    Cressa, woman of Crete, Ariadne: II.6.25

Creūsa, bride of Jason, for whom he deserted Medea: II.1.142

Crispīnus (Vettius), son of M. Vettius Bolanus: V.2.tit., 2, 162, 171

Croesus, famously wealthy king of Lydia: I.3.105. Cf. II.2.121. V.1.60

Cūlex, 'Gnat,' poem attributed to Virgil: I.epist.7. II.7.74

Cūmae, mod. Cuma on the Bay of Naples, home of the Euboean Sibyl: IV.3.65 (Cȳmē), 115. V.3.168 (Cȳmē). Cf. III.5.97. IV.3.24
    Cūmānus, adj.: IV.9.43

Cūra: I.5.12

Cūrēs, Sabine town: IV.5.56

Cūria, Senate House: I.4.41. IV.1.10. IV.5.41. V.2.27

(Curtius, M.): cf. I.1.66

Cȳaneūs, adj. from Cyaneae, clashing rocks at the entrance to the Black Sea: I.2.40

Cybelē, the Great Mother: II.2.88. V.1.223 (Cybēbē). Cf. V.3.245
    Cybelēius, adj.: I.2.176

Cȳclōpes, giants who worked in metal inside Mt Aetna, also builders of cities in Argolis:

413

INDEX

(Epicūrus): cf. 1.3.94. II.2.103
Epidaurus, in the northeast
 Peloponnese: I.4.100
  Epidaurius, adj.: I.4.61
Eratō, Muse: I.2.49. IV.7.2
(Ērigonē), daughter of Icarius,
 hanged herself in grief for his
 death: cf. V.3.74
Erīnys, Fury: V.3.195, 286. *See
 also* Furiae
Erymanthus, mountain range in
 Arcadia, home of monster
 boar captured or killed by
 Hercules: IV.6.101
Erythraeus, adj. from (mare)
 Erythraeum, Red Sea, proba-
 bly = Persian Gulf: IV 6.18
Eryx, in northwest Sicily, with
 temple of Venus: III.4.21
  Erycīnus, adj.: I.2.160
Etrusca, mother of the follow-
 ing: III.3.111, 207
Etruscus, Claudius: I.epist.29.
 I.5.tit., 14. III.epist.15.
 III.3.tit., 6, 33, 136, 149, 173.
 His father: cf. III.3 passim.
 His brother III.3.153
Euboicus, adj. from Euboea, =
 Cumanus or Neapolitanus:
 I.2.177. I.4.126. III.5.12.
 IV.3.24. IV.4.1. V.3.111.
 Euboeus, ditto: V.3.137.
 Eubois, fem. adj.: I.2.263. *See
 also* Chalcidicus
Euhān = Bacchus: I.2.17, 133,
 220. I.5.3. II.7.7. IV.2.49.
 IV.3.155. V.3.6
Eumaeus, Ulysses' faithful
 swineherd: II.6.57

Eumēlus: IV.8.49
Eumenides, Furies: V.1.28.
 V.2.95. V.3.279. *See also*
 Furiae
Euphrātēs, river of Mesopota-
 mia: II.2.122. III.2.136.
 V.1.89
Euploea, 'Fair-sail,' island in
 the Bay of Naples: II.2.79.
 III.1.149
(Euripus), strait between
 Boeotia and Euboea: cf.
 I.3.31
(Eurōpa), daughter of Agenor,
 king of Phoenicia, carried off
 to Crete by Jupiter disguised
 as a bull: cf. I.2.135. III.2.89
Eurōtās, river of Sparta: I.5.40.
 II.6.46
Eurus, East Wind: I.6.11.
 III.2.45. III.3.96
(Eurydicē), wife of Orpheus: cf.
 V.1.203. V.5.54
Eurystheus, king of Argos, Her-
 cules' taskmaster: III.1.24.
 Cf. III.3.57
Ēvander, Arcadian king, occu-
 pied the Palatine, site of fu-
 ture Rome: II.1.93. III.4.48
 Ēvandrius, adj.: IV.1.7

Fācundia: V.3.90
Falernus, adj. from Falernus,
 district in northern Campania
 famous for its wine: II.2.5
Faliscus, adj. subst. from
 Falerii, a sort of sausage:
 IV.9.35
Fāma, Fame or Rumour: I.2.28.

421

INDEX

Lūcrīnus, adj.: I.2.264.
I.3.84. III.1.150

Lūna, Moon: V.3.30. *See also*
Cynthia, Phoebe

Lūna, in Etruria: IV.2.29.
IV.4.23

Luperci, College of priests, who
celebrated their annual festival (Lupercalia) by roaming
around half-naked with whips
and striking women to bring
fertility: V.3.184

Lyaeus = Bacchus or wine:
I.4.31. I.6.95. II.2.100.
III.4.9. III.5.102. IV.2.37.
IV.5.16

Lycaeus, adj. from Lycaeus,
mountain in Arcadia: I.3.78

Lycius, adj. from Lycia, region
of southwest Asia Minor:
I.2.222

Lycophrōn, Hellenistic poet,
called 'the Obscure': V.3.157

Lycurgus, Spartan lawgiver:
II.2.90. IV.8.52

Lȳdius, adj. of Lydia, region of
eastern Asia Minor, suppos-
edly original home of the
Etruscans, hence often =
Etruscan: I.2.190. III.3.61.
IV.4.6. Lȳdus, adj. II.2.121.
III.3.191. V.1.60. Adj. subst.:
I.6.70 (Lȳdiae)

Lȳsippus, fourth-century sculptor: I.1.86. IV.6.37, 109. Cf.
I.1.103

Macetae = Macedonians:
IV.6.106

Machāonius, adj. from
Machaon, physician in the *Iliad:* I.4.114

Maecius Celer, (M.):
III.epist.12. III.2.tit., 7, 20, 82

Maenalius, adj. from Maenalus,
mountain in Arcadia: I.2.18.
Maenalis, fem. adj.: III.1.40

Maeonidēs, i.e. Homer: V.3.130,
150

Maeonius, adj. = Lydian, of
Homer: II.1.117. V.3.26

Magnus: *see* Pompeius

Maia, mother of Mercury:
V.1.233

Malēa, promontory at the
southeastern tip of Laconia,
notoriously dangerous to navigation: I.3.97

Manīlius Vopiscus: *see* Vopiscus

Mantua, mod. Mantua, *patria*
of Virgil: II.7.35. IV.2.9
Mantuānus, adj.: IV.7.27

Marathōnius, adj. from Marathon in Attica: V.3.74

Marcellus, Vitōrius: IV.epist.tit.,
1, 26. IV.4.tit., 9, 78, 99

Marcia (aqua), aqueduct: I.3.67.
I.5.27

Marcomani, German tribe:
III.3.170

Mareōticus, adj. from Mareotis,
lake and district near Alexandria, hence can = Egyptian:
III.2.24. IV.6.103. Mareōtis,
fem. adj.: = Alexandrian:
III.2.103

Marō = Virgil: II.6.20. V.3.63.
See also Vergilius

423

INDEX

bearer, buried at Misenum
(headland and town) on the
Bay of Naples): III.1.151. Cf.
II.2.77. III.5.98. IV.7.19.
V.3.167

Molorchus, peasant who put up
Hercules for the night before
he slew the Nemean lion:
III.1.29. IV.6.51

Molossī, people of Epirus with
a famous breed of dogs:
II.6.19

Monēta, the Roman mint (temple of Juno Moneta):
III.3.105

Mors, Death: III.1.172.
IV.6.103. V.1.8, 168. Mortes:
II.7.131

Mulciber = Vulcanus III.1.133

Mulvius agger, Mulvian Bridge
over the Tiber: II.1.176

Mūnychius, adj. from
Munychium, fortress of
Piraeus, the port of Athens =
Athenian: V.3.107

Mūsa, Muse: II.7.75. Mūsae:
I.5.2. I.6.2. II.7.20, 41.
III.5.65. IV.2.55. IV.4.87. Cf.
I.2.4, 8, 10, 17. V.1.25. V.3.14,
211. See also Aonides,
Aonius, Heliconis, Hyantius,
Pierius; Calliope, Clio, Erato,
Thalia. Fountains of: I.2.259.
See also Castalia, Hippo-
crene, Piplea, Pirene

Mycēnaeus, adj. from Mycenae,
ancient chief city of Argolis:
III.3.189. V.1.59

Mygdonius, adj. from Mygdon,

king of Phrygia = Phrygian:
II.2.108. V.3.245

Myrōn, famous sculptor, especially in bronze: II.2.66.
IV.6.25

Nāis, Fountain Nymph: I.2.207.
I.3.62. II.3.30, 60. III.4.42.
Nāides: I.2.264. I.5.6. II.3.7.
II.6.102. Cf. I.5.15. See also
Nymphae

Narcissus, Boeotian youth who
died of love for his own reflection: I.5.55. Cf. III.4.41

Nasamōnius, adj. from
Nasamones, people of Libya
= African or Carthaginian:
II.7.93. Nasamōniacus, ditto:
IV.6.75

Nāso, i.e. Ovid: I.2.255. Cf.
II.7.78

Nātūra: I.2.271. I.3.17. I.6.58.
II.1.34, 83. II.2.15, 52.
II.4.17. III.1.168. III.4.76.
V.3.71. V.5.22

Naxos, island in the Aegean:
I.2.131, 224

Neāpolis, Naples: III.epist.21.
IV.epist.10, 22. IV.8.6. Cf.
II.2.97. IV.8.55. See also
Chalcidicus, Euboeus,
Eubois, Parthenope;
Augustalia

Nemeā (-eē), wooded valley in
Argolis, where Hercules
killed a monstrous lion; scene
of the Nemean games: I.3.6.
III.1.30, 143, 182. IV.6.41.
V.3.52. Cf. V.3.142

425

INDEX

Nemeaeus, adj.: IV.6.58.
V.2.48

(Neoptolemus): *see* Pyrrhus

Neptūnus, Neptune, god of the
sea: III.2.5. Cf. II.2.21
Neptūnius, adj.: III.3.82

Nēreus, sea god = the sea:
II.2.75
Nēreis, daughter of
Nereus, Sea Nymph: I.2.116,
129. II.2.103. Nēreides:
III.1.144. III.2.13. Cf.
II.2.19. III.2.34

Nero, emperor: II.7.58, 119.
IV.3.8.V.2.33. Cf. II.7.61, 100.
Nerōnēus, adj.: I.5.62

Nēsis, island in the Bay of Naples, mod. Nisida: II.2.78.
III.1.148

Nestor: long-lived king of Pylos:
IV.3.150. Cf. V.3.192. *See also*
Pylius
Nestoreüs, adj.: I.3.110.
I.4.127

Nīlus, river Nile: I.6.77.
III.2.108, 115. III.3.91.
III.5.21. IV.3.157. V.1.100.
V.5.67
Nīliacus, adj.: IV.9.12

(Niobē), wife of Amphion;
turned to stone on Mt
Sipylus, her tears for her slain
children continued to flow as
a waterfall: cf. V.1.33. V.3.87

Nīsus, king of Megara, whose
life depended on his purple
lock of hair, which his daughter Scylla cut off: III.4.84

Nōbilitās: I.2.72

Nomades = Numidians: I.5.36.
II.2.92

Notus, South Wind: III.2.45.
V.1.147. noti: III.4.4

Novius Vindex: *see* Vindex

Numa, second king of Rome:
I.4.41. V.3.290

Numidae, Numidians: I.6.78.
II.4.28

Nympha, Nymph: II.2.19
(= water). II.3.44 (Pholoë).
V.3.291 (Egeria). Nymphae:
I.2.115. I.3.37, 46. I.5.23.
II.3.8. III.1.75, 101. Cf.
I.5.15. III.3.26. *See also*
Dryades, Hamadryas, Naides,
Nereides

Nȳsa, in Caria, associated with
Bacchus: I.2.221

Ōceanus, the ocean: I.4.37.
II.7.26. IV.2.53

Odrysius, adj. from Odrysii,
people of Thrace = Thracian:
V.1.203. V.3.271

Oebalidēs, son of Oebalus, king
of Sparta, i.e. Hyacinthus, fa-
vourite of Apollo: II.1.112.
Oebalius, adj. from Oebalus
= Spartan: II.6.27. III.2.10.
V.3.53. Oebalis, fem. adj.:
I.2.151

Oenomaüs, king of Pisa, who
killed his daughter's suitors
after defeating them in chariot races: I.2.42

(Oenōnē): *see* Cebrenis

Oetaeus, adj. from Oete, mountain range in Thessaly where

426

INDEX

Pollux: IV.2.48. Cf. IV.5.28.
V.3.140. *See also* Castor,
Tyndaridae
Polyclītēus, adj. from Polyclitus,
fifth-century sculptor: II.2.67.
IV.6.28
(Pompēiī). Cf. V.3.164
Pompēiānus, adj.: I.2.265
Pompēius Magnus, (Cn.):
I.4.42. II.7.69, 72, 115 (Pom-
peii). Cf. I.1.28
Ponticus, adj. from Pontus, re-
gion southeast of the Black
Sea: I.6.12
Pontica, adj. subst. neut.
plur.: V.3.188
Praeneste, in Latium, mod.
Palestrina: IV.4.15
Praenestīnus, adj.: I.3.80
Praxitelēs, fourth-century sculp-
tor: IV.6.27
Prīamidēs, son of Priam, i.e.
Hector: IV.4.105
Priamus, Priam king of Troy:
II.7.56. Cf. I.4.125. II.2.122.
II.3.73. III.4.104. V.3.256
Priscilla, wife of Abascantus:
V.epist.2, 7. V.1.tit., 3, 108,
150, 228, 249, 258
Prochyta, island off the
Campanian coast, mod.
Procida: II.2.76
Procnē, wife of Tereus, who
raped her sister Philomela
and tore out her tongue. In
revenge Procne killed their
son Itys and served him to
Tereus for dinner. Tereus,

Procne, and Philomela were
turned respectively into a
hoepoe, a swallow, and a
nightingale (on the variations
see van Dam, pp. 355f.):
II.1.140. Cf. II.4.21.
III.2.110. III.3.175. V.3.84
Propertius (Sex.), elegist: I.2.253
Prōserpina = Persephone, wife
of Pluto, queen of the Under-
world: II.6.102. V.1.254. Cf.
V.1.259. *See also* Iuno
(Prōtesilāus), first Greek to be
killed at Troy, permitted to
return from the Underworld
for one day to visit his wife
Laodamia: cf. II.7.123. *See
also* Phylaceis
Prōteus, sea god, able to change
his shape at will: I.2.129.
III.2.35
(Puteolī): *see* Dicaearchus
(Pygmaei): cf. I.6.63
Pyladēs, bosom friend of
Orestes: II.6.54. V.2.156
Pylius: adj. from Pylos in
Messene: II.2.108. III.4.104.
V.3.114, 255
Pȳramides, Pyramids: V.3.50
Pyrrhus, son of Achilles:
V.2.151. Cf. V.3.79
(Pȳthia), Apollo's prophetess at
Delphi: cf. V.1.114
(Pythian games): cf. III.1.141.
V.3.142

Quiēs: I.6.91
Quindecimvirī: IV.3.142

431

Composed in ZephGreek and ZephText by
Technologies 'N Typography, Merrimac, Massachusetts.
Printed and bound by Edwards Brothers, Ann Arbor, Michigan
on acid-free paper made by Glatfelter, Spring Grove, Pennsylvania.